DISCARDED

SCIENTIFIC EVIDENCE OF THE EXISTENCE OF THE SOUL

by

BENITO F. REYES

THE THEOSOPHICAL PUBLISHING HOUSE
Wheaton, Ill., U.S.A.
Madras, India / London, England

© Copyright Benito F. Reyes 1970

Original edition published in the Philippines
Copyright by Benito F. Reyes, Manila, Philippines, 1949

Revised edition 1970, published by
The Theosophical Publishing House, Wheaton, Illinois,
a department of The Theosophical Society in America

All rights reserved. No part of this book may be reproduced in any form without permission in writing from the author, except for the inclusion of brief quotations in a review.

Library of Congress Catalog Card Number 70-122432
ISBN: 0-8356-0192-7
Manufactured in the United States of America

SCIENTIFIC EVIDENCE OF THE EXISTENCE OF THE SOUL

For millions of people throughout the world, in both the East and the West, the existence of the soul is an accepted fact, and this view is a basic tenet in most of the great religions. Yet there are millions of others who do not accept the idea of a soul, and who have a purely mechanistic view of man as a product of evolution.

The distinguished author of this work has built up his case for the existence of the soul by drawing on many sources, including the evidence of such phenomena as memory, sleep, dreams, hypnotism, extrasensory perception, and death. He links his thesis with philosophical concepts of both East and West. The work is well documented.

This is a challenging book and it will provide absorbing reading for those who seek an answer to the meaning of man's existence.

The author, Dr. Benito F. Reyes, is the first President of the University of the City of Manila (Pamantasan ng Lungsod ng Maynila) in the Philippines. Prior to his inauguration in 1968 he was for twenty-one years a professor at the Far Eastern University in Manila. In 1951-52 he taught at Boston University as a Fulbright-Smith-Mundt professor and in 1965 he was a Fulbright-Hays philosophy professor at the State University of New York. He lectured in Harvard, Brown, and other universities. He has published a number of works on philosophy, psychology, and the quest for meaning.

TABLE OF CONTENTS

Foreword ix
Acknowledgments xi
Introduction xiii
Preface to the second edition xvii

PART I

1. Why I Use the Word *Soul* 1
2. The Legitimacy of the Soul-Problem 8
3. The Urgency of the Soul-Problem 17
4. Statement of Aims and Purposes 24
5. Humanizing the *Homo Sapiens* 31

PART II

6. The Nature of the Scientific Method 38
7. What is Fact? 45
8. An Example of Scientific Evidence 51
9. The Problem and the Technique 56

PART III

10. Evidence from the Phenomena of Consciousness 66
    A. The Nature of Consciousness
11. Evidence from the Phenomena of Consciousness 72
    B. Assumptions About Consciousness

12. Evidence from the Phenomena of Consciousness 81
    C. The Relation Between Thought and Brain

13. Evidence from the Phenomena of Consciousness 92
    D. Self-Consciousness and the Continuity
       of Consciousness

14. Evidence from the Phenomena of Memory 100

15. Evidence from the Phenomena of Sleep 117

16. Evidence from the Phenomena of Dreams 129

17. Evidence from the Phenomena of Hypnotism 141

18. Evidence from the Phenomena of
    Psychical Research 155

19. Evidence from the Phenomena of
    Psychical Research 168
    A. The Phenomena of Extrasensory
       Perception and Psychokinesis

20. Evidence from the Phenomena of
    Psychical Research 179
    B. The Phenomena of Traveling Clairvoyance

21. Evidence from the Phenomena of Psychedelics 192

22. Evidence from the Phenomena of Death 209

23. Conclusion 227

PART IV

Appendix A — Stranger-Child 236

            B — How A Dream Inspired the
                 Poem "Kubla Khan" 238

            C — The Phenomena of Reincarnation 241

Bibliography 244

Index of Names 253

Index of Subjects 256

To George and Nellie Ragan

FOREWORD

"All argument," said Samuel Johnson, "is against the appearance of the living spirit of the dead; all belief is for it."

What the learned doctor said of the immortality of the soul can be said equally of its existence.

All argument is against it, but all belief is for it.

This book has a double purpose: first, to show the invalidity of that argument and, second, to put that belief on a scientific basis. In other words, to prove, in accordance with the requirements of the fourfold scientific method, the existence of the soul.

All arguments against the existence of the soul generally originate from the confusion as to what constitutes a fact.

It is not easy to say what is the true criterion or standard for the determination of fact.

Science itself is based largely on the law of probability.

It is a fact that "roses are red" and "violets are blue." But are they to a color-blind man?

The determination of factuality, therefore, is a difficult thing. Only the ignorant think it is easy.

For this reason, several of the introductory chapters are devoted to a discussion of the meaning and nature of the scientific method, its fundamental assumptions, its specific techniques and procedures, as well as its limitations.

Throughout this book we have kept in mind the basic law of fact-evaluation enunciated by Professor Charles-Eugene Guye, namely, that it is the scale of observation which makes the phenomenon.

In the earlier part of the work, a number of chapters are dedicated to a consideration of the importance of a scientific study of the soul-problem.

It is our conviction that what is important enough for humanity to believe in through thousands of years is also important enough for science to study and investigate seriously, in order to determine once and for all whether such belief can be substantiated by fact and reason.

It is wrong for science to ignore and neglect a problem as important as the problem of the soul.

Its religious, moral, and social implications are tremendous.

We cannot leave it completely to the emotional sermonizings of pulpit orators.

We cannot abandon it solely to the airy lucubrations of speculative thinkers.

It has a right in the laboratory of science.

Let us not deny it that right.

This work constitutes, probably, the first serious attempt to gather all the available facts of science and experience pertinent to the soul-problem and to organize them, following the well-known scientific method of hypothesis, into a clear and coherent architectonic so as to lead to a necessary and inevitable conclusion.

How successfully this has been accomplished is not for the author to judge.

As we said in our concluding chapter:

"We rest our case; we pause for judgment."

BENITO F. REYES
Manila, Philippines
September 13, 1948

ACKNOWLEDGMENTS

Grateful acknowledgments are hereby made to all those authors and publishers from whose works materials were taken and permission given for inclusion in this book:

Pierre Lecomte Du Nouy, *Human Destiny* (Longmans, Green and Company, Inc., New York) 1947. Reprinted by permission of David McKay Company, Inc., New York.

Max Freedom Long, *The Secret Science Behind Miracles* (Huna Research Publications, California) 1948.

Alexis Carrel, *Man the Unknown*, (Harper and Row, Publishers, Inc., New York) 1939.

Vincent H. Gaddis, *Mysterious Fires and Lights*, (David McKay Company, Inc., New York) 1967.

P. D. Ouspensky, *Tertium Organum* (Alfred A. Knopf, Inc., New York) 1945.

Robert S. de Ropp, *Drugs and the Mind*, (St. Martin Press, Inc., New York) 1957.

Floyd W. Matson, *The Broken Image*, (George Braziller Publishing, New York) 1946.

Greenwood Press, Inc., New York, for materials from *A Philosophy of Religion* by Edgar Sheffield Brightman (Copyright, 1940, by Prentice-Hall, Inc., New York).

William Morrow and Company, Inc., for materials from *The Reach of the Mind* by J. B. Rhine (published by William Sloane Associates, Inc. Copyright, 1947, by J. B. Rhine).

George Braziller, Inc., for material from *The Broken Image* by Floyd W. Matson (Copyright, 1964, by Floyd W. Matson).

The Macmillan Company, New York, for materials by C. J. Ducasse, "The Empirical Case for Personal Survival," from *Body, Mind, and Death*, edited by Anthony Flew (copyright, 1964, by the Crowell-Collier Publishing Company).

Fawcett Publications, Inc., New York, for materials from *The LSD Story* by John Cashman, 1966.

G. P. Putnam's Sons, New York, for materials from *LSD —The Consciousness-Expanding Drug* edited by David Solomon (1964).

Fate Magazine, Highland Park, Illinois, for materials by Vincent H. Gaddis "With Brain Destroyed They Live and Think," (Vol. 1, No. 2, 1948).

The Society for Psychical Research, London, England for materials on dreams by Frederick van Eeden, *Proceedings of the Society for Psychical Research,* Vol. XXVI, 1913.

The Scotsman, "On Edge of Death: Record of Out of the Body Experience: Brought Back to Life," February 26, 1937.

Professor Delfin F. Batacan, Far Eastern University, Manila, Philippines, for "The Case of Sotera Flandez," an original manuscript.

INTRODUCTION

Dr. Benito F. Reyes, professor of philosophy, is a Filipino savant who was a welcome guest at Boston University during the academic year 1951-1952, as Fulbright Scholar. He lectured in many classrooms of the University, and mingled freely with the academic family, both faculty and students. In times when we hear too much of Iron Curtains or Bamboo Curtains dividing East and West, he has demonstrated the unity of humanity through the unity of the Spirit. He came to the United States, it is true, from an Oriental culture. His philosophical and religious convictions differ in certain respects from those current in New England. But his scholarship, his friendly personality, his respect for difference of opinion, and his constant appeals to reason and to experience have made the difference seem less important, and the ties of unity more important.

In the present book, Dr. Reyes reveals both the range of his scholarship and the depth and intensity of his personality. "The style is the man," we are told. This book is not marked by the cool and dry objectivity that characterizes most Western scientific and philosophical writing. On the contrary, personal conviction and depth of spiritual feeling are revealed on every page. Yet they are guided and checked by a wide range of scientific information and by philosophical insight, and often they are illumined by reflections from the depths of spiritual experience.

The reader of this book will experience more than a study of philosophical psychology concerned with the soul. "The soul," as a matter of fact, does not exist. Only individual souls exist; and the reader will become aware that he is becoming acquainted not only with ideas, but with a living soul — the soul of Benito F. Reyes.

The reader will also be aware of a "meeting of East and West" on a new level: not on the level of querulous fault-finding or contentious rivalry, but on the level of mutual understanding and beyond that, of the elevation of life above all geographical and political levels into the realm of spiritual values. It is thus that East and West should always meet. If the representatives of both sides had some of the qualities of Dr. Reyes, disputes would soon be settled, even if complete agreement could not be attained. His spirit is at once truth-loving and courteous; it is both intellectual and spiritual; it combines ethical idealism with competence — a combination all too rare in both East and West.

After all, what is most necessary in science and philosophy, religion and politics, is not so much complete agreement as mutual understanding; not so much surrender of difference as respect for differences. The reader of this book may perhaps find opinions expressed with which he may not fully agree; but he will never find them expressed in a spirit which he cannot admire. The objective love of truth, the respect for personality, and the search for the highest value which the human soul can experience, stand out from the pages of Dr. Reyes's book and will prove rewarding to every reader of the book.

In this book there is a fresh and sincere search for truth about the soul. The scientific method of the West is mastered and utilized. The wisdom of the East, which Dr. Reyes has studied both in the Philippines and in India, has been well digested. Not scientific and philosophical sources alone have been consulted, but the extraordinary religious experience of the East has been absorbed and woven into the texture of this work. The result is a peculiar enrichment of experience and thought which imparts a unique flavor to the book.

Dr. Reyes respects fact wherever it is found, whether seen through the microscope, experienced in everyday life, or discovered in unusual and even occult aspects of consciousness. Some readers may, perhaps, question whether all of the data referred to have been subjected to completely adequate scientific checks. But if one is to err it is better to err on the side of admitting too many facts, than too few. It is the duty of the truth-seeker to face the facts, especially when they are

Introduction   xv

embarrassing to his preconceived theories and prejudices. If one must choose between the generous inclusion of all experiences reported in this book and the narrow and pedantic veto issued by logical positivists which forbids every investigator to accept as evidential any facts other than the data of sense, the choice of the truth-seeker is clear. He will choose to include all the facts, whether they fit this formula or not.

What is needed today is a liberal and inclusive spirit — one that is receptive to new facts, new ideas, new persons. This book has the mission of breaking down the walls of scientific, philosophical, and cultural provincialism and opening the way to new possibilities. It may not solve all the problems of the soul; it invites and should receive criticism. But it should not be rejected by those who are unfamiliar with the areas of experience and meaning which it explores, without giving the facts on which it rests a reasonable hearing.

The idiom of this book is not the idiom of most current psychology; but it is the idiom of truth-seeking and this idiom always merits respect.

Edgar Sheffield Brightman
Boston University
June, 1952

PREFACE TO THE SECOND EDITION

In the process of updating this book for its second edition, (the American edition, the first being a Philippine edition) the writer became immediately aware of the long gap between 1949, when it was first published, and 1970, the year of its second publication. What surprised him really was the paucity of new data about the problem of the soul science-wise, the persistence among most scientists, of the old cerebrocentric attitude toward the question of consciousness and the continuation of the age-old human longing for survival after death.

Twenty-one years and nothing new about the immemorial question of the Sphinx: What is man? Except, perhaps, two new significant orientations, one hesitant, tentative, but quite correct — humanistic psychology; the other, exuberant, bold, but perilous — psychedelics. And they are not exactly new, except that they appear new to some people, because really they have been with us for quite a time in various guises and disguises.

When this book was written in 1949, it boldly asserted the humanistic approach to the problems of psychology; it bewailed the distortion of psychology into physiology; it assailed the physicalistic, corpocentric, cerebrocentric philosophy of man sponsored by behavioristic psychologists; it raised the question of the origin and conservation of values, as the most formidable objection to any materialistic view of man; it gave accent and vigor to autonomy, creativity, meaning, transcendental experience, personality, self-determination, and the primacy of self and consciousness in the study of human life; it sponsored valuation and evaluation as the most significant processes of human life; it rejected the compartmentalized, fragmented, elementalistic philosophy of man; it championed the total, integrated, holistic approach to the human problem; it incorporated into its attempt to understand the human condition everything that is legitimately human, following the line of thought that there is nothing, nothing at all, no subject, no idea, no concept that affects man directly or indirectly which should be considered alien to the human mind, inasmuch as, quoting Paul Valery, "When the mind is in question, everything is in question"; it emphasized particularly peak-experiences (A.H. Maslow's term) like *samadhi* of yoga-science, *satori* of Zen, and the *ecstasy* of Western mystics; but it repudiated completely and uncompromisingly the physical model of man and the cosmos taken over from physics, especially the unwarranted and illegitimate imposition of this ultra-simple physical model upon psychology and the insistence of its proponents on explaining man in terms of quanta, electrical units, chemical elements, atomic particles, and interchangeable parts interpreted elementalistically.

Probably, this book, in its first edition, was the first printed attempt to sponsor humanistic psychology consciously.

With regard to psychedelics this can be said: from very ancient times the use of drugs to stimulate sensation and cerebration has been known in India, China, the Middle East, the Near East, in South America, in Central America and even in Africa. But anyone seriously interested in the practice of yoga and the awakening of higher dimensions of awareness should read Patanjali's classic masterpiece, the *Yoga-Sutras,* and follow the *ashtanga-yoga* exercises, preferably with a reliable *guru* or teacher. Then, he might find the truth he seeks.

All in all, this second edition of *Scientific Evidence of the Existence of the Soul* has not deviated from the original idea of the book when it was first published. In fact, the updating, in terms both of additional information and greater clarification of ideas, has served only to re-emphasize it and to call greater attention to the need to do more study, more research, and more humanistic re-interpretation of available data.

It might be said here that, even in the realm of modern physics, the plausibility of soul-existence as well as of the

Preface to the second edition xix

spiritual dimensions of the universe has been greatly increased by one of its new concepts — the idea of antimatter — and on the basis of this idea the existence of nonmaterial worlds. A very interesting little book published in Stockholm, in 1966, carries this seed-idea. It is the book of Hannes Alfven of the Royal Institute of Technology, Stockholm, entitled *Worlds-Antiworlds: Antimatter in Cosmology*, released by W.H. Freeman and Company, San Francisco and London. How terribly late is this so-called new idea of Western science! For the last three thousand years the idea of nonphysical worlds interpenetrating the physical world has been a commonplace in the *Vedas* of India, especially in Vedanta and Yoga philosophy. But of course it lacks the imprimatur of Western science. Now comes from the West the idea of antimatter. Naturally it cannot be called *Anupadaka* or *Adi* as the Vedantins might call it; or *Nibbana* or *Parinibbana* as the Buddhists might term it; or simply *Spirit,* as idealistic philosophy even in the West usually labels it. It must be given a scientific name, otherwise it would not be scientific; it has to be called antimatter. My statement is not intended to be sarcastic, because I do not forget the fact that the idea of antimatter has been forced upon Western scientists by years and years of research in the inner world of the atom.

But the new conceptual dimension implied in the idea of antimatter is encouraging and stimulating. It will surely lead to greater and deeper thinking which may eventually bring about a total spiritual recrudescence in scientific thinking. Who knows but that at the ending of the twentieth century science might become both Godful and soulful.

Meanwhile, some words of appreciation and gratitude to all those people who made possible this second edition of my book must be said, and said sincerely and repeatedly:

To the late Dr. Edgar Sheffield Brightman, my professor at Boston University, who taught me accuracy, completeness, and humility. His introduction to my book is both kind and charitable.

To Prof. Valentina B. Patacsil, of the Pamantasan ng Lungsod ng Maynila (University of the City of Manila) who helped update the book, revise the footnotes and prepare both an entirely new index and a new bibliography.

And finally, to all those people whose research and studies have been used and whose works have enriched man's knowledge of himself.

To all of them: thanks without measure and without end.

BENITO F. REYES

Pamantasan ng Lungsod ng Maynila
Intramuros, Manila, Philippines
January, 1970

Chapter 1
WHY I USE THE WORD *SOUL*

The word *soul* according to most psychologists is unscientific. It has been discarded long ago, and few writers on psychology use it today. Only philosophers, ministers, and poets use it, and many of them use it apologetically.

At present, *behavior* seems a more accepted term to denote the phenomena of human personality. It carries more scientific prestige and it has the imprimatur of orthodox scientific psychology.

Even the terms *mind* and *consciousness* are regarded as being too vague and indefinite for scientific purposes. Besides, they carry over too much of the connotation of the idea of the soul.

All terminologies that smack of the soul, or even as much as approximate its traditional meaning, are usually held under suspicion. They are not scientific. They are medieval and superannuated. They belong to prescientific psychology. As far as the majority of modern doctors of psychology are concerned, such terms have no scientific usefulness.

This attitude, of course, is unfortunate because it is the product principally of a prejudice — the prejudice that favors a mechanistic interpretation of the universe and rejects almost anything otherwise.

From Psychology To Physiology

Thus, it has come to pass that psychology which started auspiciously as the "science of the soul" (*Psyche*, soul, and *logos*, word or knowledge or science) became a "science of bodily functions" or physiology. This conversion of psychology into physiology may be regarded as the greatest bathos of the twentieth century.

From the *human psyche* to the *human physique*: this is the history of modern psychology:
> From the soul to the body;
> From the mind to the brain;
> From consciousness to behavior;
> From the sublime to the ridiculous;
> This is psychology, indeed! and alas!

Classroom Psychology

Consider, for example, the ordinary classroom instruction in the so-called fundamentals of psychology. The professor is a specialist in his chosen field of study. He holds a doctorate in psychology from some reputable American university. He knows his business as the saying goes. On the other hand, there are the students — young, eager, new. They have heard about this science called psychology. They have been advised to enroll in it as a prerequisite for graduation. Credit? Three units. And what is it they want to know? They want to know what is the mind; is there a soul; what is consciousness; what is intelligence; who am I; what is the self; what is memory; why do I love? And so on.

The professor begins his lecture with the statement that psychology is a science. As such, therefore, it is based on *facts*. What are the facts? Here the professor deceives both himself and his students. He becomes involved in what Stuart Chase calls "sheer verbalism" — the tyranny of words and phrases without discoverable referents, registering a semantic blank.[1] He talks of consciousness, but discusses the nervous system. He talks of the mind, but discusses the areas and fissures of the brain. He lectures on the emotions, but explains the endocrine glands. He analyzes the personality, and reduces it to the body. He is a professor of psychology but he teaches anatomy and physiology.

Are These Facts?

What legacy of knowledge does a student inherit from such a class? If he is reflective and philosophical, he emerges more confused than before. If he is a mental blotter, absorbent but undiscriminating and uncritical, he comes out equipped with an accumulation of dogmatic and highly dubious information concerning neurones, synapses, engrams, hormones, axones, and dendrites.

Ask him what consciousness is, or the nature of the self, or the meaning of the mind, and he is as blank as a *tabula rasa*. In fact, the so-called *facts* are all theories. If there are facts at all, they are facts concerning the body and not the mind or the psyche. They are physiological, not psychological facts.

What The Student Learns

The student learns, first of all, that psychology is not a science of the psyche or soul, as its etymology implies. It is simply a science of human behavior — how man behaves.

But what is man? Here a gigantic semantic blank registers. Modern psychology does not know exactly what man is unless it dogmatically identifies him with the body. Limited by the rigors of its methodological philosophy, it finds itself compelled either to confess almost complete ignorance of man, or to assert that man is identical essentially with his body and no more.

Some scientists have taken the first alternative. Dr. Alexis Carrel is quite frank in his admission that man's ignorance of himself is profound. He states, "We do not apprehend man as a whole. We know him as composed of distinct parts. And even these parts are created by our methods. Man, as known to the specialist, is nothing but a schema, consisting of other schemata built up by the techniques of other sciences. Each of us is made up of a procession of phantoms, in the midst of which strides an unknown reality."[2] Thus, man, according to Dr. Carrel, is the Unknown.

Others have championed the second alternative, declaring that man is purely a body, a protoplasmic machine, his mind merely an epiphenomenon or by-product of the brain, "a highly attenuated material substance surrounding the cerebrum, like the halo round the head of a saint."[3]

In truth, it can be said with a large margin of safety that the ancient riddle of the Sphinx until now is unsolved.

The proper study of mankind is still man because man is still the biggest question mark in the universe. Nor has modern psychology, with all its scientific instruments and appliances, explained the true nature of man's psychological functions, his consciousness, his memory, his perception. How we see is as miraculous as how we hold a piece of stone. And it is as difficult for psychology to explain the former as it is for physics to explain the latter. Both are, from the standpoint of scientific erudition, as mysterious as the mystery of the Holy Trinity.

Just the same, the student learns dogmatically enough that he sees with his eyes, hears with his ears, smells with his nose, tastes with his tongue and thinks with his brain! Consequently, he cannot see without his eyes, hear without his ears, smell without his nose, taste without his tongue, nor think without his brain. Thus, the student learns to regard his body as himself and the brain as his mind.

Science Abolishes The Soul

The abolition of the soul concept from scientific psychology was not a sudden eradication. It was rather a gradual retrogression.

First, the soul with all its religious, moral and metaphysical implications was accepted as reality. Psychology, as its name indicates, began as the science of the soul. Psychologists, however, began doubting the scientific validity of the soul because they resented its philosophical associations. They jettisoned it and put in its place the term *mind*. Psychology became the science of the mind. But even mind was not good enough. It was as abstract and nebulous as the soul. They got rid of this and took the word *consciousness*. Psychology became the science of consciousness.

But what are we conscious of at any given moment? The structuralists came in and introduced the concept of mental states. We are, according to them, conscious only of mental states. Psychology became the science of mental states. But are there really mental states? Are there not only mental functions? The functional psychologists redefined psychology and called it the science of mental functions.

Entered Watson and his behaviorists. Mental functions, they said, are not directly observable. They are subjective. They can be reached only by introspection. And introspection is not scientific. In fact, all we can observe is behavior, the overt behavior of the organism interacting with its environment. Beyond this, we can only surmise, speculate. We cannot be scientific. In reducing psychology to the science of behavior Watson has also reduced it to physiology and anatomy.

There have been strong reactions against the limited and materialistic philosophy of behaviorism, such as Gestalt psychology, hormonic psychology, and psychoanalysis. In the main, however, modern psychology has become what Watson wanted it to be — observational, nonintrospective, mensurable, statistical, physiological, anatomical, but certainly not psychological.

The Watsonian attitude is similar to that of the materialistic scientist who, in order to find out what made Goethe's novel *Werther* cause an epidemic of suicides, begins to study its first edition according to the method of exact, positive science. He weighs the book, measures it by the most precise instruments, notes the number of its pages, makes a chemical analysis of the paper, the number of letters, and even how many times the letter *A* is repeated, how many times the letter *B*, and how many times the interrogation mark, the period, the comma are used and so on. Now, on the basis of his very careful investigations, he writes an erudite treatise on the relationship of the letter *A* of the German *alaphabet* to suicide.[4]

Behaviorism is effective in the study of animal psychology because animals are not self-analytic. Their minds are inaccessible. Only their overt behavior can be observed. But this is certainly not adequate in the study of human psychology.

It is lamentable to discover that in spite of the emergence of other schools of psychological thought, behaviorism is still the dominant psychological philosophy of the century.

From soul-psychology to behaviorism — that was the retrogression, the devolution, the materialization of the sci-

ence of psychology:
  The science of the soul.
  The science of the mind.
  The science of consciousness.
  The science of mental states.
  The science of mental functions.
  The science of behavior.
  The science of the body.

When psychology discovered the body, it immediately abolished the soul.

C.G. Jung and the depth psychologists may have begun to reverse this trend, but academic psychology still clings to the physical interpretation, and so perpetuates a soul-science without a soul.

I Use The Word Soul

Hence, I use the word *soul* deliberately, intentionally, and purposely.

I use it, because to me the soul is no less real than any so-called scientific fact, like the revolution of the earth or the existence of the electrons.

I use it, because to permit the continuance of its banishment from the field of science is to perpetuate the tyranny of a method that cannot soar above the limitations of inert matter and the illusions of the sense organs.

I use it, because a psychology without a soul completely deprives man of the true basis of the moral life.

I use it, because under different names, like old wine in new bottles, the soul-concept is coming into its own.

Names By Which The Soul Has Been Called

McDougall, the dynamic psychologist, employs the word *soul*. The Gestaltists call it "total configuration." Frederick Myers calls it "subliminal consciousness." P.D. Ouspensky employs the term "fourth dimensional consciousness." Dr. R.M. Bucke and Edward Carpenter name it "cosmic consciousness." The Freudians call it the ego, sometimes the "subconscious."

Why I Use the Word Soul

In the East where the psychology of the soul has never lost its charms for either the scientist or the philosopher, the soul is called by various names. The Vedantist calls it *Atman,* and identifies it with Divine Essence or Brahman. The Sankhya names it *Purusha.* The Jaina gives it the name *Jiva.*

But by whatever name it may pass, the soul is regarded in the East as a unitary and multi-dimensional consciousness which uses the body as a vehicle or instrument of manifestation in the physical universe. It is distinct from the body. It relinquishes the body at death. But even before death, it may, if it wants, emancipate itself from the limitations of the body by the practice of yoga. The soul is the "I Am," the man himself; the body is only his garment.

None of the terminologies mentioned gives the full meaning of the word *soul.* Each of them emphasizes one aspect, but none has the richness, the comprehensiveness, the completeness of the ancient word *soul* or *psyche.*

That is why I use the word *soul.*

References

[1] Stuart Chase, *The Tyranny of Words* (New York: Harcourt, Brace and Co., 1938), p. 21.

[2] Alexis Carrel, *Man the Unknown* (New York: Harper and Brothers, 1939) pp. 3-4.

[3] C. M. Joad, *Introduction to Modern Philosophy* (Oxford: Clarendon Press, 1958) p. 90.

[4] P. D. Ouspensky, *Tertium Organum, The Third Cannon of Thought, A key to the Enigmas of the World,* translated from the Russian by Nicholas Bessaraboff and Claude Bragdon. Third American Edition, (New York: Alfred A. Knoff, 1945) p. 128.

Chapter 2

THE LEGITIMACY OF THE SOUL-PROBLEM

The Soul-Problem Is Intrinsically Human

The problem of the soul, in all its various aspects, is a legitimate problem of man. As such, it is a primary problem of science. It arose almost simultaneously with the birth of man's mind. Up to the present time its importance has not appreciably diminished.

The problem is intrinsically human. It is inextricably interwoven with everything that is truly human in man:

His desire for truth.
His search for God.
His fear of death.
His yearning for immortality.
His hope for salvation.
His vision of perfection.

All questions concerning God, death, survival, immortality, salvation, morality, perfection, origin and destiny, education, knowledge and values will probably remain unanswered until the more fundamental question "What is Man?" is answered first. If the answer is "Man is the Body — a physical being," then a materialistic civilization will result. If, on the other hand, the answer is "Man is the Soul — a spiritual being," then a different civilization will develop.

For the individual man, as for humanity as a whole, the problem is so basic in its significance and so far-reaching in its implications that it becomes our duty to face it and to try to solve it as best we can.

The Soul-Problem Is Empirical

The soul-problem is not academically spurious. It is a legitimate problem of human existence. It developed not from the dialectical exigencies of classroom discussion, but from the sweat and blood of man's daily living. Its practical importance is as salty as tears and as vital as protoplasm. It underlies man's thinking and feeling and acting.

Somehow, in one way or the other, man lives according to the body or according to the spirit. In the language of philosophy, he is either materialistic or idealistic. The man who thinks he is the body and perceives no reality beyond the bounds of the flesh will have a philosophy of life peculiar to his own beliefs. His moral criteria, his religious standards, his norms of daily living will differ markedly from those of the man whose perception enables him to see beyond the veil of flesh that constitutes his body.

This distinction holds true not only for individual men but also for groups of men, for families, for nations, for whole cultures and civilizations.

The East is, for instance, fundamentally spiritual in outlook. The West, on the other hand, is largely materialistic in orientation. To the Western mind, the soul must be proved, and it must be regarded as untrue or unreal until proven true or real; the body is self-evident, incontestably true and real. The general Eastern attitude may be described as soul-oriented, while the Western attitude is body-oriented.

This does not mean that the East necessarily ignores the body or that the West necessarily repudiates the soul. It does mean, however, that generally the East regards the body as only an instrument of the soul, whereas the West regards the body as the all important reality and the soul as only an assumption that is yet to be proved as true.

The result is that to a great extent the East looks at the things of matter with the eyes of Spirit, whereas the West looks at the things of the Spirit with the eyes of matter. The further result is that the East is materially less but spiritually more advanced than the West.

In the sciences of matter, such as physics and chemistry, it may be conceded that the West is far ahead of the East.

But it cannot be denied, too, that in the spiritual and psychological sciences, the West has much to learn from the East.

In the science of psychology alone, there are depths and heights in the Eastern "science of the soul" or *Atma-Vidya* (*atma*, spirit, *vidya*, knowledge) that the European and the American psychologists are just beginning to discover. The vastly important question, of course, is what humanity should try to achieve. Should it be a spiritually advanced civilization like that of the East, or a materially advanced civilization like that of the West? Or should we have a happy and well-balanced integration of the two? The answer is not easy. But whatever be humanity's choice for its future, it must be conditioned by the answer to the problem of the soul, the question Job asked Jehovah but which Jehovah did not answer: "What is man?"

The Soul-Problem Is Fundamental

The soul-problem is a fundamental problem, because it underlies many other problems:
1. The problem of religion.
2. The problem of morality.
3. The problem of education.
4. The problem of death and immortality.

These are general, basic problems. The theoretical and practical details they involve are multifarious.

The Problem Of Religion

Religion is one of the primary aspects of civilization. It is almost instinctive in man. Before man was a philosopher or a scientist, he was first a worshipper. In other words, before he was a thinker or an experimenter, he was first a believer. He believed in a spiritual order of reality which he regarded sometimes monistically, sometimes dualistically, and at other times, pluralistically.

Whatever else religion may be, it is above all a spiritual concern. It is, said Schleiermacher, "the feeling of absolute dependence upon the unseen determiner of our destiny,

The Legitimacy of the Soul-Problem 11

accompanied by the conscious desire to come into harmonious relations with it." It is, said Matthew Arnold, "the belief in a power not ourselves which moves to righteousness, together with the conscious desire to enter into friendly relations with it." It is, said Emerson, "communion with the Over-soul; the divinity within us reaching up to the Divinity above."

All religions, living and dead, teach the existence of the soul, the spiritual substratum of man, of which the body is only a temporary physical manifestation. Furthermore, the soul is generally regarded as one in essence with the Divine.

The following list gives the terminologies for soul, or what is possibly equivalent for soul, in some of the different religions and religious sects of the world:

1. Hinduism: *purusha; jiva; atma; manas; jivatma; aham*
2. Buddhism: *nirmanakaya; skandhas*
3. Yoga: *vijnanamayakosha; anandamayakosha*
4. Raja Yoga: *karana-sharira*
5. Judaism: *ruah, neshamah;* heavenly man (Zohar)
6. Islam: *ruh; nafs-i-natica*
7. Jainism: *karana-sharira*
8. Christianity: soul, spirit
9. Sufi: *tabiyat-i-kul; nafs-i-kul*
10. Zoroastrianism: *farohars, fravashis; ahmi*
11. Taoism: Tao; *lin won*
12. Confucianism: Tao; *lin won*
13. Shinto: *Kan-nagara* (Inazo Nitobe)
14. Primitive religions: *tanaora* (Poso-Alfures of Celebes); *idhlozi* (Zulus of Africa); *itongo* (Berbers)
15. Extinct religion: *Ka* or *Ra; Ba* (Egyptian Book of the Dead)
16. Tagalog (Christian): *Kaluluwa*

The Tagalog word for soul, *kaluluwa* is striking. Its first syllable is exactly the word for soul, "ka," and its last three syllables, "luluwa," constitute the Hebrew word for "all beautiful." Literally, the term *kaluluwa* means, therefore, "all beautiful soul."

The preceding list of terms to designate the concept of the soul is highly significant in that it shows the persistence, the universality, and the deep-rootedness of mankind's belief in the existence of the soul.

When orthodox science abolished the soul-concept from psychology, it accomplished two things both undesirable: it struck at one of humanity's most vital beliefs, religion; and it has arbitrarily and unnecessarily widened the gulf between religion and science.

There can be no humanity without religion. But there can be no religion without the soul. How shall it be, then? Shall it be religion without science? Or science without religion? Religion is primarily a belief in a spiritual order. Science is *par excellence* a procedure, a method.

Is there no way, then, of proving scientifically the reality of the spiritual order that constitutes the essence of religion? If this could be done, it would be possible for religion and science to join hands.

The possibility may be found in the field of psychology. It can be shown by strict scientific procedure that the soul is a psychological reality. In other words, it can be shown that psychology is really the "science of the soul."

The Moral Problem

The relation between ethics and psychology is very close. Moral conduct springs from the instincts, the needs, the desires, the emotions, and the intelligence of man. It is true that there can be no ethics without psychology, because there can be no moral nature without human nature. It is equally true, therefore, that psychology which arbitrarily ignores the spiritual nature of man cannot provide foundations for true ethics.

A system of ethics based on physiology is, at best, only extreme sensationalism such as Hobbes' materialism and opportunism. At its worst, it eradicates the very essence of the moral life — the moral consciousness itself. The body can be neither good nor bad. It is simply animal, with no moral significance.

Morality involves personality, choice, will, the consciousness of right and wrong, the sense of moral obligation or

The Legitimacy of the Soul-Problem

duty, conscience. The body has no conscience, no sense of moral obligation, no consciousness of right and wrong. It has only irritability, motility, reproductivity and the other properties of protoplasm. True ethics cannot grow on purely physical soil. The body cannot give birth to the moral imperative. On the contrary, since it is protoplasmic, it must be motivated by the elemental protoplasmic urges which are essentially selfish, acquisitive, and centripetal.

Ethics is based on several necessary assumptions. These necessary assumptions are technically called postulates in science. Among the important ethical postulates are:

1. The postulate of individuality — that man is a real personality capable of self-determination and choice.

2. The postulate of freedom — that man is a free-willing personality who can be held responsible for all his actions. This is known sometimes as the doctrine of free will.

These two postulates of ethics, without which the science of morality is not possible, are inexplicable on the basis of body-psychology.

In the first place, body-psychology is incompatible with the reality of the human personality. It can logically accept only the mechanistic concept of man according to which man is a machine and all his activities are functions of atoms interacting blindly in a physicochemical way. This nullifies completely the first moral postulate.

In the second place, body-psychology is completely irreconcilable with the concept of free will. If man is not a personality capable of spontaneous acts of choice, if he is nothing but a machine operating according to the laws of physics and chemistry, then none of his actions are free, all are predetermined according to the fixed laws of "atoms moving in empty space." As such, man cannot be held accountable for his actions. He is no better than a billiard ball which moves blindly by external propulsion. This doctrine is known as determinism and it is the only doctrine with which body-psychology is compatible. And determinism destroys the second moral postulate.

To accept body-psychology, therefore, is to deny the moral life and to deny the moral life is to reduce man to an animal. There is hardly anything more alarming to the welfare of society than this reduction of man to a cunning but completely unscrupulous and irresponsible beast!

The Educational Problem

The danger is particularly alarming in the field of education. Education is psychology in action. And if our schools produce cunning but unscrupulous men and women whose thinking and living are motivated solely by selfish ends, we can hardly blame the educator at all. We should, rather, blame the psychologist who lays the foundations for all educational philosophies. He should be able to explain what the human mind really is and how it works with the brain; what thought is and how it is produced; what instinct is and how it may be properly polarized; what emotions are and how they may be harmoniously integrated.

But he has no certain knowledge concerning the mind. He has not even a "theory." *He has,* Dr. J.B. Rhine, formerly of Duke University, says, *only beliefs and nothing more,* and his beliefs are frighteningly materialistic.

His psychology is body-psychology; man is entirely physical in nature; the mind is an epiphenomenon or a halo of cerebration; thinking is a function of cerebral physics, and the emotions are only glandular secretions.

What kind of educational philosophy can be built upon such foundations? Only a materialistic, cerebrocentric, sense-bound, sense-fulfilling, stomach-oriented, protoplasmic, hunger- and sex-satisfying philosophy.

Thus, because the psychologist is confused, the educator also is confused. And because the educator is confused, the students are confused. Now, because education, in general, is confused, civilization is confused.

We do not know what we are educating. We are not sure what to study or what to teach. We do not know what we are looking for. We do not know exactly what we want.

At a conference of the Association of Private Universities held in Manila a few years ago, some of the country's leading educators met to establish a philosophy of education based on moral rehabilitation. Character education, they declared, is what we need.

The Legitimacy of the Soul-Problem 15

One of the prominent psychologists of the country was asked to discuss the psychological basis of moral education. Personality, he said, is the pivot of all educational aims and procedures. But what is personality? Well, he talked of emotions, glands, clothes, intelligence, possessions and other things. But what is the substratum of personality? He was clear and precise: *Body*. His point of view was clearly representative of the brain-centered, conservative, official psychology of the present century.

That the body is the substratum of personality was the most ridiculous assertion in the conference. But nobody seemed to have noticed it. Or if anyone did notice, he was indifferent; or he was afraid to contradict the prominent psychologist. The assertion was allowed to pass unquestioned.

Here now is the question: Can the body be made moral, that is, good in the ethical sense? Can the body be morally educated? Is there such a thing as the moral education of the body?

Dr. J. B. Rhine, who conducted extensive experiments in extrasensory perception during his tenure in the Psychology Department of Duke University in North Carolina, made one very apt and true observation that should make psychologists revamp their attitude. He said:

> Our social institutions are founded on the mind-centered or psychocentric view of man. Present-day psychology on the other hand is largely cerebrocentric, with its focus on the dynamics of the brain. And the schism between these two concepts is deep and radical. Our culture assumes, for instance, that the mind is sufficiently different from the physical body to allow for free will. . . . The physicalistic view of personality, on the other hand, makes every act subject to physical law and leaves no room at all for freedom.[1]

It is important for us, therefore, to determine which is true: the cerebrocentric or the psychocentric view of man?

If the first is true, it is useless to talk of character and moral education. They simply cannot be. Without free will, there can be no morality, no real democracy, not even scientific research.

If on the other hand, the second is true, then moral improvement is possible and character education as an educational aim becomes imperative.

The time has come for psychologists to work, study, and decide on this issue.

The Problem Of Death And Immortality

The desire for immortality springs ever anew in the heart of man, but the cold fact of death is a brutal reminder that protoplasmic life is only a temporary earthly sojourn.

Modern psychology, with its dogmatic and arbitrary materialism, completely ignores the problem of death and immortality, because it understands clearly enough its inability to solve it. This inability arises from the fact that its method precludes right from the start the recognition that man is a personality distinct from his perishable physical body. In other words, it is not quite possible to solve the problem of death and immortality unless the problem of the soul is solved first.

In ignoring these problems, modern psychology seems to have become somewhat unmindful of man's legitimate and practical needs. Both are legitimate. Both are practical. Psychology that deliberately confines itself to scientific academism is useless, or is destined to become useless.

Psychology has a responsibility to man. It has no right to repudiate any problem concerning human life and personality just because it is difficult to solve or cannot be solved by the orthodox methods of investigation.

It is hoped that psychologists do not forget at least two things: 1. That every legitimate problem of human life and personality is a legitimate psychological problem, and 2. That the purpose of science is the discovery of truth, not the justification of a pet theory, however beloved, or a favorite method, however well-tried. If the theory has become obsolete, it should be discarded. If the method has become inefficient, it should be superseded.

Reference
[1] J. B. Rhine, *The Reach of the Mind*, (New York: William Sloane Associates, Inc., 1947) pp. 8-9.

Chapter 3

THE URGENCY OF THE SOUL-PROBLEM

The problem of the soul is not only legitimate. It is urgent. Its urgency arises from the perplexity and confusion that physicalistic psychology has produced in society.

Every year universities graduate thousands of students who are indoctrinated with the unproved idea that mental life is purely a function of the brain and that man possesses no reality beyond the limits of his physical body.

Every day thousands of newspapers and magazines use the printed word to mold public opinion and direct the flow of human thought in accordance with the materialistic view that man is wholly and purely a physical organism belonging to class mammalia and to kingdom animalia.

The result is that men usually treat each other like animals. They live according to the Darwinian principle of struggle for existence, and they behave as if the be-all and end-all of their lives were the promotion of their protoplasmic existence.

The Art Of Social Intercourse

The fact is that we do not even know how to deal with people. The art of social intercourse either is a lost art to us or is still an undiscovered art. We distrust each other. We fear each other. We treat everyone as a potential enemy. For this reason, we bar our windows and bolt our doors.

Once in a while the mysterious emotion of love lifts the pall of fear and distrust from our hearts and we awaken into a brighter and happier realization of our true nature, but only temporarily. The pall settles down again. We reassume our imprisonments, and we are as before, selfish, fearful, distrustful, suspicious.

Expand the situation from our individual selves into the nations, into the world itself, and what do we have? Nations that fear other nations. A world afraid of its own self, a civilization that knows not what it wants and knows not where it is going. For how can men who know themselves only as their bodies build a world of mutual respect, moral responsibility, and justice? How can men who proudly trace their physical ancestry to the extinct bodies of the Mesozoic reptiles create a civilization which demands the fairest virtues of their souls? We are a terribly confused people.

Confusion In Religion

Official psychology solemnly tells us we are only bodies and all our mental life has its springs in the physical cells of our brains.

Official anthropology declares that our earliest ancestors lie buried in the rocks of the Cenozoic period, or in those of the higher Mesozoic.

Man, then, is an animal, a descendant of the dinosaurs, a nephew of the gibbons, a distant cousin of the orangutan and the gorilla. All these statements are probably quite true. Science has proofs and science is reliable.

It may be true that *our bodies* trace their physical ancestry to the extinct animals of the Cenozoic and the Mesozoic ages. It may be true that our bodies are relatives of the apes. But these are our *bodies,* not *us.* And the gross error of official science lies precisely in the dogmatic assertion that *we are our bodies* and that our total reality as human beings does not extend beyond the periphery of our protoplasmic shells. That, let us repeat, is a dogmatic assertion. Science has no proof to substantiate it, and it is an assertion that goes against the experience of mankind.

Religion teaches the spiritual nature of man.

Five thousand years of religious teachings cannot be absolutely wrong. It is quite possible to reconcile science and religion if we can show that man is both spiritual and material, a soul expressing itself through a body. This is a task for psychology, and it is a very urgent one.

The Urgency of the Soul-Problem

Confusion In Society

The confusion in society arising from man's lack of true knowledge concerning himself is even greater. Consider, for example, a number of the pressing issues that confront us today.

In the Philippines what should be our attitude toward the Japanese, the Chinese, the Moslems, the Huks? Should we give amnesty to all the Huks? How should we deal with the divorce problem, prostitution, the gangster problem, crime, unemployment, the slums, the squatter problem?

Internationally and generally, what should be our attitude toward Communism? racial minorities? the Negro problem? the Vietnam problem? the Arab-Israel problem? conquered peoples? trade competition? tariff barriers? religious intolerance? migration of peoples? miscegenation? trade unionism? feminism? birth control? the pill? sterilization of the unfit? crime? capital punishment? poverty? starvation amidst plenty? nationalism? socialism? social problems? population explosion? the H-bomb? distribution of goods? labor and capital?

We do not know just what the right answers are. There are probably as many answers as there are men, and all of them are simply opinions, mere beliefs, not based on certain knowledge.

From this welter of opinions and beliefs, the confusion develops. The confusion leads to prejudices, doubt, fear, distrust, suspicion. War becomes inevitable at the end.

It is urgent, therefore, that there must be some sort of stock-taking among ourselves. And it must start with the question of human nature itself. Without a clear and unprejudiced knowledge of ourselves, we cannot solve the multifarious problems that make our planetary life a continuous harassment of anxiety, fear, hunger, and despair. To know ourselves is to know our problems as well as their solutions. In fact, it can be said that all our problems arise from our very ignorance of ourselves — our true nature, our needs, our purposes and our goals.

Confusion In Politics

The confusion in politics, both national and international, is particularly ludicrous. For instance, is the "cold war" really a conflict between communism and democracy? How we make terms fight for us! We arm them with high sounding, passion-charged propaganda and soon enough the communists say democracy is imperialistic and the democracies denounce communism as atheistic.

Who is imperialistic? The democracies? No! It is men who are imperialistic — men who understand only one ideal: conquest and lust for power. There are imperialists in every country.

And who is atheistic? Communist nations? No! It is men who are atheistic — men who have lost their spiritual moorings. There are atheists in every country also.

In fact, both communism and democracy are essentially pro-people philosophies. Both are committed to the welfare of the people, but here is the trouble: communist countries are committed to the welfare of their own people only, and democracies to the welfare of their own people.

The whole confusion, then, is due to misunderstanding. Nations with conflicting ideologies do not know how to treat each other properly. Would it not be wiser to revamp our philosophy of human nature in order to bring about a reorientation in our philosophy of human relationships?

Everyman's Philosophy Of Human Relationships

The ordinary man looks at the world dualistically. There is the material world of which he is aware with his senses, and there is the non-material world which he dimly feels also to be real. Therefore, he behaves dualistically, He acts physically in a world of physical things and events, but at the same time he knows himself to be the nonphysical self-determining, free-willing cause of all his actions. For this reason he regards himself as responsible for all his voluntary actions. Society accepts this principle. Ethics assumes it. Law is based on it. All human relationships operate according to it.

The Urgency of the Soul-Problem

What monkey wrench of confusion has psychology thrown into this situation? The consequences are appalling. They are,
    1. In the realm of religion: atheism, left-hand existentialism, agnosticism.
    2. In the field of philosophy and science: materialism and logical positivism.
    3. In the economic and political life of man: dialectical materialism or economic determinism.
    4. In morals: egoistic hedonism.
    5. In society: pessimism and cynicism.
    6. In general: the philosophy of defeatism and confusion.
The result is unhappiness.

The Sad State Of Man

Man on earth is a very unhappy creature. It makes very little difference whether he is rich or poor, high or low, educated or uneducated. He is simply unhappy. And all the palliative attempts to cure the sickness of unhappiness, such as the movies, television, nightclubs, the cabarets, and the thousand other distractions seem to make him all the more unhappy. Why?

The reason is that he has lost his spiritual moorings and is now a sort of spiritual jetsam. The general materialism of science has confused him. Knowledge, indeed, seems to have increased, but wisdom seems to have decreased correspondingly. Detailed information is almost beyond human capacity to assimilate, but there is lack of orthogenetic direction of human thought.

We do not know where we are going, nor why, nor how to reach there. Just the same, we all seem to be in a hurry to get somewhere else. We do not know what we want, nor why nor how to get it. Just the same, we all seem terribly engrossed in trying to get it. We do not know who we are, nor why, nor how we came about. Just the same, we all seem to feel comfortably well informed about ourselves. The truth, however, is that we are not. We know more about the stars than we do about our cerebrum. We can manufacture beer, but can we make a simple drop of human blood?

Both our origin and our destiny are shrouded in profoundest darkness. We are, as it were, sandwiched between two areas of ignorance — our ignorance of our past and our ignorance of our future. And what is between is also ignorance — our ignorance of ourselves.

But this ignorance is of an insidious variety. It is not simply the *absence of knowledge* or nescience. It is the presence of a dogmatic and unproved assertion which is made to pass for true knowledge.

It is the assertion that man is the body.

Such a philosophy of human nature naturally has no room for the belief in God. It cannot but be atheistic. At best, it must be agnostic. Because it is physically oriented, it must be hedonistic and egoistic. It must sponsor the benefits of the body. It must be selfish.

Because it is egoistic and body-centered, it can be compatible with only one type of social philosophy, the materialistic philosophy of economic determinism. Economics is the supreme science. Civilization is purely the product of economic forces. Man is largely an economic animal. All his motivation and actuations proceed from his stomach and his genitals. Individually, he is hunger; racially, he is sex.

With this as his basic philosophy of life, man becomes a marauding animal. He must struggle. He must fight. And he must kill. He must fight for planetary space because his body has to occupy space. He must fight for bread, because man lives by bread alone and his life is not more than meat. He must fight for clothes, because clothes make the man and his body is not more than raiment. (Matt. 4:4; 6:25.) The earth thus becomes a bloody battleground and life itself becomes internecine warfare that begins at the cradle and ends in the grave.

Peace, brotherhood, and prosperity, therefore, become ideals completely inaccessible to man. They cannot be expected to develop from conditions that preclude them right from the start. Man must change his outlook on life. This can be done only by a proper knowledge of himself, his nature, his needs, his purposes and aims.

As Dr. Rhine puts it:

> Reflective men today must decide which is the control center of the individual's personal world — his subjective, experiencing mind, or his objective, organic brain. But only by research can it be determined which is correct, the mind-centered or *psychocentric* view of man, or the brain-centered or *cerebrocentric* conception. It cannot be settled by authority of any kind. Mere beliefs, of whatever type, are no longer sufficient for the guidance of humanity.[1]

Reference
[1] J. B. Rhine, *The Reach of the Mind,* (New York: William Sloane Associates, Inc., 1947) p. 7.

Chapter 4
STATEMENT OF AIMS AND PURPOSES

The preceding chapters show clearly that the soul-problem is important — important in its inherent legitimacy, important in its frightening urgency; it cannot be lightly brushed aside.

Science and philosophy have a serious duty to discharge, and that is, to guide human thought along channels that will enable man to know the truth, to achieve freedom, and to attain peace and happiness. This duty is particularly imperative with regard to the question of human nature.

It is disconcerting, even alarming, to know that about man, the knower, man knows nothing at all. He merely has beliefs.

This, in effect, is Alexis Carrel's lament for "man's profound ignorance of man." This, too, is Lecomte du Nouy's similar jeremiad in his thought-provoking book, *Human Destiny*.

Dr. J.B. Rhine is even more brutally frank in his book, *The Reach of the Mind,* when he says about man: ". . . . there isn't even a 'theory.' Such ignorance about the very knower himself is scarcely credible."[1]

General And Specific Purposes Of This Book

Along with other books intended to bring about a realignment of human thought with regard to the problem of man, this book is designed to help build an enlightened philosophy of human nature that will answer impartially, steadily, and it is hoped, totally, the age-old question, "What is man?"

Statement of Aims and Purposes

Specifically, however, the purpose of this book is to show both experimentally and nonexperimentally the reality of a *nonphysical element* in man by whatever name it might be called. Some call it simply *mind*. I prefer to call it *soul*. If this purpose could be realized, then the machine concept of man would be overthrown; we would be able to establish a true foundation for the social, political, economic, educational, moral, and religious life of mankind.

Specific Aims

Aside from the general and specific purposes of this book, however, there are other aims which are not necessarily minor in significance or implication. It is not possible perhaps to realize or fulfill completely all of these aims, but, it is nevertheless quite possible to point a way, or indicate a direction by which others may satisfactorily fulfill them. Each of these aims represents a need which is vital to mankind, individually and collectively. Let us consider some of the more important ones.

The Soul Problem

There is need to revive in the minds of psychologists the important question of the existence of the soul, a question that science has tried consistently to ignore as unscientific. This attitude should not be allowed to persist because it is a manifestation of "scientific dogmatism."

It is unwise and impractical to leave in the care of speculative philosophy or of dogmatic theology, a problem as highly charged with tremendous human implications as the problem of the soul. This is a problem for science, not a theme for philosophical disputation or pulpit oratory. It has a legitimate right in the laboratory. Let us not deny it that right.

Parapsychological And Metapsychical Phenomena

There is need to organize the large and almost unwieldy mass of facts of human life and mind concerning certain unusual forms of behavior which until now have not been satisfactorily explained or interpreted. These facts are primary data of human experience. As such, they are primary data for scientific investigation.

Among the most unusual available examples are the facts of yoga and mysticism and those of parapsychology (J.B. Rhine) and metapsychics (Charles Richet).

Yoga is a recognized institution in India and China. It is a philosophy, a science, and a way of life. The facts connected with it are real; but so far, Western science has found no clear way of explaining them, although it has not necessarily repudiated them, nor has it rejected the alleged yogic phenomena. On the contrary more and more books on yoga by European and American writers and practitioners are appearing regularly. One of the latest gives yoga a stamp of Catholic approval, the book of Father Dechanet entitled *Christian Yoga.*

Perhaps, if and when official psychology accepts the existence of a non-physical principle in man, it will be possible for the Western mind to understand the startling phenomena connected with Eastern yoga, such as mass hypnosis, the voluntary control of all metabolic processes, levitation, and many other things.

Mysticism is the Western equivalent of Eastern yoga. The difference, however, is that in the West mysticism is usually regarded as a vague and uncontrolled process, while in the East, yoga is a highly developed science and art. Just the same, mystical phenomena among the Western mystics such as those of St. Theresa, Swedenborg, Boehme, and others parallel those of the *yogis* in India.

The facts of parapsychology and psychical research are many and they are very interesting. Telepathy, clairvoyance, psychometry, traveling clairvoyance, somnambulism, somniloquism, prophetic dreams, and other phenomena are facts. But how can they be explained? How do they happen? What are the *modus vivendi,* the *modus operandi?*

Salvaging Psychology

There is need to salvage modern psychology.

The history of psychology has been a continuous process of materialization. This is due to the fallacious attempts

Statement of Aims and Purposes

of psychologists to explain the multitudinous and highly complex phenomena of life and mind by means of a few concepts found useful in the physical and chemical sciences. The error consists in the unwarranted importation into these concepts of meanings they do not have in their respective spheres.

Physical and chemical concepts are intended to explain and unify the facts of the physical universe. To use them in explaining the phenomena of life and mind is to reduce psychology to a physical science which gives ontological priority to the body in the interpretation of psychological phenomena.

This is exactly what is happening now. Modern psychology is completely cerebrocentric. To be sure there are some psychologists who have reacted against this attitude. Their voices, however, are lost in the wilderness.

A typical modern psychologist of the physicalistic school told me one day that as a Christian he believes in the existence of the soul, but that as a psychologist it is not his business to talk about it. It is "unscientific," according to him, to have anything to do with it.

Here then is a good representative case of a scientist who apparently *believes* in something he regards as *unscientific* and therefore, *false*. He has divided life into the scientific and unscientific. By scientific he means conformity to the dogma of science and, by unscientific, non-conformity. To him the soul is something unscientific because it does not lend itself to test-tube analysis or to the blood-precipitin test. Nevertheless, he confesses frankly enough that he believes in it.

Is it not the duty of science to prove the truth or falsity of any belief? Without benefit of proof, however, psychology has already rejected the problem of the soul.

There is, according to Dr. J.B. Rhine, "antipathy among psychologists for any claim that suggested the presence of a nonphysical factor in man... One can only conclude that Science, too, can be functionally blind when it would shock her complacency to see. Science can be *very* human."[2]

In fact, psychologists have been trying hard to get the mind "explained" by integrating psychical processes with physical ones. But this could be done only if perception were limited to the physical sense organs. The soul, or whatever one might call the nonphysical factor in man, has no place in the dynamics of the nervous system. It does not fit into the physical picture of the universe. "It is intolerable to the ways of thinking that had now become orthodox."[3]

Therefore the soul had to go. But in rejecting the soul or nonphysical element in man, psychology has also rejected all religion, all morality, all spirituality. It has reduced itself to pure physiology that still parades as the "science of the soul."

Psychology, the science of sciences because it is supposed to study that which studies all the other sciences, has become completely materialistic.

Eastern And Western Psychology

There is need to awaken interest among Western psychologists in the highly spiritual but no less highly scientific psychology of the East with the hope of bringing about a rapprochement between Eastern and Western cultures.

Eastern psychology is very old and well developed. It constitutes the basis or substratum of all systems of Eastern philosophy and religion. *It differs from Western psychology in that it has always been the "science of the soul" or Atma-Vidya.* It is precisely for this reason that it has studied levels of consciousness still completely unknown to Western psychology.

Western psychology studies largely the waking consciousness of man. This is known as *jagrat* in India. It is only lately that *depth psychology,* or *level psychology* or *holistic psychology* has developed in Europe and America.

The Eastern psychologists talk of consciousness, subliminal consciousness (subconsciousness), and supraliminal consciousness (supraconsciousness). T. Subba Row, in his book *Esoteric Writings,* gives the following list of the different levels of consciousness known in *Atma-Vidya*:

I. Jagrat   Jagrat of Jagrat — Waking Consciousness
                   Svapna of Jagrat — Dreaming
                   Sushupti of Jagrat — Dreamless Sleep

II. Svapna	Jagrat of Svapna — Waking Clairvoyance
Svapna of Svapna — Somnambulic Clairvoyance
Sushupti of Svapna — Fourth Dimensional Clairvoyance (Kamaloka)
III. Sushupti	Jagrat of Sushupti — Devachan
Svapna of Sushupti — Between Planets
Sushupti of Sushupti — Between Universes
IV. Turiya	Cosmic or Total Consciousness.

These terms would hardly mean anything to a Western psychologist. But if he had witnessed the pragmatic manifestations of Eastern psychology among the yogis of the East, he would agree with Shakespeare that "there are more things in heaven and earth than are dreamt of" in Western psychology.

Science And Religion

There is urgent need to bring about reconciliation between science and religion, and thus to eradicate the conflicts that rage in the hearts and minds of men regarding questions of morality, education, social relationships, government, God, soul, death and immortality.

This task of bridge-building can be begun with psychology which, after all, is a sort of link between the physical sciences, such as physics and chemistry, and such nonphysical sciences as religion, ethics, and politics.

If the physical and nonphysical sciences are not reconciled, man will always find himself in a sort of emotional and intellectual riptide that may ultimately destroy him and his civilization.

Physics and chemistry give us a mechanical interpretation of man and his behavior. Man is a machine. All his actions are simply blind manifestations of physiochemical laws that operate without will or morality. Intelligence is only an epiphenomenon of the brain. Personality is only a term. It has no reality.

The nonphysical sciences, however, regard man as a personality capable of free will, free choice, and self-determination.

Which interpretation should man follow? The choice is not easy. The consequences are cataclysmic in significance. Here, then, lies the great and grave task of psychology.

Man demands an answer, and time is pressing. Already we have seen what the intellect of man has done in Hiroshima, in Nagasaki, in Bikini.

If that intelligence is not guided by morality, by spiritual wisdom, what will it do to itself and to the civilization it has gradually and painfully developed through the years? What is your answer, Psychology?

References
[1] J. B. Rhine, *The Reach of the Mind,* (New York: William Sloane Associates, Inc., 1947) p. 3.
[2] *Ibid.,* pp. 24-25.
[3] *Ibid.,* p. 25.

Chapter 5

HUMANIZING THE *HOMO SAPIENS*

The Dehumanizing Of Man

In an urgent plea for sanity, Lewis C. Mumford writes, "Not the Power Man, not the Profit Man; not the Mechanical Man, but the Whole Man, Man in Person, so to say, must be the central actor in the new drama of civilization."[1]

No message, ever written or spoken, seems to be more appropriate, more timely, more appealing and urgent than this. The past three centuries, closely allied and identified, as it were, with the advances and progress made in industry, in the sciences, and in automation, have witnessed and left in their wake a broken, shattered, and dehumanized image of *Homo sapiens*.

Economically, the Economic Man has emerged, conquering the wilderness, increasing production, scouring the market-place, raising the standard of living, and building sky-scrapers and cities.

Politically, the strong man, the Power Man has come out more boldly than ever, conquering small nations, strengthening governments, tightening sovereign control over both man and nations, now exploring and conquering outer space.

Psychologically, out of the science of behaviorism and inspired by the excrescences of industrialization and automation, has emerged the Mechanical Man, devoid of feeling, and emotion, but skillfully, automatically and artistically contrived — working, thinking, computing, with clock-like precision, or so it seems.

Man, poor man, despite all the affluence, the excitement, the rigors of a life mathematically computed and scientifically planned, has emerged hapless, confused, unhappy, lonely, and more desolate than ever before. He has ceased to be humanly interesting. He has become alienated from himself. He has even become his most dangerous enemy.

How account for this brazen incongruity? The scientific cosmology created by Newton, Galileo, and Pascal during the past centuries has permeated and revolutionized all areas and modes of life, thinking and activity.

The dictum of the century was: Only the experimentable, quantifiable, and mensurable by the methods and techniques of science were considered real. All other experiences — perceptual, affective, qualitative, subjective, and personal — were, in effect, considered unreal, untrue, nonexistent.

Thus, did the world of physics, chemistry, and mathematics, home of these great minds, lord it mightily over the other areas of intellectual pursuits.

The fascination attached to forms and numbers, atoms and molecules, energy and life, has resulted in the unraveling, to all and sundry, of the once hitherto unknown mysteries and complexities of the physical universe, of the human organism.

Magnet-like, the physical and natural sciences attracted men from all areas and fields of endeavor: philosophers, artists, writers, humanists, economists, politicians, and social scientists.

From these fields and through these great minds emerged the despiritualization of man.

Hobbes mechanized philosophy and to him, through gray-colored lenses, man became an artificial animal:

> For seeing life is but a motion of limbs, the beginning whereof is in some principal part within; why may we not say, that all *automata* (engines that move themselves by springs and wheels as doth a watch) have an artificial life? For what is the heart, but a spring; and the nerves, but so many strings; and the joints, but so many wheels, giving motion to the whole body, such as was intended by the artificer.[2]

Or Descartes who, following a reflective dream, wrote his famous treatise, *Discourse on Method,* wherein was projected nothing less than the Science of Sciences — the Universal mechanism underlying and illuminating all reality. To Descartes, space or extension became the fundamental reality, motion the point of all departure, and mathematics the language of its revelation.[3]

Humanizing the Homo Sapiens

Nor was the French political writer, Voltaire, spared. He took up the interpretation of Newtonian cosmology in his *English Letters* and *Elements of Newtonian Philosophy*. Rousseau, another French political writer, philosopher, and educator, is said to have composed a tract on the laws of chemistry. Diderot wrote on the elements of physiology, and Montesquieu's early work was involved with physical and physiological problems.[4]

But the greatest bane of all was the involvement of psychology — conservatively defined as the study of the soul and more popularly known today as the science of human behavior — in the thick of Newtonian and Galilean cosmology, in the intricacies of scientific and laboratory measurement and experimentation.

Thus was born Watson's school of behaviorism and the classic statement, "Give me the baby and my world to bring it up in and I'll make it climb and use its hands in constructing buildings of stone or wood; I'll make it a thief, a gunman, or a dope fiend. The possibility of shaping in any direction is almost endless."

Is it any wonder, then, that modern man is mechanical, restless, irrational, unhappy; that he has become humanly uninteresting, has alienated himself from himself, has even arisen as his most dangerous enemy; that in the words of Hobbes, he has become solitary, poor, nasty, brutish, and short?

Without being unnecessarily optimistic, we must insist that man's nature and condition are not at all hopeless. The understanding of man starts with man himself. Let us look at him other than as a packet of atoms and molecules, a quantifiable amount of energy, a bundle of nerves and adapting mechanism, a structure of bones and muscles. Let us stop looking at him as merely a body. Let us explore the innermost recesses of his heart, his feelings and emotions, his capacities for love, his will and inner freedom, his mind, his values and potentialities. Let us look for that spark of divinity in him and his capacity for transcendence. Let us look at man from the other side of the coin. Let us look at him as a spiritual creature, a soul, a true human being.

The Need For Psychological Reorientation

Man stands at the crossroads, indecisive and uncertain. Shall it be further mechanization, damnation, or salvation? Time is of the essence. And that time is now. For each of us, and for all fields concerned with the study of the nature and condition of man, the moment of truth and renewal has come.

People in all fields of endeavor, without any exception, should rise up in arms against the Goliath that has swallowed up and demeaned the pride, the dignity and the stature of man.

Fortunately and most opportunely, psychology is slowly awakening from the state of lethargy and somnolence in which it has been in the past century. It has slowly caught up with this challenge and, with renewed affirmation in the worth of the individual, is now undergoing a rebirth with the emerging trend toward a more humanistic psychology.

Also known as the "third force" between behaviorism and psychoanalysis, this new orientation attempts to examine critically the theories, assumptions, and methodologies employed in the study of man; from here a theory and a method capable of fully explaining the unity of the human personality as well as the primacy of the self and its inner desires and strivings have begun to emerge.

The first edition of this book published twenty-one years ago, was in a sense almost a prophecy of the present humanistic attempt to examine, analyze, and synthesize that which the "third force" is trying to do now. Essentially and unquestionably humanistic in approach and orientation, it has endeavored to study man from the truly psychological standpoint. It has analyzed the scientific method and the theory of probability, and through much scientific evidence has painstakingly illustrated what to many scientists is a controversial and touchy subject — the existence of the soul.

For a complete understanding of man, the corpocentric theory alone does not hold. Neither could the human personality be explained by the quantum assumptions of science alone. Necessarily then, a critical re-examination of the content and issues of psychology is imperative.

It is now admissible that a reliance upon science and the scientific method will not do. Enclosed in its ivory tower and further restrained by its rigid methods and standards, science in the study of man cannot consider him only as being in and part of the material world; neither can it give full justice to the richness, the breadth and the fullness of his experience. For if it were so, there would be no controversy, no quarrel between science and the humanities, no "third force" or humanistic attempt to bridge the gap that has remained unbridged and unsettled in these past centuries.

Up to the present, the sciences have sought only limited answers to limited and isolated problems. They have stuck to objectivism, shied away from the obscure and undecipherable world of subjective experiences, and in so doing, have denied and neglected the greater and more wonderful aspect of man's existence — his emotion, his spirituality, his very humanity.

The operations of the mind, just like the affective components of man, his desire for freedom and transcendence, while not subject to measurement and scientific analysis, are no less real than the workings of his heart, his liver, his hands.

How does one propose to bridge the gap? What is the proper study of man? What does it involve?

Again, the proper study of man must start with man himself. This is a moment of renewal, of reorientation, of awakening. The change must start in the minds and hearts of men of all walks of life, in all fields of endeavor. If I may use the terminology of C. J. Jung, the approach is a "wholesouled" encounter, the understanding of the individual in the totality and wholeness of his being. Because psychology's primary mission is the understanding of man, his wholeness and uniqueness, a return to the study of man is therefore inevitable.

By entering into the inner sanctum of the individual, his private intentions and needs, his desires and longings, his values and his dreams, psychology can no longer regard him as a means or an experimental datum, but as an end: the subject and not the object; the whole man, not the part man; the human man, not the structural man.

Through cumulative evidence from psychobiology, perception, psychoanalysis, psychotherapy, and existential psychology, the groundwork for a new and reconstructive science of human behavior — an alternative to "behavioral science" — is now emerging. The main outlines of that science are now identifiable.[5]

It will be a science whose guiding purpose is not the measurement of organic mechanisms or the manipulation of conditioned responses but the understanding of personal experience in its complementary wholeness: a science which, in Riezler's words, begins with "respect for the subject-matter"—and ends in vindication of that respect.

It will be a science activated, not by a rage for order, but by a passion for freedom.

It will be a science which regards men as actors as well as spectators, and accordingly perceives its own task as one primarily of participation (intersubjectivity) and only secondarily of observation (objectivity). In short, it will recognize with Tillich that "detachment" is only one element within the embracing act of cognitive participation.[6]

It will be a science which, in seeking to comprehend human nature and conduct, takes men's reasons and reasoning into account as seriously as it does nature's causes; one that makes of its inquiry into truth and understanding a reasonable dialogue, in which the other partner (the observed) has an equal right to be heard and even to be trusted—not because this is a generous thing to do, but because it is indispensable to the inquiry. For the inquiry of this humane science will be predicated on the outrageous hypothesis, as proposed by the author of *The Organization Man,* "that people often do what they do for the reasons they think they do."

The constructive science of behavior will dare to look upon all men as moral agents, and upon their behavior as the expression of a choice—in agreement with Sartre that "this decision is human, and I shall carry the entire responsibility for it."[7]

And it will agree with Socrates, in his final words to his scientific friends, that even in the last extremity the mind of man has reasons that his organic machinery knows not of:

> For, by the Dog! these bones and sinews, I think, would have been somewhere near Megara and Boeotia long ago, carried there by an opinion of what is best, if I had not believed it better and more just to submit to any sentence which my city gives than to take to my heels and run. But to call such things causes is strange indeed. If one should say that unless I had such things, bones and sinews and all the rest I have, I should not have been able to do what I thought best, that would be true; but to say that these, and not my choice of the best, are the causes of my doing what I do . . . would be a very far-fetched and slovenly way of speaking.[8]

When all of these things shall have come to pass, we shall have restored to man his dignity, his worth, his individuality, his spirit, his all.

We shall have differentiated him from all other creatures. We shall have recognized in him God's greatest gift — a divine personality, possible only if we look at him not only as a physical entity, a functioning body, but as a soul.

In all this new approach to the problem of man's existence, which is now called Humanistic Psychology, we see principally a rediscovery of one of the greatest intuitions of past civilization, the very core of the human person, the reality, actuality, and factuality of the nonphysical element or factor in man, the existence of the human soul.

References

[1] Floyd W. Matson, *The Broken Image,* New York: George Braziller, 1964, (inside cover flap).

[2] Thomas Hobbes, *Leviathan* in *The English Philosophers from Bacon to Mill,* Edwin A. Burtt (Editor) New York: The Modern Library, 1939, p. 129.

[3] Matson, *op. cit.,* p. 22.

[4] Augusto Pi Suner, *The Bridge of Life.* New York: The Macmillan Company, 1951, pp. 171-172.

[5] Matson, *op. cit.,* pp. 241-242.

[6] Paul Tillich, *The Courage to Be.* New Haven: Yale University Press, 1959, p. 124.

[7] Jean-Paul Sartre, *Existentialism and Human Emotions.* New York: Wisdom Library, 1957, p. 53.

[8] Plato, *Phaedo,* in *Great Dialogues of Plato.* New York: Mentor Books, 1956.

Chapter 6

THE NATURE OF THE SCIENTIFIC METHOD

Why Science Rejected The Soul

In truth and in fact, in the choice of what should be studied and what should be regarded as fact in the field of psychological phenomena, scientists have proceeded arbitrarily due to the inordinate predilection for a method which divides the world into the observable and nonobservable, the experimentable and the nonexperimentable, the quantitative and the qualitative. They declared dogmatically that only the former in each pair of alternatives is real, while all else is unreal.

The result of this excessive love for the analytical methods of science has been the elimination from the field of psychological investigation of all data not susceptible to scientific observation, experimentation and measurement, a method obviously fallacious. If this were true, the world of microorganisms would never have existed until the invention of the microscope. In other words, the microscope created the world of microorganisms. If it were true, it would be only an assumption that the earth is revolving around the sun, since to attest to such a fact has been until recently beyond all possibility of human observation.

Similarly, the soul-concept is beyond human observation, scientific analysis, and experimentation. It does not seem to fit into the physical picture of the universe that science has created for itself. Hence, under this methodological imperative, the soul had to go. Science rejected it because the soul cannot be observed nor experimented upon; because it cannot be put into a test tube to discover its color and its chemical constituents: because it cannot be measured to ascertain its length, breadth and height; because it cannot be put on a scale to determine its weight in grams or in pounds. Science rejected it because it cannot be seen, smelled or heard, or touched directly. There is no scientific room at all for the soul!

In rejecting the soul, science has committed treason against humanity.

Is It True?

The rejection of the soul-concept represents an attempt by science to explain the universe and its multitudinous phenomena in terms of a completely physical hypothesis which assumes that atoms moving in empty space constitute the fundamental reality of the entire cosmos. Although complex in its innumerable details, this hypothesis is, in the main, a masterpiece of utter simplicity.

It depicts the universe as essentially a highly integrated machine which operates in blind obedience to the laws of physics and chemistry; all things in this universe — matter, life, mind, even human personality — are only manifestations of physico-chemical laws. There is no room in such a theory for free will, for choice, for moral responsibility.

This materialistic interpretation of the universe has been adopted by science as its standard of truth. But is this a true standard? By what shall we measure its correctness?

The answer of science is clear and precise: This materialistic interpretation is largely the product of the scientific method. In other words, any judgment of the interpretation is a judgment of the scientific method, because the interpretation was made necessary by the employment of that method.

The Scientific Method

The scientific method as generally employed in modern science consists of four well-recognized steps, namely:
1. *The appreciation of the problem.* The problem is the phenomenon under investigation. It is generally a fact or an occurrence which is apprehended as peculiar, that is, as not being familiar in a familiar complex situation; and since it is *unfamiliar*, there arises the need of explaining it, or connecting it with the universe of familiar facts and occurrences.
2. *The formation of a hypothesis* which will connect the unfamiliar fact or occurrence with the universe of familiar facts and occurrences.
3. *The deductive development of the hypothesis* whereby using the hypothesis as a premise, we deduce cer-

tain consequences, the truth of which we determine by appealing to the observable facts of experience.
4. *The process of verification* by observation and experimentation.

The scientific method as outlined above is both deductive and inductive. It follows a definite sequence; thus, it is deductive. But it is essentially inductive in that it is based on the Baconian process of accumulating, analyzing, and classifying facts and of drawing some general conclusions from these facts on the basis of resemblances and differences.

In other words, induction constitutes the very heart of the scientific method.

The Nature Of Induction

According to John Stuart Mill, "Induction is that operation of the mind by which we infer that what we know to be true in some particular case or cases, will be true in all cases resembling the former in certain assignable aspects. In other words, induction is the process by which we conclude that what is true of certain individuals of a class is true of the whole class, or that what is true at certain times will be true in similar circumstances at all times. Induction, as above defined, is a process of inference; it proceeds from the known to the unknown, and any process in which what seems the conclusion is no wider than the premises from which it is drawn, does not fall within the meaning of the term."[1]

From this classic definition of induction by Mill we gather the following essential characteristics of inductive reasoning:
1. The premises of inductive inference are the particular facts of experience. These facts of experience are considered *true* in the sense of being actual, objective, and real. They are not merely projected creations of the mind.
2. The conclusion of inductive inference is a generalization. It is regarded as applicable not only to the facts of experience enumerated in the premises but also to other facts which resemble the known set of facts. In other words, an inductive conclusion is always more general than any of the premises or all

of them taken together. Being more general, it is, therefore, relatively unknown. Hence, Mill regarded induction as the passage from the particular to the general, an inferential transition from the relatively known to the relatively unknown.
3. Unlike that of deduction which is only formally true, or valid, the conclusion of induction is both formally true and materially true, that is, both valid and true. It is consistent with its premises, hence, valid. It is also faithful to facts; hence, true.

Induction And Fact

The essential characteristics of induction give rise to several questions upon the answer to which depends the whole validity of the inductive method.

In the first place, what is fact? Superficially this is a very simple question. Upon closer analysis, however, we realize that it is a highly metaphysical one.

The *Dictionary of Philosophy*[2] gives some amusing definitions. For example:
1. That which simply is, as contrasted with that which is necessarily.
2. That which is actual, as contrasted with that which is merely possible.
3. That which is, regardless of its value.
4. That which is nonfictive.
5. Actual individual occurrence.
6. An indubitable truth of actuality.
7. A brute event.

Induction And Probability

The second question that arises with regard to the characteristics of induction is: How reliable is an inductive generalization?

It is a well-known fact that the truth of induction rests on the principle of probability. The reliability of an inductive generalization, therefore, depends on the reliability of this principle which is just a high-sounding name for the principle of chance. This, it appears then, is that on which the truth of induction rests.

The principle of probability or chance means simply that our knowledge of the universe is never absolutely certain. There is always the possibility that what we know might be wrong.

Let us consider, for example, the inductive generalization, "All men are mortal." Is it absolutely true that all men are mortal? Empirically, we may answer yes; scientifically, however, we have to answer no.

Strictly logically, as long as one man remains alive, by that one not *all* men are mortal. But when that last man dies, knowledge, too, dies with him.

Furthermore, the inductive statement, "All men are mortal," is really only a general conclusion drawn by analogy from individual cases of death in the past. It is absolutely true as far as those men who have died are concerned; it is only *highly* probable as far as those who are still living and those who will yet be born are concerned. In the future some men *may* be born who will not die. It is even possible that some men still living *may* not die. We can never tell. Our ignorance is profound.

In fact, we cannot even be sure, scientifically speaking, that today will be followed by tomorrow, despite the fact that in the past experience of mankind, today has always been followed by tomorrow. All that the scientific law of probability permits us to say is that the degree of probability is *very high,* since tomorrow has followed today innumerable times in the past. But tonight a planetary collision may occur, and tomorrow is forever; it will never happen to us!

Science Cannot Be Too Sure

Our analysis of the inductive method, which constitutes the heart of the scientific method, makes us realize several important things.

In the first place, we come to realize that we can neither demand nor expect absolute certainty from the inductive method. All that we can have from it is a high degree of preponderance of probability.

In the second place, we come to know that scientific conclusions, based on inductive generalizations, are always tentative. They possess no permanency of truth. They can be superseded, replaced, changed.

The realization of this fact should engender a healthy attitude of humility among scientists. They cannot be too cocksure of their assertions. They should not forget that the history of science has always been a history of discarded theories. No theory, law, nor even so-called facts are secure. As man grows, develops and improves himself, he will discover new truths, new facts that will force him to modify, time and again, his interpretation of the universe.

No one, not even science itself, with all the prestige it has earned through years of honest, careful, and patient research, can declare, "This is the final truth, this is the last word in human knowledge."

Science And The Soul

The physicalistic interpretation of the universe, therefore, which repudiates the existence of the soul, free choice, and moral responsibility, should be regarded only as a hypothesis. It cannot even be said to have a high degree of probability.

Those cerebrocentric scientists who reject the reality of a nonphysical factor in the human personality, simply because it does not conform to the requirements of an antiquated and materialistic interpretation of man, should not forget the following points:

1. That the physicalistic interpretation of the human personality is merely the product of a method that is not necessarily infallible;
2. That the scientific method is based on the principle of probability which, in turn, is based on the presumption of man's ignorance concerning the total possibility that exists in a universe still largely mysterious to us;
3. That this method, further, dogmatically assumes a criterion of knowledge which declares that only that is fact which is observable, experimentable, and measurable in accordance with what science regards as its standard of observation, experimentation and measurement;
4. That this standard is not an absolute but a changing

standard, so that as it changes, it changes also what we shall regard as fact or not fact;
5. That it is this standard, *this scale of observation which creates the phenomenon, so that every time we change the scale of observation, we encounter new phenomena;*[3]
6. That, therefore, it may be possible to prove the existence of the soul, inductively and scientifically, *provided we change our scale of observation;*
7. That this is precisely what some progressive scientists such as Dr. J.B. Rhine and his colleagues at Duke University, Dr. Pierre Janet of the Sorbonne, Edmund Curney of Cambridge University, Dr. Hans Bender of the University of Colorado, and many others, have been doing.[4] *They have changed their scale of observation from ordinary sense-perception to extrasensory perception or ESP, including both clairvoyance and telepathy.*

The result of this change of the scale of observation in the employment of the scientific method with regard to the problem of human personality is revolutionary.

Let Dr. Rhine speak:

The results suggested that the cerebrocentric idea of man was only a scientific artifact and had no true foundation.[5]

Therefore, as things stand today, extrasensory perception must admittedly transcend the laws of physics with regard to space, and hence be essentially extraphysical. Even clairvoyance .... has been demonstrated to be free of spatial dependence. ... There is more to the mind of man than physical law can encompass.[6]

References
[1] John Stuart Mill, *A System of Logic,* (London: Longmans, Green Publishing Company, 1952) p. 188.
[2] Dagobert D. Runes, *The Dictionary of Philosophy,* (New York: Philosophical Library, 1942) p. 107.
[3] Lecomet du Nouy, *Human Destiny,* (London: Longmans, Green and Company, Ltd., 1947) p. 11.
[4] J. B. Rhine, *The Reach of the Mind,* (New York: William Sloane Associates, Inc., 1947) pp. 14-15, 38, 40.
[5] *Ibid.,* p. 49.
[6] *Ibid.,* pp. 63-64.

Chapter 7
WHAT IS FACT?

Science, sponsored and championed by orthodox cerebrocentric scientists, seems quite sure that the soul is not a fact; that there is no such thing as soul, that it does not exist.

This assertion is, of course, only an assumption based largely on prejudice.

The burden of proof rests, naturally, on the shoulders of the soul-idea proponents. It is their function to prove that the soul does exist.

Science, asked why it rejects unqualifiedly the existence of the soul, must have some sort of criterion to determine what exists and what does not, what is factual and what is not.

Millions of people believe that the soul exists. The soul-idea is a persistent one. The primitive peoples of the earth believe in it in one form or another. All religions, extinct and extant, teach it. Many modern psychologists accept it. William McDougall sponsors it. William James endorses it. The psychic experience of thousands of people corroborate it.

Of course it is not proposed here that simply because many people believe something exists, therefore, it exists. Epistemic existence is not necessarily identical with ontologic existence. Thought and being are not necessarily one. But we propose here that what millions of people everywhere and at all times have believed as true must be regarded as a primary datum of scientific interest. It must be given its day in the court of science. And the question we submit to this court may be expressed thus: Have all the people who have believed in the existence of the soul from the past to the present, all over the world, been altogether wrong? Are they *all* wrong, *all* the time, *everywhere?*

"Quod Semper, Quod Ubique"

If we should test the probability of the existence of the soul on the basis of the famous maxim of Vincentius Lirenensis (Vincent of Lirens, 5th century A.D.), it would appear that a good case has been established for accepting it.

This maxim, enunciated in Vincent's treatise, entitled *Commonitorium,* may be regarded as an axiom by which we may test the *probability,* at least, of all sorts of beliefs and traditions.

It is stated thus: *"Quod semper, quod ubique, quod ab omnibus traditum est."*[1] Translated freely, it means that we are to believe whatever tradition has been handed down at *all times, in all places,* and *by all persons.*

In other words, what has always been believed as true everywhere and by all cannot be altogether false, *even if official science should say so.* It must have some foundation in truth; its probability, at least, cannot be denied.

Lincoln paraphrased this axiom in a simpler and more emphatic way. He said that you can fool all the people some of the time, some of the people all the time, but *not all the people all the time.* It would seem, in the scientific view, that belief in the existence of the soul has deceived all men, all the time, everywhere. Or is the belief true, after all? The character of the soul-idea, its persistence in the minds of men, its universality, and its ubiquity seem completely to satisfy the requirements of Vincent's famous maxim.

The Fallacy Of Science

The maxim of Vincentius Lirenensis does not, of course, prove conclusively that the soul exists, but it establishes rather a strong point in favor of, or the probability of, its existence.

Even on this ground alone, science has no right to reject the soul-idea as unscientific. It could have accepted it at least as a datum or subject for study and investigation. But it did exactly the opposite because, says science, the idea of the soul or anything resembling it is not a fact; it is only an assumption without proof, a belief without foundation in the real, the existential; in brief, it does not exist.

How does science know that it does not exist? Because its existence cannot be verified. This identification of verifiability with existentiality is about the most prejudiced way of establishing factuality, because scientific verifiability is essentially of a sensorial nature.

Why does science say there is no soul? Because it cannot be touched, seen, heard, tasted, smelled, observed or experienced by means of the senses. It is thus, in the technical language of science, *unverifiable*.

What science does not seem to understand here, of course, is that the soul cannot be touched, seen, heard, tasted, smelled, weighed, or observed, because it is, itself the toucher, the seer, the hearer, the taster, the smeller, the weigher, and the observer.

Here, then, lies the greatest fallacy of orthodox science; that assuming a criterion for determining what is fact and what is not fact *based solely on one scale of observation, largely the sensory and physical scale,* it considers all other criteria, *based on other scales of observation,* as false.

From the sensory and physical scale of observation, the soul is not a fact. From the extrasensory (ESP) and superphysical scale, however, it is a fact. A fact, in other words, is largely a matter of the scale of observation. In the words of Lecomte du Nouy, "It is the scale of observation which creates the phenomenon."[2]

Charles-Eugene Guye's Principle

This fundamental idea that it is the scale of observation which creates the phenomenon was first pointed out by Professor Charles-Eugene Guye, a brilliant Swiss physicist, who died in 1942.

It is probably one of the most basic principles of knowledge enunciated in the twentieth century.

And it is, sadly enough, the one principle that many orthodox scientists often forget.

Let Lecomte du Nouy explain it:

> Certain of our mental illusions are due to the fact that we consider a phenomenon, as we observe it, in the frame of our current life. Motion in a straight line, for

instance, is real with respect to the earth, and false with respect to the universe. *This does not apply only to sensory illusions. It applies to all our human observations which are always relative to the system of reference chosen. By system of reference we simply mean the scale of observation.*[3] This demands an explanation.

Let us suppose that we have at our disposal two powders. One white (flour) and the other black (finely crushed charcoal or soot). If we mix them we obtain a gray powder which will be lighter in color if it contains more flour and darker if it contains more soot. If the mixture is perfect, *on our scale of observation* (that is, without the help of a microscope), the phenomenon studied will always be a gray powder. But let us suppose that an insect of the size of the grains of flour or of soot moves around in this powder. For him there will be no gray powder, but only black or white boulders. On his scale of observation, the phenomenon, "gray powder," *does not exist.*

The same is true of any print or engraving. When examined with a magnifying glass, the nose of George Washington will look to us like a succession of black and white points. Under the microscope, we will see nothing but the grain of the paper, gray, black, or white according to whether it has been covered by ink or not. The principal phenomenon, the design, the portrait of Washington, has disappeared. It only existed *on our normal scale of observation.*

In other words, one can say that from the standpoint of man *it is the scale of observation which creates the phenomenon.* Every time we change the scale of observation we encounter new phenomena.

On our scale of human observation, as pointed out before, the edge of a razor blade, is a continuous line. On the microscopic scale, it is a broken but solid line. On the chemical scale we have atoms of iron and carbon. On the sub-atomic scale we have electrons in perpetual motion which travel at the rate of several thousand miles per second. All these phenomena are in reality the manifestations of the same basic phenomenon, the motions of the electrons. The only difference which exists between them is the scale of observation.[4]

The Congenital Deaf-Mute And Color-Blind

There are many facts within human experience that attest to the universality of Charles-Eugene Guye's principle. Colors, which are real enough to people with normal eyes, are completely nonexistent to congenitally color-blind people to whom they are simply not facts. To a congenital deaf-mute sounds do not exist. As the color-blind man lives in a gray, colorless world, so the deaf-mute lives in a strangely silent world.

The normal man, the color-blind, and the deaf-mute do not live in three different worlds. The other normal senses of the last two confirm to them that they live also in the same world in which the normal man lives. There is only one world for all of them. *But they perceive this world from three different scales of observation.*

If we should use the language of psychology instead of Guye's language of physics, we would say that our three types of men perceive the world from three different levels or states of consciousness, the first from the normal level and the last two from two different abnormal levels. Because of this difference of scale of observation or level of consciousness, they naturally will have different interpretations of what is fact and what is not fact.

The Physical And The Nonphysical

From the standpoint of Charles-Eugene Guye's principle, it would be illogical and wrong to reject anything as false, *just because it is nonexistent on a given scale of observation.*

It would be wrong for the color-blind and the deaf-mute to reject color and sound as false, just because these phenomena are nonexistent on their abnormal scales of observation.

Therefore, it is wrong for science to reject the soul as false, just because it is nonexistent on the sensory and physical scale of observation.

The soul is not a physical fact. Therefore, we cannot expect our physical sense organs, which are, by nature and by habit, capable of perceiving only physical facts, to perceive it. It is, none the less, a fact, although a nonphysical one. As such, it can reasonably be supposed to be perceivable by the use of nonphysical sense organs, such as clairvoyance, telepathy, precognition, and other nonphysical organs of perception which now pass under the well-known name coined by Dr. J.B. Rhine, ESP, or extrasensory perception.

Any proof of the existence of the soul, therefore, to be reasonable, just and fair, must proceed along extrasensory and nonphysical scales of observation and not along sensory and physical scales.

To demand that the soul be seen or touched or smelled or tasted before its reality can be accepted is to demand that our consciousness or intelligence be seen or smelled or touched or tasted before we accept its undeniable reality.

The important question, then, is the following: Is there a way of proving the existence of the soul along the well-recognized four steps of the scientific method, provided we change our scale of observation, from the sensory to the extrasensory, from the physical to the non-physical as Lecomte du Nouy suggested and in accordance with the principle of Charles-Eugene Guye?

References
[1] Robert Ingham Clegg 33°, *Mackey's Symbolism of Freemasonry. Its Science, Philosophy, Legends, Myths and Symbols*, (Chicago, New York and London: The Masonic History Company, 1921) pp. 54-55.
[2] Lecomte du Nouy, *Human Destiny*, (London: Longmans, Green and Co., Ltd., 1947) p. 11.
[3] Author's italics.
[4] *Ibid.*, pp. 10-11.

Chapter 8

AN EXAMPLE OF SCIENTIFIC EVIDENCE

The Meaning Of Scientific Evidence

We have explained the four steps of the scientific method. It is the purpose of this chapter to point out a way whereby, using these steps, credence may be established regarding the existence of the soul.

An evidence may be regarded as anything that is capable of eliciting conviction or belief, or producing credence that a certain proposition corresponds to reality or truth. Its aim, therefore, is the attainment of truth; its appeal is to fact; its materials are proofs or statements of fact.

Scientific evidence is a type of proof designed to produce conviction or belief or credence by the use of the fourfold scientific method of hypothesis and verification based on the mathematical principle of preponderance of probability.

This principle demands that if the evidence brought forth weighs more heavily in favor of a given assertion or proposition, the one so favored will be regarded as possessing a higher degree of probability than any other. In other words, it possesses preponderance of probability, a term which, in science is regarded as the basis of the acceptance that a given statement is true.

An Example

A good example of the use of the scientific method to prove the truth of a given proposition is afforded by the historical case of the conflict between the geocentric hypothesis of Ptolemy and the heliocentric theory of Copernicus, now regarded as fact.

The earlier and, at the time, more favored theory was the Ptolemaic theory of geocentricity of the solar system. The earth, according to this theory, is the center of the universe and the sun and all the stars revolve around it. The Copernican theory, on the other hand, proposes that the sun is the center of the solar system and the earth revolves around it. Hence, it is called heliocentric.

The question to be settled is: Which is true? Which corresponds to fact or reality: that the sun revolves around the earth or that the earth revolves around the sun?

The majority of men during the time of Copernicus believed in the geocentric theory. It was not only unpopular to sponsor another theory; it was dangerous. Galileo was forced to recant publicly his endorsement of the heliocentric theory. Giordano Bruno was burned at the stake for championing it.

By what cogent reasoning did Copernicus prove the heliocentricity of the solar system despite the militant prejudice against it and despite the actual testimony of the senses that it is the sun which seems to be actually moving around an apparently unmoving earth?

Copernicus proved his point by the scientific method of hypothesis and verification. He proved to the satisfaction of the world that his theory of heliocentricity is simpler, more consistent, and more complete than the geocentric theory of Ptolemy. He was able to verify his theory, that is, correlate harmoniously all solar phenomena and build up a coherent, rational explanation of the behavior of heavenly bodies in terms of the heliocentricity of the solar system.

First, he accumulated facts, such as the alternation of night and day, the succession of the seasons, solar and lunar eclipses, the phases of the moon and of the interior planets, the behavior of gyroscopes, the flattening of the earth at the poles, the precession of the equinoxes, and many others.

Then he asked himself the question: Which hypothesis can explain these facts better, the geocentric or the heliocentric? Next, he developed each hypothesis deductively with the fundamental idea of each as a sort of major assumption or premise in order to determine the validity of the conclusion that followed.

An Example of Scientific Evidence 53

At the end, he discovered that all the facts were explainable in a simple, systematic, and orderly way in terms of the heliocentric hypothesis, but that they could be explained in terms of the geocentric hypothesis only if special assumptions, difficult to prove and not systematically related to the original geocentric fundamental, were made. In other words, Copernicus was able to establish a preponderance of probability in favor of heliocentricity *despite the obvious report of the eyes that the sun moves around the earth.*

There is neither time nor space to consider all the facts enumerated. Let us, however, apply the Copernican procedure to the alternation of night and day.

Obviously, both hypotheses can explain the alternation of night and day on earth. But which of them can explain it better, that is, more simply, more coherently and more comprehensively without giving rise to further problems difficult of solution?

The earth completes one rotation around its axis in twenty-four hours. This movement, according to the Copernican theory, together with its revolution around the sun accounts for the alternation of night and day.

On the other hand, if the geocentric theory were true, then the sun, together with the other heavenly bodies, would have to complete one revolution around the earth in twenty-four hours in order to account for the alternation of night and day on the earth's surface. This would mean that the sun, approximately 93,000,000 miles from the earth would have to move at a speed of around 25,000,000 miles an hour, or about 7,222 miles per second in order to complete one revolution around the earth, an orbit of about 6,000,000,000 miles; while the nearest star, Alpha Centauri, which is approximately 4.5 light years or 23,695,632,000,000 miles from the earth would have to travel at the physically impossible rate of 172,319,900 miles per second, *a speed almost one thousand times that of light* (186,300 miles per second) in order to complete one revolution around the earth, an orbit of about 148,884,393,982,400 miles.

In other words, the assumption of the geocentric theory, in order to explain the alternation of night and day on the earth's surface, would lead to absurd and scientifically untenable conclusions.

Probability

Two important things should be noticed with regard to the scientific acceptance of the heliocentric theory on the basis of the Copernican inductive-deductive procedure.

In the first place, greater probative weight is given to consistency and logicality of reasoning rather than to the bare report of the senses.

Nobody has ever seen the earth rotating around its axis or revolving around the sun. Even space travel to the moon or the use of satellites sending back pictures do not alter this statement for the earth still cannot be "seen" to revolve. In fact, nobody has ever seen the earth moving at all. On the contrary, it is the sun which seems to be moving. That the "earth revolves around the sun" is a fact established by "scientific inference." Factuality, in science, is established by the scientific method and the nonsensory report of reason. Factuality is not necessarily established by "seeing" or through the report of the other senses.

"Seeing is believing," in other words, is not a scientifically reliable basis of judgment. One should not believe in what he sees; he should rather believe in what he understands. It is, in fact, dangerous to believe in what one sees. Seen by the naked eyes, the stars are small; but who among our astronomers would assert that they are? They are gigantic bodies, some of them bigger than the sun. Seen in the ordinary way, the surface of the earth seems flat; but where is the educated man now who would declare that it is so?

This particular observation is significant because, in proving the existence of the soul, we are dealing with a nonsensory phenomenon which cannot and should not be judged in terms of sensory criteria.

In the second place, the basis for the acceptance of the heliocentric theory is largely preponderance of probability. This is, after all, the basis for the acceptance of the so-called scientific truths. There is no other. This, too, by the way, is the basis for the acceptance of truth in court.

An Example of Scientific Evidence

There may be other more empirical bases for acceptance of truth. Intuition or direct perception is one of them. Mysticism is another. These methods, in fact, are regarded in the East as more reliable than the scientific procedure of circumstantial evidence, especially in dealing with problems of a nonphysical, nonsensory nature such as the existence of the soul. "No one who is clairvoyant," says C. W. Leadbeater, "can be atheistic. The evidence is too overwhelming."

But science repudiates all other methods except its own. No doubt this is rather dogmatic, but like a good general, we shall conquer science on its own ground. We shall prove the existence of the soul in accordance with the fourfold scientific method of hypothesis and preponderance of probability.

Chapter 9

THE PROBLEM AND THE TECHNIQUE

The Technique

In proving the existence of the soul, we shall follow a procedure similar to that of Copernicus in proving the heliocentricity of the solar system. We will state the problem as simply and as clearly as possible, defining all terms, explaining all the issues involved. Then we will formulate the most probable hypothesis and, by a deductive development of each, determine which can solve the problem in the most scientific and logical manner.

To do this, we will gather as comprehensively and exhaustively as possible all the available pertinent facts of man's life as man and then accurately and carefully find out which of the rival hypotheses can explain them all most simply, coherently, comprehensively, and without giving rise to further problems that are difficult of solution.

Finally, we will determine which hypothesis has the preponderance of probability, and this hypothesis shall be declared true on the scientific basis of truth-acceptance.

Basis Of Truth-Acceptance

In general, there are five main criteria or bases of truth-acceptance. They are:
1. Sense-Experience (Sensation)
2. Intuition (Mysticism)
3. Correspondence
4. Practical results (Pragmatism)
5. Coherence

All these criteria will be used wherever and whenever possible. They are not mutually exclusive. On the basis of Charles-Eugene Guye's principle of the scale of observation, each can be used validly according to the nature of the problem being solved. In the verification of problems involving *observable natural processes,* the criteria of sense-experience, correspondence, practical results, and coherence can be used. In problems involving *mathematical and logical* systems, however, practical results and sense-experience will not generally apply.

Now, in problems such as soul existence, involving the *existence of minds,* almost all the criteria will apply provided we do not forget that we are dealing with a nonphysical problem in the solution of which it is necessary to change our scale of observation and interpretation.

In using all the criteria, however, there is implied the assumption that none alone is sufficient. In fact, none of them is.

There is no doubt that sense-experience is one of the real sources of knowledge. The saltiness of salt can be verified by tasting it. But how shall we verify facts inaccessible to our sense-organs? Ideas are real, but who can sense them? They are nonphysical, but they are none the less real. The reader of this page has certainly a mind, but I accept this fact not because I see his mind or taste it or hear it or in any way sense it; I accept it by analogy from his behavior or by communication through language.

Sense-experience is a true criterion, but we must recognize the limits of its applicability. What many scientists would probably consider as the best criterion is the pragmatic test of truth, or the test of practical results. An idea, according to this standard, is true if it works, or has practical consequences.

Now, there is no question that if an idea is true, it will work, it will yield practical results. But if an idea yields practical results, is it necessarily true? What is meant by practical results? As Brightman aptly puts it:

> . . . . every idea that we can fool ourselves or others with may be said to work to that extent. Belief in transubstantiation works among Catholics; it does not work among Methodists or Quakers; it is utter nonsense to Mohammedans or Shintoists. The belief in the omnipotence of God may work for the purpose of explaining concrete evils in the world. Belief in the efficacy of the bones of a saint may work until it is found that his skull is on exhibition at several different shrines.[1]

Our Criterion

Our criterion will be the well-established one of coherence which, in its comprehensive application, will involve the use of all other criteria, *provided we use it on the basis of Guye's fundamental principle that it is the scale of observation that makes the phenomenon.*

The combination of these two principles will, it appears to us, offer a universal test of truth, the application of which is both exhaustive and comprehensive.

According to these combined criteria of coherence and scale of observation, an idea is true if, levels of consciousness and scales of observation being properly recognized and adjusted:

1. It is self-consistent;
2. It is consistent with all the known facts of experience based on both a physical, sensory scale and a nonphysical, nonsensory scale of observation;
3. It is consistent with all other ideas or propositions regarded or accepted as true;
4. It establishes explanatory and interpretative relations between various parts of experience;
5. It correlates itself harmoniously with all known aspects of experience individually and as a whole.

The Problem Stated And Explained

The statement of any problem, to be logical and scientific, must start with the given. This given, whatever it is, must constitute a minimum essential. With regard to the problem of the soul, what minimum essential may we assume as the given from which we may start our investigation?

Brightman in discussing the nature of scientific experiment and philosophical interpretation, said that experiments do not occur in a vacuum; they are initiated, observed, and reported by a mind. Every experiment, according to him, presupposes among other things, a self or person and the unity of the self during the entire experiment.

As in every experiment, and in every human task, so in the problem of the soul, the basic presupposition is the reality of the self or the "I am." It is the given in every problem.

Our minimum essential, therefore, will be the self or ego, the "I am." The self, the "I am," is the indubitable fact. It is the scientific minimum. It is the philosophical substratum. It is the indispensable first basis of all knowledge, all science, all truth. It is not only indubitable. It is undeniable because it is the basis of all affirmation and negation. No one doubts "am I or am I not."[2] In fact, it would be illogical and abnormal to declare, "I am not."

The self cannot be denied. Its denial is its affirmation. To doubt it is to believe in it. To deny it is to affirm it.

"*Cogito, ergo sum,*" said Descartes. "I think, therefore I am."

Accordingly, the reality of the self, the indispensable, indubitable, undeniable "I am" will be the basis for the statement of our problem. I am; I exist; I am real. This affirmation is the basis of everything I think, or feel, or do. For example: I read; I philosophize; I love; I hate; I worship; I write. I am proving scientifically the existence of the soul. And so on, *ad infinitum*.

And let not the semanticists confuse the issue by saying that the "I am" is not real after all; that it is only a term, a sort of verbal counter or symbol that we find expedient to use for purposes of efficient knowledge-communication.

No, it is not. It is something real enough. In fact, it is so real that Brightman, among many others, is constrained by force of sheer empiricism to declare the self as the only true experience, the Situation Experienced, all other situations being only *Situation Believed-in*.[3]

Now, the next question is: Who am I? What is the self? To what exactly do I refer when I affirm myself?

Am I the soul, as religion teaches? Am I the body or any part of the body, as some physicalistic scientists declare?

When my stomach contracts, I feel hungry. Am I the stomach? When my brain operates, I think. Am I the brain? I feel hungry when my stomach contracts. I feel thirsty when my throat is parched. Therefore, wrongly or rightly, I say, I am hungry, I am thirsty.

Now, with what do I feel when I am happy? With what do I feel sympathy when I sympathize?

The eyes to see, the nose to smell, the ears to hear, the tongue to taste. What organ do we use to hate, to love, to worship, to rejoice, to aspire?

An over-simple person might suggest that I am Mr. Reyes. This, however, is puerile. Mr. Reyes is only a name, an accident of circumstance. I could call myself Mr. Santos and the self that I am remains unaffected and unchanged.

So, the problem remains: Who am I? What am I? To what exactly do I refer when I say, "I am"?

Theories Of The Self

There are a number of theories or hypotheses proposed to answer the question. The well-known ones are the following:

1. I am the Body
2. I am the Body with a Soul
3. I am the Soul with a Body
4. I am the combination or compound of Body and Soul

For purposes of this book, these four hypotheses may be resolved into two: the materialistic Body-Hypothesis and the spiritual Soul-Hypothesis. It matters little, as far as the general intention of this book is concerned, whether our Soul-Hypothesis is in the form of the Body-with-a-Soul, or the Soul-with-a-Body, or the Body-Soul combination theory; although it can be said that of these three principal types of the Soul-Hypothesis, the most logical and coherent one is the Soul-with-a-Body theory.

In general, all three assume the existence of the soul, and as such, they are all opposed to the corpocentric I-am-the-Body hypothesis.

Our main purpose is to prove scientifically the existence of the soul. For the present, therefore, we shall regard it simply as a matter of emphasis whether the Soul-Hypothesis is stated in one way or the other.

This difference of emphasis takes on importance only from the standpoint of strict philosophical interpretation. With that, however, we have for the moment, nothing to do. We have, just now, a definite task to perform.

Recapitulation

We have before us, therefore, two diametrically opposed hypotheses:

1. The idealistic, spiritual, psychocentric Soul-Hypothesis which declares that man is primarily nonphysical, a soul who, while living on earth, uses a physical body as an instrument or vehicle of expression. He is definitely not the body.

2. The materialistic, physical, cerebrocentric Body-Hypothesis which declares that man is essentially the body and no more. All his actuations originate from his nervous system. There is nothing non-physical in him. His mind is his brain. He thinks with this brain. He is, in a sense, this brain. At any rate, he is definitely the body; and all his functions, including the so-called mental and emotional, originate from his body.

Now, the question is: Which of these two rival hypotheses is true? Which will the actual facts of human life and behavior sustain? Which of them will explain more simply, more coherently, more comprehensively, and without giving rise to additional problems, the multifarious facts of human behavior, including the physical, the emotional, the mental, the moral, and the religious, the Soul-Hypothesis or the Body-Hypothesis?

The Facts To Be Explained

How shall we proceed to answer the question? Following the inductive procedure, we first gather all the pertinent facts available concerning human behavior. They are multitudinous, and it is not easy to classify them. For this reason we cannot be exhaustive. We can try, however, to be at least comprehensive.

The facts available for our study may be grouped under the following categories:
1. The facts of consciousness, self-consciousness, and the identity and continuity of consciousness
2. The phenomena of memory
3. The phenomena of sleep
4. The phenomena of dreams
5. The phenomena of death
6. The facts of psychical research

7. The phenomena of ESP (extra-sensory perception)
8. The phenomena of traveling clairvoyance
9. The phenomena of hypnotism
10. The phenomena of mysticism (Western) and of yoga (Eastern)
11. The phenomena of psychedelic experience

These are facts. They are not assumptions. With some exceptions all of them are within the normal everyday experience of all men. Although they fall within the realm of normal everyday occurrence, they are none the less among the unsolved problems of science. Psychology has no definite answers to them. It has only theories.

What is consciousness? What is self-consciousness? Are they epiphenomena of the brain? How do we preserve the identity and continuity of our consciousness?

What is memory? How do we remember? Do we really forget? Why do we remember what we forget? Who remembers? What remembers?

What is sleep? Who sleeps? What sleeps: the body, the consciousness? Why do we wake up from sleep when we are called? Do we hear, asleep? Why does a sleeping person wake up when he is touched? What is the process of "falling asleep?" Are we partially awake when sleeping? partially sleeping when awake? how about hypnagogy? hypnopompy? how about somniloquism or sleep-talking? and somnambulism or sleep-walking?

And dreams, what are they? Who dreams? How explain dreams within dreams, or double, even treble dreams, serial dreams, prophetic dreams?

Finally, what is death, the most frightening, because the most mysterious problem of all? Who dies? What dies? What is death? What happens to consciousness at death, to thoughts, to emotions? They are forms of energy. The first law of thermodynamics, or the law of conservation of energy, does not permit their total annihilation. Where do they go? To what are they transformed?

How about the after-death experiences of resurrected persons? Are they all hallucination? How about so-called ghosts? Must they all be dismissed as superstitions? How about the Eastern theory of death, as exemplified, for instance, in the theory of Shankara's temporary occupancy of the physical body of the dead King Amaraka?[4]

With reference to the last six phenomena given in the list, this much can be said, that only the uninformed are not acquainted with them.

Hundreds of books have been written about them. Psychical Research is now regarded as a science and thousands of researchers throughout the world are daily engaged in its study, numbering among them some of the keenest minds of the century, such as Dr. J.B. Rhine of the Duke University, Professor H.H. Price, Wykeham Professor of Logic at the University of Oxford, Professor C.D. Broad, Knightsbridge Professor of Moral Philosophy at the University of Cambridge, Dr. Robert H. Thouless of the Department of Education, University of Cambridge, and Mr. G.N. Tyrrell, outstanding investigator and writer in the field of psychical research, and many others. A good list of psychical research investigations may be found in Dr. J.B. Rhine's book, *The Reach of the Mind.*

The phenomena of hypnotism, including posthypnotic phenomena, are so well known that only the uninformed and indifferent ignore them today. Hypnotism is a recognized therapeutic method in psychoanalysis. It is given as a regular course in some universities and colleges; in the medical colleges of Salpetriere and of Nancy in France, the medical student is required to complete a course in hypnotism before his medical degree is conferred upon him.

Mysticism and yoga are genuine experiences of mankind. These terms stand for the same series of phenomena connected with man's experience of the superior or spiritual life. Careful studies of the psychology of mysticism have been written by James,[5] Leuba,[6] and Hocking.[7]

Yoga is both a science and an art in the East. It is the science of union with the Higher Consciousness, ordinarily called God. It is the art of attaining peace and happiness through spiritual maturing. One of the most enlightening books on yoga for the Western world is Yogananda Paramahansa's *An Autobiography of a Yogi.*[8] A book more acceptable to Catholic readers is Father Dechanet's *Christian Yoga.*

The phenomena of psychedelic experience through such "mind-expanding" drugs as peyote, mescaline, and d-lysergic acid diethylamide tartrate (LSD, for short) have aroused public interest. LSD was described as early as 1938 by Hofmann who accidentally stumbled on this ergot derivative in his laboratory. Serious clinical experimentation on LSD has, however, been intensified only in the late 1950's. Since then, volumes of learned medical papers have been written on this subject. Among the outstanding experients of the psychedelic phenomena was writer Aldous Huxley. Former Harvard professors and psychologists Timothy Leary and Richard Alpert, poets Robert Graves and Allen Ginsberg, and philosopher, writer and minister Alan Watts are among other psychedelic experients who testify to the interesting similarity between yogic and psychedelic phenomena.

What Is The Best Explanation?

How shall we explain all these facts? It is the duty and function of science to explain. And science is not supposed to quarrel with facts, even if the facts are stubbornly mysterious and unpleasantly disturbing to dogmatic complacency.

Shall we explain them in terms of the cerebrocentric Body-Hypothesis which regards the body and its nervous system as the seat and origin of all human behavior or on the basis of the idealistic Soul-Hypothesis which centers all human behavior around the psyche or soul or consciousness as the spring of human life and conduct and as the basic origin of all activities of the human organism?

Man the Body or Man the Soul? Which theory or hypothesis is more probable? Which is simpler, more coherent, more exhaustive, more comprehensive? Which gives rise to fewer unproved assumptions, to more valid conclusions, to more thorough, more logical interpretations? Which explains better individual experience, as well as total experience? Which serves as a better principle of ever-increasing reorganization of human knowledge and interpretation of life, considering the fact that both science and experience are not fixed and static, but dynamic and constantly growing: Man the Body or Man the Soul?

The Principle Of Minimum Meaning

The answer will be given in the subsequent chapter, using the well-tried method of science we have already explained, the deductive development or elaboration of each hypothesis in relation to all the facts of human behavior enumerated in our list; but one word more; in what sense do we use the word soul? We give it a minimum meaning. *The nonphysical principle in man, or, more accurately, man himself as a nonphysical entity or being.*

It is not our responsibility to discover the nature of the soul. Our primary preoccupation is to prove scientifically that it exists, that it is a fact. We cannot logically consider *what a thing is,* unless first we prove that *it is.*

Therefore, the principle of minimum meaning stands valid in all pioneer investigations of anything. Occam's Law of Parsimony does not permit an assumption more than the minimum given.[9]

At any rate, at the risk of philosophical discussion, the word *soul* as used here may be regarded, from a general standpoint, as a synonym for mind or consciousness including its various levels of subconsciousness and supraconsciousness. It should be constantly kept in mind, though, that its minimum meaning is retained: Man regarded as a nonphysical entity or being, Man, the Soul.

References

[1] Edgar Sheffield Brightman, *A Philosophy of Religion,* (New York: Prentice Hall, Inc., 1946) pp. 127-128.

[2] Bhagavan Das, *The Science of Peace,* (Benares: The Indian Book Shop, 1948) p. 22.

[3] Brightman, *op. cit.,* p. 347.

[4] Adams Beck, *The Story of Oriental Philosophy,* (New York: Farrar and Rhinehart, Inc., 1928) pp. 69-71.

[5] William James, *The Varieties of Religious Experience,* (New York: Longmans, Green and Co., 1921).

[6] James H. Leuba, *A Psychological Study of Religion,* (New York: The Macmillan Co., 1912).

[7] William Ernest Hocking, *The Meaning of God in Human Experience* (New Haven and London: Yale University Press c. 1921), Fourth Printing, 1963.

[8] Paramahansa Yogananda, *Autobiography of a Yogi,* (New York: The Philosophical Library, 1946).

[9] Occam's Law: "Entia non sunt multiplicanda praeter necessitatem." Entities should not be multiplied beyond necessity.

Chapter 10
EVIDENCES FROM THE PHENOMENA OF CONSCIOUSNESS
A. The Nature Of Consciousness
Indefinability Of Consciousness

The most fundamental fact of human experience is consciousness. It is also the most mysterious. Nothing is more intimate, or more immediate; but nothing also is more illusive. One cannot quite fix it. It forever escapes definition. Why? Sir William Hamilton, in his *Lectures on Metaphysics,* gave the reason. He said:

> Consciousness cannot be defined: We may be ourselves fully aware what consciousness is, but we cannot without confusion convey to others a definition of what we ourselves clearly apprehend. The reason is plain: consciousness lies at the root of all knowledge.[1]

The difficulty of defining consciousness lies at the root of the definition itself. That is, to define consciousness is to be conscious of consciousness; and apparently when that is done, we discover, to our dismay, that it has escaped us, because we realize that we are still using consciousness to think of consciousness; we are using consciousness to define consciousness.

Would that not be a sort of psychological *circulus in definiendo,* or defining in a circle?

The Fact Of Consciousness

For purposes of this book, only three phenomena of consciousness will be discussed: namely, the fact of consciousness itself, the nature of self-consciousness, and the identity-continuity of consciousness.

Let us consider the first, the fact of consciousness. To begin, let us by a process of introspection, attempt to analyze the two following questions:

Am I, can I be, conscious of my body, or any portion of it, like my legs, my hands, or my head? The answer is obviously yes. I can be conscious of my body, or any part of it, its size, its shape, its pleasures, its pains. This is a fact within the easy observation of any normal person.

Let us analyze the second question: Can the body — my body, for instance, be conscious of itself? At first thought I might answer immediately: No, my body cannot be conscious of itself; rather, I can be, I am, conscious of my body. And this answer is empirically, essentially correct. Strict logicality, however, demands a more accurate answer. And the more accurate answer would be: I do not know, I cannot tell, because, empirically, there is no way of answering the question at all.

If one should be asked, for example, whether the pen he is using, or the tie he is wearing, is conscious of itself, the only answer he could give is: I do not know, I cannot tell. Ask the pen, ask the tie, if they can answer.

Similarly, I would not know, I cannot tell whether my finger is conscious of itself, or my leg, or my ear, or my nose, or even the brain, or my entire body itself. They cannot tell, neither individually nor as a whole, because none of them is a self, a personality. They are, in fact, empirically, the same thing. Consciousness is personality and personality is consciousness.[2]

Now, my finger is not a person. Neither is my leg, my ear, my nose, nor even my brain, nor my entire body. None of them possesses self-experience. It is I experiencing through them and in them. If, for example, something touches my leg, it would not be exactly right, empirically speaking, to say that my leg is conscious of the stimulation. It is I, through my leg and in my leg, by a process of identification, not my leg itself, who am conscious of the touch.

It is also through this process of self-identification with the various parts of the body, as for example, the stomach, that a man is able to say he is hungry, when, as a matter of fact, it is his stomach, not he himself, which is demanding food.

The expression, "I am hungry," means I, the self, the personality, am conscious of the contractions of my stomach. If, however, my stomach be locally anesthetized, then the process of self-identification with the stomach is broken, and I cease to be conscious of its contractions. In other words, I am not hungry any more.

Empirically, therefore, it is permissible to say that neither the body as a whole nor any of its parts is really self-conscious; if not self-conscious, then not a personality, not a self, not an I-am. If it is not a personality, not a self, not an I-am, then it is as completely unwarranted to say, "I am the body," as it is to say, "I am the stomach," or "I am the leg."

The only logical thing to say, without violating the testimony of experience, is, "I am conscious of my body, or my stomach, or my leg."

If it is unwarranted to say, "I am the body," because the body is not a personality, not an I-am, how then explain my selfhood, my consciousness of egoity, my I-am-ness?

The only other alternative is that I am myself the consciousness, or using the word we have advisedly chosen to use, the soul. I am the soul, using the body, conscious of it as a whole and as composed of parts.

I am the real thinker, feeler, and actor behind my body. I think through the brain and, through the nervous system, I motivate all parts of the body. I am not the brain nor the nervous system any more than the pianist is the piano he uses. As the pianist produces music through his appropriate instrument, the piano, so do I, the thinker, produce thoughts through my appropriate instrument, the brain.

If the piano is destroyed, the pianist is not thereby also destroyed. But he is thus incapacitated to produce music. If my body is destroyed, am I thereby destroyed also? Analogically, no.

The piano-brain or the pianist-soul analogy, however, stops here. If the piano is destroyed, the pianist is unable to produce music, unless he takes another piano. If the body is destroyed, does the soul become incapacitated, thereby, to produce thought? We shall see in subsequent chapters that the new science of psychical research and the phenomena of hypnotism answer this question in the negative.

If one can think without using the brain, if, in addition, mentation without cerebration could be demonstrated by actual experiment, here, then, is a positive evidence that mind and brain are not the same. Here, indeed, is a clincher-proof that man is not the body, but a nonphysical mind, a spaceless center of consciousness, a personality, a soul!

Am I The Brain?

This question would seem superfluous after the analysis of consciousness given in the preceding section. This, however, is the last-ditch stand of corpocentric psychologists; from this position, too, they must be dislodged.

Philosophically, it is illogical to identify the self with the brain. I cannot be the brain. In the first place, I can think of my brain, as I can think of a chair, or a table, or a pencil. This fact immediately establishes a distinction between me and my brain. I am the thinker; my brain is the object of my thought. In the second place, can my brain think of me? In fact, can it think at all? It cannot answer, it cannot tell. Therefore, I am not the brain. For if I were the brain, then it should be able to answer, it should be able to tell, because I am able to answer, to tell; I am able to think, not only of my brain, but also of myself as a personality, as a consciousness.

I am a self-thinking being. Is my brain a self-thinking organ? Can it think without me?

If it can, why cannot a corpse think if its brain is organically intact? Obviously, because it is dead. That is, it is only body; it is only the brain. The thinker is no longer there. How can the brain think, if the thinker is no longer there?

The radical empiricists, such as Brightman, for example, would even go to the extreme of saying that the brain is not a Situation-Experienced. It is only an object of belief or a Situation-Believed-in.

Only personal consciousness is experience. All other things, all bodies, all brains, all organs are only objects of belief, or Situations-Believed-in. Why?

Brightman says:

> It is necessary to distinguish between Situations-Experienced and Situations-Believed-in. A "situation" means any state of affairs. No situation is Situation-Experienced unless it is actually present in consciousness. Experience is given only as a conscious state of affairs. To experience is to be aware. A man cannot properly say that he is experiencing a fire in his house merely because the fire is going on; he experiences the fire only when it makes a perceptible difference to his conscious experience. More exactly, the man can never say he is experiencing the fire, even when perceptions of its odor or heat occur; yes, even when the fire burns his body, the Situation-Experienced is excruciating pain, not actual fire. The fire is always a Situation-Believed-in, no matter how painfully well-grounded the belief may be.
>
> The only Situation-Experienced by anyone is his own consciousness. From this, if he is able to observe and reason even in an elementary way, he is able to infer with varying degrees of accuracy, the presence in his environment of fire. . . . The only basis we have for any knowledge, belief, faith, truth, or error, is to be found in Situations-Experienced. Whatever is not in the Situation Experienced is a Situation-Believed-in or Disbelieved-in; for example, a person's brain, or the bottom of the ocean, or God. A Situation-Experienced is a self, a person, or an experient because it is a self-experiencing whole which includes thinking, remembering, anticipating, and purposing, as well as feeling and sensing . . .
>
> *No portion of an experient's nervous system nor any part of his body has ever been or can be a Situation-Experienced by that experient.*[3] When I see my hand, for example, the hand is not itself actually in my consciousness. The Situation-Experienced consists of a whole within which there is observed a certain pattern of sense data. That pattern is a part of a personal Situation-Experienced; the hand itself is a Situation-Believed-in.[4]

This radical empiricism of Brightman means simply that there is a sharp distinction between actual experience and the beliefs to which it gives rise. Now, since to experience means to be aware, and to be aware means to be actually present in consciousness, it follows logically that personal consciousness alone is experience, and all bodies, all nervous systems, all brains are only objects of belief.

Therefore, it follows, further, that man is not the body nor the nervous system, nor the brain, nor a combination of all these. For if he were so, that is, if man had no soul, and his personality is the product purely of the physicochemical structures and functions of the nervous system, particularly the brain, he would indeed be a perfect "thinking machine" but still very much less the human being he actually is; and he is what he is now, a human being, because he is not just a perfect "thinking machine" or servo-mechanism — he is a person, and a person is more, much more, than just the totality of his physical parts. He is not just a total of his parts, because his parts are the products of his initial wholeness, and not the other way around.

References
[1] Dagobert D. Runes, *The Dictionary of Philosophy*, (New York: Philosophical Library, 1942) p. 64.

[2] Edgar Sheffield Brightman, in his book *A Philosophy of Religion*, (New York: Prentice-Hall, Inc. 1940, pp. 342-370) chapter on 'Problem of Human Personality," listed, among four others, the following significant characteristics of a *minimum self* or simplest possible consciousness: (a) *Self-Experience* (or consciousness of itself) — a unified complexity of consciousness (Stern's *unitas multiplex*). (b) *Process and conation* — all selves are in a constant process of change, including the *striving of ends*. (c) *Awareness of meaning* — the simplest self treats its experience as signs of further experience. The humblest paramecium experiences objective reference in all its pursuits and avoidances. (d) *Privacy* — every self is directly experienced only by itself. "The monads," said Leibnitz, "have no windows."

[3] Author's italics.

[4] Brightman, *ibid.*, pp. 347-348.

Chapter 11

EVIDENCES FROM THE PHENOMENA OF CONSCIOUSNESS

B. Assumptions About Consciousness

Psychology And Physiology

These two sciences are very closely interrelated. In fact, there exists a branch of psychology called physiological psychology. It investigates the functions of the nervous system, receptors and effectors in their bearing on behavior and mental processes.[1]

The existence of this specialized branch of psychology implies the heavy dependence of psychology on physiology. Can there be no psychology without physiology? Considering the corpocentric attitude of modern scientists, it is natural to expect a negative answer to that question.

However, since there exists the science of physiological psychology, why should not there be a science of psychological physiology? It should be interesting to find out how much dependence physiology has on psychology. Is there such dependence, in the first place? Both psychologists and physiologists would probably say *no*. At any rate, why should physiology be given precedence over psychology? In other words, why should the brain be regarded as the basis of the mind?

Should the science of psychological physiology some day come into existence, it should be defined as, "the study or the investigation of the bearing of thought or consciousness on the functions of the nervous system, the receptors and the effectors." This idea may seem ridiculous to positivistic and materialistic scientists. There is, however, something even more ridiculous than this. It is the peculiar relation between physiology and psychology.

Evidence from the Phenomena of Consciousness 73

Physiology is the science of organic functions. It deals with the modes of operation of an organism, or any part of it.[2] Applied to man, it is especially concerned with the functions of the nervous system, particularly the brain. *Yet, as a science, it consistently and anomalously ignores the most important function connected with the nervous system, namely, consciousness.*

In fact physiologists such as Winston and Bayliss frankly admit the inability of physiology to answer this highly perplexing problem. They state, "Physiology has nothing to say about the nature of consciousness except that it is something that seems to accompany the most elaborate reactions of an animal to its environment. It may mean that some fundamentally different kind of process is occurring or it may not."[3] What this fundamentally different kind of process is, the authors did not specify.

Assumptions About Consciousness

It is very clear, then, that we cannot make any intelligent remarks about consciousness. In the first place, some scientists refuse to say anything about the exact nature of consciousness and the relation between the brain, on the one hand, and the various phenomena of consciousness, on the other. In the second place, scientists do not exactly know what specific region of the brain is associated with the phenomena of consciousness, thought, and memory.

Thus, the relationship between brain and consciousness has become as muddled and mysterious as ever. The only statements we are able to get from scientists regarding the particular area of the brain where consciousness resides (if it resides there at all) are the following confusing and contradictory assumptions:

> That there must be connection between the mind and brain is clear, but what it is remains a mystery.[4]
>
> There is a physicochemical mechanism in the brain matter which is capable of giving us a reaction in consciousness.[5]
>
> Psychical activity in man is associated with the cortical matter of the cerebrum.[6]

> It is most likely that the reticular substance is the oldest coordinating mechanism, and therefore probably the oldest seat of consciousness.[7]
>
> It is natural to regard the neocortex as the "seat of consciousness" in the sense that impulses must reach cortical cells before awareness is evoked.[8]
>
> Mind liaison with brain occurs primarily in the cerebral cortex, though diencephalic centers may also be concerned, particularly as continued bombardment by impulses therefrom is necessary for sustaining activity in the cerebral cortex. Presumably this explanation accounts for the finding that experimental interferences with the diencephalon causes loss of consciousness.[9]
>
> We are fairly sure that it (consciousness) does not reside in the cortex, for we (or a disease) can take part of the cortex away without our becoming aware of it — a state known as anosognosia. But clinical experience and animal experimentation, have, however, shown that consciousness appears to be connected somehow with the mid-brain and the brain stem. Operations near the quadrigeminal bodies lead almost invariably to a loss of consciousness. Consciousness may be restored after manipulations in that region, or it may never come back — the patient may become a vegetable. . . . Experimentally it was shown in dogs that pressure on the brain stem can abolish consciousness, but not manipulations of the cortex.[10]
>
> . . . . the large portion of the frontal lobes anterior to the premotor areas is chiefly concerned with consciousness, memory, judgment, and intellectual processes in general.[11]

Dr. Wiggers, nevertheless, is of the opinion, "that the frontal lobes are not a *sine qua non* for intellect."[12] He cites the example of Dandy who found "that the complete surgical removal of the right hemisphere above the basal ganglia or of both frontal lobes had no significant effects upon the mentality of patients."[13]

In fact, analysis of the physical defects following from extensive damage to the frontal lobes during World War II indicated clearly to German clinicians that disturbances of attention, memory, performance, will, and feeling which do occur are not isolated phenomena but part and parcel of a generally disturbed *function change*. Jacobsen studied the effect of extirpating the frontal lobes trained in behavioral tests and found that unilateral extirpations cause no impairment of performance in any test. Complete bilateral extirpations did not affect reactions in which the essential cues were provided in the animal's immediate sensory experience, but they resulted in stereotyped performance when the essential cues had to be wholly or partly recalled from the animal's past experience."[14]

Rene Descartes once declared that the soul interacts with the body through the pineal gland. It would seem that modern science is gradually vindicating his statement.

Studies at Cornell University seem to indicate that consciousness and the emotions originate in a ring-shaped structure of four parts deep in the middle of the brain near the area regarded by the ancients as the seat of the soul. These four parts, mysterious both as to structure and function, are the hypothalamus, the mammillary body, the gyrus cinguli, and the hippocampus — the latter probably the source of electrical waves, known as the Berger rhythm, pulsing through the cerebral cortex. This structure, however, is only the vortex through which the multi-dimensional energy of the soul pours into our three-dimensional body.

In the East, it is called the coronal or *Brahmarandra chakra*. Through it streams the energy of *Atman*, the soul, for the sustenance of man's earthly life. Through it, the soul escapes, as it were, either temporarily as in the case of traveling clairvoyance, or permanently at death, when soul and body separate from each other, the body to disintegrate into its constituent elements and the soul to transfocalize itself into the higher dimensional universe.

The above contradictory and confusing assumptions about consciousness point to the embarrassing helplessness of science to resolve the mysterious relationship between brain and consciousness. The utmost that any fair-minded physiologist can say is that "the nature of this relation constitutes the most difficult problem of physiology and psychology, a problem which perhaps is beyond the possibility of a satisfactory scientific explanation."[15]

What science, then, is now charged with the duty of investigating the phenomenon of consciousness which, according to Fulton, is neither matter nor energy, and therefore, beyond the scope of physiological and scientific explanations? Evidently, the science of psychology, and here lies the paradox.

Physiologists plainly recognize the nonphysical nature of consciousness. As such, it is not, according to them, susceptible to investigation by the use of physiological methods. But what do we find?

Psychologists insist on dissecting consciousness with the surgeon's scalpel and stubbornly persist in the physiological study of psychology. The result is the identification of the mind with the brain and the reduction of the man to the body.

The Brain Is Not The Seat Of Consciousness

It is simpler to state that the brain is not the seat of consciousness because human brains are not conscious in the first place. As such, therefore, both the existence and the nature of consciousness neither wholly depend on nor necessitate the presence of a functioning nervous system.

The brain, then, is only an instrument with which to start thought, a sort of intellectual switchboard the tuning of which permits the flowing in of movement and life, and the closing of which checks the manifestations of both sensations and ideas.

Questions: Who or what is the consciousness itself? Who sits at the brain switchboard to turn it off and on, as it were? Who starts thought? Who perceives phenomena or sensations and transforms them into noumena or ideas?

Answer: Man, the soul, the personality, the consciousness. All mental, emotional, and physical life emanates from him, but it courses through the brain and the entire nervous system for expression and manifestation.

Consciousness Without Brain

Is it possible to think without using the brain? Our answer is yes. It is possible to think without using the *brain,*

Evidence from the Phenomena of Consciousness

but not necessarily without using the *mind*.

The mind, thus, must be regarded as something completely different from the brain. It is nonphysical, whereas the brain is physical. This non-physical reality in man we choose to call *soul*.

The clincher proof to show that thinking is possible without the brain, or, in other words, that mentation (function of the mind) is possible without cerebration (function of the brain) will be given in the chapter on hypnotism.

In this chapter, however, we will give actual examples of persons who, with their brains either partially or wholly destroyed, continued to live and think normally.

Many of these examples were taken from the article of Vincent H. Gaddis, "With Brain Destroyed They Live and Think" in the summer issue of *Fate* magazine, Vol. I, No. 2, 1948.[16]

The first startling case is that of Phineas Gage, a railroad foreman who, while charging a hole with powder preparatory to blasting, suffered the accident of having a tamping-bar, three and a half feet long, driven completely through his skull. The bar "passed through the left anterior lobe of the cerebrum and made its exit at the junction of the coronal and saggital sutures, fracturing the parietal and frontal bones and breaking up considerable portion of the brain." Removal of the bar left a hole three and a half inches in diameter.

Gage did not lose consciousness. In fact he walked a considerable distance for medical aid. He remained completely rational until recovery and lived normally for many years afterward.

Today, the original bar, together with a cast of the patient's skull, is on exhibition in the Harvard University Medical Museum.

The next startling case we cite is that of a male infant born at St. Vincent's Hospital, NewYork City, in 1935. He lived 27 days without a brain, "but defied all orthodox concepts of physiology by eating, crying, and reacting to pain and other stimuli." There was no indication that the baby was abnormal until an autopsy was performed when it was discovered that the cranial cavity contained only fluid.

Professor G.W. Surya reported the case of a man, insane for years, who suddenly became normal shortly before his death. "The autopsy revealed that there was practically nothing of the brain left in his brain-pan. A pathological process had gradually destroyed its substance, but the mystery of his return to normalcy remained unexplained.

Dr. Hufeland, the German physician, tells of a man whose skull was found to contain nothing but a little water, but whose mental faculties remained normal until death.

That memory remains unaffected despite brain destruction is demonstrated in the case of a man reported by Dr. Gould and Dr. Pyle. He suffered from a cerebral tumor that ultimately caused his death. Autopsy revealed a cavity in the brain at least five inches in length. The patient, nevertheless, not only had his sense and locomotor muscles in perfect control up to the instant of death, but also revealed excellence of memory retention by steadily memorizing poems to within two weeks of his passing.

Sometimes surgical removal of brain substance, instead of producing the expected impairment of mental functions, actually brings about the opposite effect. The American Psychiatric Association reports the case of a woman who, after one operation involving the extirpation of the entire right prefrontal lobe and most of the left lobe, became more even-tempered, more retentive in memory and more powerful in concentration.

More cases of this kind can be found in Dr. Gustave Geley's book *From the Unconscious to the Conscious*. One of the most remarkable phenomena mentioned in this book is that of a young boy who died in full possession of his mental faculties, although the encephalic mass was completely detached from the bulb (a condition equivalent to literal decapitation) due to an active abscess involving the entire cerebellum.

Problem And Solution

How did these persons manage to retain their intellectual faculties, despite the widespread and sometimes complete

Evidence from the Phenomena of Consciousness 79

destruction of their brains? This is the problem. But what is the solution?

It is clear that the materialistic hypothesis that the mind is the epiphenomenon of the brain cannot solve this problem. Rather, it is becoming more and more evident even to positivistic scientists themselves that the brain is only a secondary organ directed by a deeper, more subtle, nonphysical source.

Prof. G.W. Surya believes that:

> when the brain is destroyed, the mind (I would say the soul: *Author*) through neurocenters or ganglia, floods the nervous system of the physical body. If the mind (soul) is the primary source of mental energy, then the brain is the switchboard and the nervous system transmits power to the various secondary motors. When the switchboard is destroyed, emergency lines are laid from the mind (soul) to the various secondary motors, the injured brain is by-passed, and thus full command of the faculties is retained.[17]

It is interesting to note, in connection with Professor Surya's explanation, that Dr. Roland Davis and Dr. William Shaw, of the psychology department of Columbia University, have demonstrated by the oscillograph that we think with the entire nervous system and not only with the brain.

This fact will also explain how the amoeba, brainless as it is, is yet able to react to stimulation, as if it were aware or conscious of its environment.

In other words, it appears, on the basis of the experiments of Davis and Shaw, that consciousness is really co-extensive with life itself, as Bergson, in all his lectures and writings, intimated years ago.

As Dr. Geley says:

> It seems impossible to explain mental by cerebral activity, and to reduce the former to the latter. In fact, each time that the thinking being is not limited to repetition, but acquires some new thing, he transcends the mechanism resident in him . . . . he combines what has already been acquired with the new impressions; and this implies an increase of activity on his part. The

cerebral mechanism lags behind the intelligence . . . . therefore there is no strict parallelism between the biological and the psychological sequences; the latter transcends the former . . . . psychological activity appears indeed as a synthesis, but this synthesis is different from the elements of which it is composed — it is other than those elements.[18]

References
[1] Howard Warren, *Dictionary of Psychology*, (Cambridge: Houghton Mifflin Co., The Riverside Press, 1934) p. 202.
[2] *Ibid.*, p. 202.
[3] F. R. Winston and L. E. Bayliss, *Human Physiology*, (5th Edition, Little Brown and Co., Boston, 1962) p. 417.
[4] Gerhardt von Bonin, "Brain and Mind" in *Humanistic Viewpoints in Psychology* Frank T. Severin, Editor (New York: McGraw Hill Book Company, 1965) p. 150.
[5] John F. Fulton (Editor), *Howell's Textbook of Physiology*, (Philadelphia and London: W. B. Saunders Company, 1946) p. 255.
[6] *Ibid.*
[7] von Bonin, *op. cit.*, p. 158.
[8] W. Penfield and H. Jasper, *Epilepsy and the Functional Anatomy of the Human Brain*, (Boston: Little Brown Co., 1954) p. 1184.
[9] John Eccles Carew, *The Neurological Basis of Mind*, (Oxford: At the Clarendon Press, 1965) pp. 264-267.
[10] von Bonin, *op. cit.*, pp. 148-149.
[11] Carl J. Wiggers. *Physiology in Health and Disease*, (Philadelphia: Lea and Febiger) p. 192.
[12] *Ibid.*
[13] *Ibid.*, p. 193.
[14] *Ibid.*, p. 192.
[15] John F. Fulton, *op. cit.*, p. 255.
[16] Vincent H. Gaddis, "With Brain Destroyed They Live and Think." *Fate*, (Vol. 1, No. 2, Summer, 1948) p. 81. By special permission from *Fate* magazine.
[17] Quoted by Vincent H. Gaddis, *op. cit.*
[18] Quoted by Vincent H. Gaddis, *op. cit.*

Chapter 12
EVIDENCES FROM THE PHENOMENA OF CONSCIOUSNESS
C. The Relation Between Thought And Brain
Does The Brain Think?

From the standpoint of our discussion in the preceding chapter, the answer to this question should be obvious.

If I am not the brain, and my brain is only a part of my functional environment, if further, thinking is a function of an experient, a personality, however high or low, and the brain, however complex, is not an experient, not a personality, it is clear that the brain does not think, that it is I, the personality, who thinks, using the brain as an instrument of thought; or, as Ouspensky puts it, the "necessary prism, passing through which part of the psyche manifests to us as intellect, the mirror, reflecting psychic life in our three-dimensional section of the world."[1]

The question, however, is worth considering from another point of view; the relation between brain and thought. Thinking is one of the proudest functions of man. It is also one of the most mysterious. As I write, I think. Who thinks? Is it I, or is it my brain?

What is thought? Is it an epiphenomenon of the brain, a by-product of brain activity? What are ideas? Are they, as Carl Vogt once said, secretions of the brain as the bile is a secretion of the liver?[2]

These questions carry far-reaching experimental significance, and ultimately they can be answered conclusively only by experiment.

To experiment on thought and brain, however, requires a change in the scientific scale of observation. Thought is not a physical fact, therefore, it can be studied only by its results or effects. It invariably escapes sensory analysis. On the other hand, any conclusion about the nature of thought, or its generation and behavior, based solely on the study of brain structure, is altogether unreliable. It is purely theoretical. It is not even logical.

This unreliability, this illogicality is due to the existence of a radical incompatibility between the nature and the structure of the physical brain as we study it.

Thought is nonphysical, or metaphysical; and it does not conform to physicochemical laws. The brain is physical, and it operates according to the laws of physics and chemistry. This is the incompatibility. It is a chasm not easy to bridge. How can a physical organ, like the brain, produce such metaphysical realities as ideas?

Various Theories On Brain-Thought Relation

Before it can be reasonably accepted that the brain produces thoughts or ideas, that is, that the brain thinks, it must first be proved that ideas or thoughts are physical. Otherwise, we have to swing to the other alternative that ideas and thoughts are not real after all, that they are only sensaions. In both cases, however, the act of thinking is abolished.

In the first case, it is not an experimentally proven fact that the brain produces ideas. *This is only a theory.* That ideas exist is a fact. That they are produced by the brain is only a theory.

No one, no scientist, living or dead, has opened the cranium of any man and seen, directly or indirectly, the brain actually producing ideas or thought or images or engrams or neurograms or whatever science might choose to call them.

That the phenomenon of thought is connected with the cerebrum is acceptable enough. But this is only a connection. What kind of connection it is, no scientist knows exactly. None has the right to legislate. One can only theorize.

On the other hand, there are those who would assert that "thought or consciousness" is but another name for subvocal speech, or for some other form of behavior, or for molecular processes in the tissues of the brain. This assertion is, of course, untenable, if not illogical. Ducasse quotes Paulsen and others who have pointed out that:

> .... no evidence ever is or can be offered to support that assertion, because it is in fact but a disguised proposal to make the words "thought," "feeling," "sensation," "desire," and so on, denote facts quite different from those which these words are commonly employed to denote. To say that those words are but other names for certain chemical or behavioral events is as grossly arbitrary as it would be to say that "wood" is but another name for glass, or "potato" but another name for cabbage. What thought, desire, sensation, and other mental states are like, each of us can observe directly by introspection; and what introspection reveals is that they do not in the least resemble muscular contraction, or glandular secretion, or any other known bodily events. No tampering with language can alter the observable fact that thinking is one thing and muttering quite another; that the feeling called anger has no resemblance to the bodily behavior which usually goes with it; or that an act of will is not in the least like anything we find when we open the skull and examine the brain. Certain mental events are doubtless connected in some way with certain bodily events, but they are not those bodily events themselves. The connection is not identity.[3]

It may be said then that the cerebrum is only a sort of prism, as Ouspensky suggested, and thoughts are the broken white light of psychic energy passing through it. But where does the light come from and who is the generator?

It may be said that the cerebrum is merely the central switchboard of a mighty system of communication from which the different parts of the body are controlled. But who is the operator that sits at the controls?

It may be, as Sir Charles Sherrington declared in a lecture at Oxford University, that "grown up with the animal, the brain fits the motor mechanism of the animal as a key fits its lock."[4] The question, however, is, "Who turns the key?"

Are Ideas Only Sensations?

In the second case we have a theory that is currently popular among orthodox psychologists. This is the theory that ideas are essentially sensations. Physiologically, according to these theories, ideas are merely centrally aroused sensations, as differentiated from real sensations which are peripherally aroused.

This theory, however, does not explain the nature of ideas. It merely localizes their point of origin. To say that they are essentially sensations does not explain how they are transformed from a peripheral to a cerebral phenomenon and *what or who does the transforming*. Is it the brain? Is it the whole nervous system?

Therefore, we are back to the original problem. Only, instead of asking, Who thinks? we now ask, Who transforms?

If ideas are only sensations, then there are no ideas. If there are no ideas, then man does not think. He merely senses. Man, therefore, is not a thinker. He is only a sensor. Empirically, however, all of these assertions are groundless and unwarranted.

In the first place, we do think. Somehow, we can create nonphysical images called ideas. Whoever denies this plain fact denies even this denial which, after all, is a system of ideas.

In the second place, it is not completely correct to say that all ideas are sensations. Sensations do constitute raw materials for thinking. But the mind has power to reconstitute them into ideas. Sensations and ideas, perceptions and conceptions are different orders of psychological phenomena.

Locke was wrong, said Kant, when he said, "There is nothing in the mind which was not first in the sense."[5] Leibnitz was right when he added, "nothing, except the mind itself."[6]

Furthermore, we have ideas of space, time and number. What sensations exactly correspond to each of these? What sensation for instance, is number 1 or 2 or 3? What sensation is zero?

In the third place, it is a well-known fact that the cerebrum itself registers no sensation. It cannot sense. It cannot, for example, feel pain or pressure. Whatever pain or pressure is felt near the cerebral regions is definitely localizable in the endosteum, the inner fibrous membrane of the cranium which is not a part of the cerebrum at all. In other words, the cerebrum is not a sensory organ. It is, therefore, completely meaningless to say that ideas are centrally aroused sensations. No sensations can be aroused in the cerebrum. Ideas are ideas and sensations are sensations. How sensations become apparently transformed into ideas is, until now, unexplained. That ideas are transformed sensations is only hypothetical. Who or what transforms sensations into ideas is a larger mystery.

It can be said with a fair degree of certainty that with regard to the phenomena of the cerebrum, science is in a state of befuddled uncertainty. There are no ascertained facts at all. There are only theories. And these theories are not convincing.

In the fourth place, to explain ideas and their origin in terms of sensations and their generation is to assume that we understand what sensations are and how they are produced and developed. In sober truth, we do not. The genesis of sensation is as mysterious as the evolution of ideas.

How Do We See?

Consider, for example, what to us is probably the most important sensation of all, sight. How do we see? Who sees? What sees?

Modern psychologists and physiologists will find it interesting to read the acutely fine analysis of visual perception given in the *Surangama Sutra* of Buddhism.[7] In sheer logicality of reasoning and utter perspicacity of insight into the real nature of perception, this Mahayana treatise far surpasses both Locke's *Essay Concerning Human Understanding* and Hume's *Enquiry into Human Understanding*.

Let us repeat the question the Buddha asked his favorite disciple, Ananda: "What was it that gave you the sensation of seeing? What was it that experienced the sensation"? In short, what, or who sees, when I see?

To start, we can say that it is definitely not the eye as a whole that sees; for even if the eye is structurally, histologically, and functionally intact, if either the optic nerve or the optic lobe is diseased or out of order, the eye cannot see.

Elder quotes the case of an Australian soldier at Gallipoli who was firing through an embrasure when bullets struck several times near his head. He could no longer see with his eye, although the tissues were perfectly normal. The condition was interpreted as an instinctive protest against further damage.[8] In other words, we have here a case of functional blindness. Eye, optic nerve, and optic lobe were completely unimpaired. The soldier, nevertheless, was blind. Pillsbury attributes the blindness to a natural "instinctive protest against further danger." Very well, but who protests, what protests?

To protest implies the presence of personality, consciousness, will, ego. Shall we call it soul, for the sake of simplicity and truth? It is evident, therefore, that it is not the eye as a whole, nor the optic nerve, nor the optic lobe that sees. Is it, then, any of their parts, or combination of them? Is it the retina, for example?

It is most inaccurate to say that the real seeing portion of the eye is the retina. Actually, the retina is only a structure that transforms light waves into nervous impulse. That is its real function. How this transformation is effected nobody really knows. This nervous impulse is carried by the optic nerve to the occipital lobe in the brain, and there another mysterious transformation occurs: the nervous impulse somehow becomes what psychologically is called visual image, the real sensation.

From light vibrations to nerve impulse; from nerve impulse to visual image — this is seeing. But who sees?

It is not the eye. It is not the optic nerve. It is not the occipital lobe. It is not any of their individual parts, or combination of them. Is it, then, all of them combined? If all of them combined, how explain functional blindness where there is no apparent organic or histological injury in the total visual mechanism?

Furthermore, why cannot a corpse see, even if all its organs, including both the brain and the eyes, are intact? The expected answer would be: Because the man is dead. In other words, there is no life.

Shall we say, then, that it is the life in a living man that enables him to see and to think, since by Mill's Method of Difference, the absence of life results in the absence of seeing and thinking?

Now, if life is a form of energy, biotic energy as Benjamin Moore[9] and J.M. Macfarlane[10] call it, shall we say, then, that it is energy that sees, that feels, that thinks, that worships, that aspires? Would such a statement be more logical, more scientific, more acceptable than to say that it is personality, it is soul that sees, feels, thinks, worships, and aspires, using the body and its various organs as a means of manifestation and expression?

Do we ever logically and empirically connect or associate the functions of seeing, feeling, thinking, worshipping, and aspiring with blind energy? Or do we find such functions connected or associated only with personality, in fact, *produced only by personality?*

If such be the case, then, if empirically, functions like seeing and thinking are associated with personality only, if it is neither the eyes that see, nor the brain that thinks, we can conclude — we have the right to conclude — that it is the personality that sees and thinks, not the body.

It is I that sees, that thinks. And I am consciousness; I am soul. It is the soul that sees through the visual mechanism, the eyes. It is the soul that thinks through the thinking mechanism, the brain.

The Nature Of Ideas

That thinking is not a function of the brain, but of the mind or psyche or soul working through the brain can be shown in yet another way.

Ouspensky, in *Tertium Organum,* talks of different modes of existence. There is, according to him, *physical* existence, recognized by certain sorts of actions and functions, and there is *metaphysical* existence recognized by other sorts of actions and functions.

The Neo-Realists, Meinong, Husserl, and Russell, would rather call the first simply *existence,* and the second, *sub-*

sistence.¹¹ I think that Ouspensky's distinction is more empirical, and, therefore, more verifiable.

Says Ouspensky:

> A *house exists* and the *idea of good and evil* exists. But they do not exist in like manner. One and the same method of proof of existence does not suffice for the proof of the existence of an idea. A house is a *physical fact,* an idea is a *metaphysical* fact. Physical and metaphysical facts exist, but they exist differently.
>
> Our relations to an idea and to a house are quite different. It is possible by a certain effort to destroy a house — to burn, to wreck it. The house will cease to exist. But suppose you attempt to destroy, by an effort, an idea. The more you try to contest, argue, refute, ridicule, the more the idea is likely to spread, grow, strengthen. And contrariwise, silence, oblivion, *non-action,* "non-resistance" will exterminate, or in any case weaken an idea. Silence, oblivion, will not wreck a house, will not hurt a stone. It is clear that the existence of a house and that of an idea are quite different existences.
>
> Of such *different existences* we know very many. A book exists and also the *contents of a book.* Notes exist, and so does *the music that the notes combine to make.* A coin *exists,* and so does the *purchasing* value of a coin. A *word* exists, and the *energy* which it contains.
>
> We discern on the one hand, a whole series of *physical facts,* and on the other hand, a series of *metaphysical facts*.¹²

The existence of ideas is an indubitable declaration of human experience. In fact, to prove that they exist, it is enough to think of them, and their reality or existence is thereby already sufficiently established. Knowledge is the best proof of the existence of ideas, because knowledge is essentially a system of ideas.

But ideas are not physical existences. They are, as Ouspensky insistently points out, *metaphysical existences.* Now, it is precisely for the reason that ideas are metaphysical existences that it would be erroneous to regard them as functions or products of the *physical brain.* If they were products or functions of physical substance as is the brain, we should expect them to behave in the manner of physical substance.

But They Do Not

First, they are spaceless and timeless. They do not occupy space. They are not destroyed or emasculated by time.

Second, they are relatively permanent and indestructible. You can destroy a house, but you cannot destroy the idea of a house.

Third, like knowledge and unlike physical substance, they increase by expenditure. If I have one hundred pesos and I give some away, I diminish the amount of money I have. But if I have knowledge and I give it away, not only do I not diminish my own, but I even increase the number of knowing minds.

Fourth, they are infinite. Now, if the cerebrocentric theory of psychology is true, namely, that each idea corresponds to some synaptic connection in the brain, then there should be as many synapses as there are ideas. In other words, synapses, too, like ideas, should be infinite.

If we should count, for instance, from one and go on counting ad infinitum, the process to be undertaken continuously by successive generations of men, would there be enough synapses to answer for every number that the mind could think of? Surprisingly, the neurological capacities of the human brain are simply astronomical. We possess, each of us, around ten billion brain cells. This is several times the number of human beings in the world. Any one brain cell can be in relationship with as many as 25,000 others. The number of possible associations is of the order of ten billion to the twenty-five thousandth power, a quantity larger than the number of atoms in the universe.[13]

The anatomical structure of consciousness is, indeed, inconceivable in its complexity. And because the mind can count to ten raised to the power of infinity, the number of numbers that the mind can think of becomes infinite.

Evidently, ideas are neither functions nor products of the brain. Their spacelessness and timelessness, their relative indestructibility and permanency, their inaccessibility to physicochemical laws — all point to a source equally and similarly spaceless and timeless, equally indestructible and permanent, equally infinite in function, equally inaccessible to physicochemical laws, equally immediate to consciousness — and that is consciousness itself, the spaceless, timeless, indestructible nonphysical self, the personality, the soul!

Experimental Evidence

We have shown coherently the illogicality and untenability of the theory of epiphenomenalism which regards thought or consciousness as the effect or by-product of brain activity. The theory is based on insufficient physiological knowledge of the brain, in the first place. Furthermore, it lacks the authority of actual experience. It is not empirically verifiable. Finally, it is self-contradictory.

It is self-contradictory, because, as Brightman indicated, "all experimentation presupposes a unified and identical self as observer and interpreter of the experiment. Physiological psychology *(which is the proponent of the epiphenomenalistic hypothesis)*, therefore, insofar as it is experimental, presupposes the unitary self which epiphenomenalism denies. The theory is, therefore, self-contradictory."[14]

There is yet, however, the question of experimental evidence to be considered. Are there facts to prove that man can think even if the brain, especially the cerebrum, be diseased or injured, for example? Can it be experimentally demonstrated that man can think even if the brain be functionally inactive? These decisive questions will be answered in subsequent chapters, particularly the chapters on self-consciousness and the continuity of consciousness, on dreams, on somniloquism, and on hypnotic phenomena.

References

[1] P. D. Ouspensky, *Tertium Organum. The Third Cannon of Thought. A Key to the Enigmas of the World*. Translated from the Russian by Nicholas Bessaraboff and Claude Bragdon, (Third American Edition, New York: Alfred A. Knopf 1945) p. 164.

[2] Annie Besant. *Psychology*, (2nd Edition, Los Angeles, California: Theosophical Publishing House, 1919.) p. 36.

[3] C. J. Ducasse, "The Empirical Case For Personal Survival," in *Body, Mind, and Death*, (New York: The Cromwell Publishing Company, 1964) pp. 223-224.

[4] Vincent H. Gaddis, "With Brain Destroyed — They Live and Think!" *Fate*. Vol. 1, No. 2, p. 82, Summer, 1948.

[5] Locke's famous dictum which is the basis of modern sensationalistic philosophy: "Nihil est in intellectu quod no prius fuerit in sensu."

[6] Will Durant, *The Story of Philosophy*, (New York: Garden City Publishing Co., Inc. 1943) p. 206.

[7] Lin Yutang has a good English extract of Hume's *Enquiry into Human Understanding* in his book *The Wisdom of China and India*. (New York: Modern Library. Seventh Printing. 1942.)

[8] W. B. Pillsbury, *The Essentials of Psychology*, (New York: The Macmillan Company, 1930) pp. 335-336.

[9] Benjamin Moore, *The Origin and Nature of Life*. (Home University Library, Henry Holt and Company) pp. 225-226.

[10] John Muirhead Macfarlane, *The Causes and Course of Organic Evolution*. Chapters IV-VI.

[11] R. G. Fuller, *A History of Philosophy*, (New York: Henry Holt and Company, 1945) pp. 482-491.

[12] P. D. Ouspensky, *op. cit.*, p. 23.

[13] Quoted from the Introduction by Timothy Leary in *LSD — The Consciousness-Expanding Drug*, edited by David Solomon, (New York: G. P. Putnam's Sons, 1964) p. 8; from Robert Campbell, "The Circuit of the Senses," (Part IV), *Life*, Vol. 54, no. 26 (June 28, 1963).

[14] Edgar S. Brightman, *A Philosophy of Religion*, (New York: Prentice-Hall, Inc., 1946) pp. 356-357.

Chapter 13
EVIDENCES FROM THE PHENOMENA OF CONSCIOUSNESS
D. Self-Consciousness And The Continuity Of Consciousness

The Nature Of Self-Consciousness

How, for example, can we study the nature of self-consciousness by the objective methods of science, how measure it, how analyze?

It is, nevertheless, something very real. It is empirically undeniable.

I am conscious of this paper. But I can be, I am also conscious of myself being conscious of this paper. This is the fact of self-consciousness. And it is a proof that I am not the brain. For if I am the brain, and I can think of myself, therefore the brain can think of itself.

This, however, is not true to fact. This, we discover, is empirically unreal. To deny the autonomy and fundamentality of consciousness by making it an epiphenomenon of the brain is to get involved in a mass of contradictions. Consider, for instance, the famous argument of Hume in the fifth and sixth sections of his *Treatise of Human Nature*, Part IV. It is fairly representative of a purely physiological interpretation of self-consciousness.

Here is the argument:

> For my part, when I enter most intimately into what I call *myself,* I always stumble on some particular perception or other, of heat or cold, light or shade, pain or pleasure. I never can catch *myself* at any time without a perception. When my perceptions are re-

moved for any time, as by sound sleep, so long am I insensible of myself, and may truly be said not to exist. And were all my perceptions removed by death, and I could neither think nor feel, nor see, nor love, nor hate, after the dissolution of my body, I should be entirely annihilated, nor can I conceive what is further necessary to make me a perfect non-entity. If anyone, upon superior and unprejudiced reflection, thinks he has a different notion of *himself,* I must confess I can no longer be with him. All I can allow him is, that he may be in the right as well as I, and that we are essentially different in this particular. He may, perhaps, perceive something simple and continued which he calls himself; though I am certain there is no such principle in me. I may venture to affirm of the rest of mankind, that they are nothing but a bundle or collection of different perceptions, which succeed each other with inconceivable rapidity, and are in a perpetual flux and movement.

We must admit that Hume tried to be thoroughly empirical. But his empiricism was prejudiced from the very start. It was prejudiced against the existence of the Perceiver of his perceptions. His declaration that man is "nothing but a bundle or a collection of different perceptions," is a masterpiece of physiological naiveté. Did he ever ask, for example, who was analyzing whom or what when he was analyzing himself?

The fact of self-consciousness proved the greatest stumbling block on the path of Hume's biased self examination. It was the most obvious, because it was the most immediate and intimate. But it was the one thing Hume failed to observe.

For if I, as Hume very categorically affirms, am nothing but a *bundle of perceptions,* who then, is analyzing myself when I am analyzing myself? Evidently, I, the bundle of perceptions, am analyzing myself, the bundle of perceptions. In other words, the bundle of perceptions is analyzing the bundle of perceptions. This, therefore, constitutes Hume's definition of self-consciousness: perception perceiving perception; sensation sensing sensation; idea ideating idea. It is self-consciousness with neither self nor consciousness at all. It is really non-self-non-consciousness. It is an uncompromising and completely dogmatic denial of the most fundamental fact of human experience — the experiencer himself, the perceiver of perception, the sensor of sensations, the ideator of ideas, the personality, the self, the ego, the soul.

In reading the illogical analysis of Hume, it is impossible to escape noticing the self-contradictory nature of the expressions used.

"When I enter . . . . I always stumble . . . . I never can catch myself . . . . I can conceive . . . . all I can allow . . . . I may venture . . . . etc."

If we were to use Hume's definition of the "I" in his analysis, we would be reducing it to a terrible absurdity.

Thus: When the *bundle of perceptions* enters into what the *bundle of perceptions* calls the *bundle of perceptions,* the *bundle of perceptions* always stumbles on some particular perception . . . . The *bundle of perceptions* never can catch the *bundle of perceptions* at any time without a perception. When my perceptions are removed for any time, as by sound sleep, so long is the *bundle of perceptions* insensible of the *bundle of perceptions,* and may truly be said not to exist. And were all my perceptions removed by death, and the *bundle of perceptions* could neither think nor feel, nor see, nor love, nor hate, after the dissolution of my body, the *bundle of perceptions* would be entirely annihilated; nor can the *bundle of perceptions* conceive what is further necessary to make the *bundle of perceptions* a perfect non-entity, and so on.

The extreme insouciance of Mr. Hume, the English bundle of perceptions, is highly amusing, to me a Filipino bundle of perceptions. It is an utter disregard of the fundamental first basis of knowledge — the self, the knower.

The priority, the fundamentality, the primacy of the self cannot be brushed aside without endangering the very validity of all knowledge, all science, all philosophy. The indispensability of the self, the knower and experiencer, is shown by the fact that Hume himself could not escape from the consciousness that he was other than his perceptions. This universal result of introspection, the consciousness of the

Evidence from the Phenomena of Consciousness

"I," otherwise called self-consciousness, betrays itself in the very argument aimed at its annihilation.

We cannot quite succeed in proving the unreality of self-consciousness without arriving at exactly the opposite conclusion, its inevitable reality.

Annie Besant states:

> Let anyone experiment on himself; let him shut himself in, free from all interruption from without; let him patiently and steadily investigate his mental processes; he will find that the shifting contents of his consciousness are not *he*; that he is other than the feelings, the perceptions, the conceptions that pass before him; that they are his, not he, and that he can drive them away, can empty his mind of all save Self-consciousness; can, in the words of Patanjali, become a "spectator without a spectacle."[1]

We may, therefore, conclude that the very act of knowing as well as the fact of knowledge itself, attests to the incontrovertible reality of self-consciousness; and that the fact of self-consciousness presupposes, in an equally incontestable way, the existence of the self, the knower, the perceiver, the experiencer, the ego, the soul amid all the flux of percepts and concepts and objects in the world.

The Identity And Continuity Of Consciousness

The fact of self-consciousness implies yet another important thing, the continuous identity of self-consciousness with itself. And this, the identity and continuity of consciousness, is yet another proof of the existence of the soul — of man the soul as distinguished from his body the instrument, "a local habitation and a name."

At this juncture, one cannot help remembering Carlyle's explosive question when, looking at himself in the mirror and noticing how, at the age of 80, his face had become completely wrinkled, he thundered:

"Who the hell then am I?"

Yes, that is the mighty question. Who am I?

One of the curious phenomena observable regarding the relation between consciousness and the body is the fact that they seem to belong to two entirely different levels of reality, notwithstanding the more obvious fact that they are proceeding along parallel directions. The body ages; the consciousness, the mind does not, though of course it matures.

The body tires; the consciousness does not, though probably, it gets bored. The first tires and ages with the years; the consciousness, or the mind, only becomes wiser. In the first case, there is the exhaustion of physical energy; in the second case, the inexhaustibleness of psychical energy. Physical strength wanes with time; psychic energy, like love, for example, may even grow stronger with the years. The heart grows weaker with age; the power to love, even to hate, may strengthen with time.

Evidently, body and consciousness, two entirely different processes, do not operate on the same level of reality. As such, they cannot be studied from the same level of observation and they cannot be understood according to the same scale or standard of measurement.

There is no adequate way whereby we can reliably interpret consciousness on the basis of the phenomena of the body, as behaviorists insist and persist in trying to do. They represent two different sets of facts, one physical, and the other metaphysical. The first is corruptible, as the Bible says; the other is incorruptible. The first is cellular and molecular, as science says; the other, psychic and spiritual. The first is body, as we insist on saying; the other is soul.

Consider, for instance, the utter inexplicability of the identity and continuity of consciousness in terms of physical data.

The science of physiology tells us that the cells of our bodies are constantly changing, so that after a period of time, approximately seven years, not a single cell I had seven years ago is now in my body.[2]

Now, how shall we explain the identity and continuity of the "I am" in terms of the cerebral cells? They get completely changed every seven years. On the other hand, my consciousness of myself as an identical and continuous personality from the age of seven, for example, to fourteen, to twenty-one, to twenty-eight, has remained unchanged and unbroken.

Of course, it may be argued here by neurologists that the brain cells are not actually replaced, that they only undergo change. The question is, how many changes constitute replacement? And if a cell undergoes a certain change from cell X_1 to cell X_2, has not cell X_2 actually replaced cell X_1?

Now how can an unbroken and continuous personality be based on the behavior of periodically changing cells?

As far as my consciousness is concerned, as far as I am concerned, I feel the same person now that I was seven, fourteen, twenty-one, twenty-eight years ago. I am what I was, with knowledge increased, with experiences gathered. My body now, however, is not exactly the same body I had seven, fourteen, twenty-one, twenty-eight years ago. It has undergone at least four or five complete renovations, during which every cell in my brain has been changed.

How, on the basis of these two sets of irreconcilable facts, shall we explain the fact of the identity and continuity of human consciousness? To explain it in terms of the overlapping of mental states, as William James proposed, is to assume we know what we are talking about.

What is a mental state? Is it a cerebral condition or a state of consciousness? If it is a state of consciousness, then we have a case of *circulus in probando*.

A mental state is a state of consciousness. To explain the continuity of consciousness by the overlapping of states of consciousness is to say the same thing in two different ways. If on the other hand, it is a cerebral state, then we have an assumption that no physiologist would dare make: namely, that a state of consciousness is a cerebral state; in other words, that the brain produces consciousness.

As a matter of fact, no physiologist, no psychologist has any scientific warrant to say that the brain produces consciousness, only for the reason that they are closely associated with each other. It would be like saying that the piano produces music, only for the reason that piano and music are closely associated with each other. We would be ignoring or forgetting completely the efficient cause of music, the pianist. Are we not, therefore, completely forgetting in the former case the efficient cause of consciousness, the personality, the self, the soul?

Soul As Identical And Continuous Self-Consciousness

The complete incompatibility between the empirically incontrovertible fact of the identity and continuity of consciousness and the equally empirically indubitable fact of the constantly changing structure and substance of brain and body leaves us but one alternative explanation: namely, that there is in man something "that varies not nor changes in the midst of things that vary and change."[3]

It is the soul, call it by what name you will: mind, personality, consciousness, self-consciousness, subliminal consciousness, ego, self, experient, or simply, "I am."

Bhagavan Das, elucidating on the identity and continuity of self-consciousness, states:

> It persists unchanged and one, throughout all the changes of the material body and of all its surroundings. "I" who played and leaped and slept as an infant in my parent's lap so many years ago have no infants in mind. What unchanged and persistent particle of matter continues throughout these years in my physical organism? What identity is there between that infantine body and this aged body of mine? But the "I" has not changed. It is the same. Talking of myself I always name myself "I" and nothing more or less. The sheaths in which I am always enwrapping the "I" — thus: I am happy, I am miserable, I am rich, I am poor, I am sick, I am strong, I am young, I am old, I am black, I am white — these are accidents and incidents in the continuity of the "I." They are passing and varying. The "I" remains the same. Conditions change, but they always surround the same "I," the unchanging amid the changing; and anything that changes is at first instinctively, and later, deliberately rejected from the "I," as no part of itself.
>
> Again what is true of the "I" with regard to the body is also true of it with regard to all other things. The house, the town, the country, the earth, the solar system, which "I" live in and identify and connect with myself persisting unchanged through all their changes. *"I" am never and can never be conscious of myself having ever been born or of dying, of experiencing a beginning or an end.*[4] In all the endless months, years,

and small and great cycles, past and to come, this Self-luminous consciousness alone neither arises nor ever sets. But as regards all the things other than "I," that "I" am conscious of, "I" am or can become conscious also of their beginnings and endings, their changes.

Never has the cessation of consciousness been *experienced,* been witnessed directly; or if it has been, then witness, the experiencer himself still remains behind as the continued embodiment of that same consciousness.[5]

References
[1] Annie Besant, *Psychology,* 2nd Edition, (Los Angeles, California: Theosophical Publishing House, 1919) pp. 231-232.
[2] *Ibid.,* p. 4.
[3] *Bhamati;* quoted by Bhagavan Das, *The Science of Peace, An Attempt at an Exposition of the First Principles of the Science of the Self.* Adhyatma-Vidya, (London and Benares: Theosophical Publishing Society, 1904) p. 20.
[4] Author's italics.
[5] Bhagavan Das, *op. cit.,* pp. 20-23.

Chapter 14

EVIDENCES FROM THE PHENOMENA OF MEMORY

The Problem

Memory is one of the commonest experiences of living organisms, particularly of human beings. Mysterious like all other phenomena of mind and consciousness, it is none the less one of the most undeniable facts of life. It is, in fact, as indubitable as consciousness itself.

The important thing to consider, however, is, What is memory? That is the question. That is the problem. What is memory? How does it operate? Who remembers? What remembers? Is memory a function of the brain? Or is it a function of the mind, the personality, the soul? Can memory operate without the brain? What happens when we forget? Is memory always associated with brain substance? Can we remember even when the brain is inactive?

Ultimately, all these questions resolve themselves into one fundamental problem involving two opposing theories: Is memory a brain-function or a soul-function?

Brain And Memory

One thing can be conceded at once, that memory is generally associated with brain substance. But this is only a connection the nature of which is completely unknown. It should not be regarded as a causal connection, one way or the other. It would be unwarranted, in other words, to assume that brain substance produces memory, or that memory produces brain substance. There is nothing more than a connection, an association, a correlation, and it is not even a *necessary* connection. It is only a *general* or *usual* connection. In other words, memory is *not always* associated with brain substance. We cannot, logically or empirically, attribute memory only to living beings which have brain, and deny it to those who have none. We cannot, without violating experience, limit memory only to living organisms with brain.

To do so would be, quoting Bergson:

> .... just as though we should say that because in ourselves digestion is directly connected with a stomach, therefore, only living beings with stomachs can digest. An amoeba digests, although it is an almost undifferentiated mass of protoplasm. What is true is that in proportion to the complexity and perfection of the organism, there is a division of labor; special organs are assigned special functions, and the faculty of digesting is localized in the stomach, or rather in a general digestive apparatus, which works better because it is confined to that one function alone.[1]

In like manner, it would be incorrect to say that there can be no memory without the brain, just for the reason that in ourselves we discover memory directly connected with the brain.

The amoeba has no brain. Neither has it any special organ for remembering. But it can remember just as well, in its own primitive and unspecialized way, to promote its own primitive and unspecialized mode of life. That it can remember is shown by the fact that it can learn; and learning is the first stage in the memory process. It can learn, after several repetitions, to approach foods and avoid irritants. It has, according to Jennings, the power of "getting used" to certain stimulations.[2] In fact, he is inclined to think that this process of "getting used" to certain stimulations is very suggestive of memory in a higher type of mind. Mast and Pusch, in their work, *Modification of Response in the Amoeba,* reported a possible case of learning in the amoeba similar to that of Jennings in his book, *Behavior of Lower Organisms.*

Memory And Consciousness

Does memory explain the continuity of consciousness? This is the theory of most psychologists, Pillsbury, for example.[3] Memory, however, is as mysterious as consciousness itself. We can probably describe how we remember, but we cannot adequately understand *why* we remember at all. Why do we remember? What enables us to remember? What is the basis for memory? Why, it may be asked, does memory appear, as in the case of the amoeba, even in the absence of any specialized organ like the brain?

The answer is obvious enough. Memory is not a function of the brain. It cannot, logically, be a function of the brain since it occurs even in the absence of the brain.

"Nothing," says Joseph, in his *Introduction to Logic*, "is the cause of a phenomenon in the absence of which it nevertheless occurs".[4]

This is the well-known scientific Method of Agreement formulated by Mill on the basis of the Baconian Method of Varying the Circumstances.

If, further, we consider the fact that memory may not occur even in the presence of the brain, as in the case of a corpse whose brain is histologically intact, or even in the ordinary case of amnesia, then the ground for rejecting the brain as the seat of memory is thereby made firmer.

"Nothing," continues Joseph, "is the cause of a phenomenon in the presence of which it nevertheless fails to occur."[5] This is the clincher method of scientific experiment known as the Method of Difference.

Now, therefore, since the phenomenon of memory occurs irrespective of whether there is brain or not, we have logically the right to conclude that there is no causal connection between the two. Memory, in brief, is not a function of the brain. It can, however, be said, that memory is a function of consciousness, both in its simplest and most primitive stage in the amoeba and in its highest and most complex manifestation in man. Without consciousness there can be no memory. Therefore, consciousness is the seat of memory.

Evidence from the Phenomena of Memory 103

It should not be forgotten at this juncture that consciousness in man is not the brain, but the self, the ego, the soul, the "I am," the user of the brain.

Memory, in other words, points to the existence of the soul. Its phenomena are completely inexplicable in terms of brain substance and brain physics. They are explicable only in terms of soul-substance and metaphysics. Let us analyze some of the interesting phenomena of memory in the light of our two opposing theories, the soul-theory and the body-theory.

Why Cannot A Dead Man Remember?

This question may seem trite and the answer to it is very obvious. But the fact that it is trite and obvious, is the very reason why we insist on asking it and on demanding only logically inevitable answers.

A corpse does not remember, even though the brain, the whole nervous system, nay, the whole corporal body is intact, because it is no longer alive. And it is no longer alive, because, evidently, something is no longer there. What is absent in a corpse that is present in a living man? "Life," answers the cautious scientist. And we agree, but consciousness, too; and therefore, also memory.

Life, consciousness, memory — they are coextensive, as Henri Bergson said.[6] Life is consciousness and consciousness is life. Life is consciousness turned inward. Consciousness is life turned outward. And memory is a function of consiousness, not of the brain.

The brain is merely a system of neurones and reaction patterns. Consciousness is the recall of images and the choice of reactions; in other words, consciousness is memory. How can we remember, unless first we are conscious?

To Bergson, therefore, mind is not identical with brain. If consciousness depends upon the brain, it will naturally fall with it; but so does a coat fall with the nail on which it hangs. This does not prove, however, that the coat is an "epiphenomenon" or an ornamental ectoplasm of the nail.[7]

Why, then, does a corpse not remember? Despite the high-sounding technical terminology of science, the simple, unpretentious, ancient answer of religion is still correct: because the soul is no longer there.

The Permanence Of Memory

One of the remarkable discoveries (I would say rediscoveries, because the East, particularly India, has known it all along) due mainly to psychoanalysis and depth psychology is the relative permanence of memory. According to this school of psychological thought, the mind does not really forget and there is no such thing as forgetting in the ordinary acceptation of the word.

Forgetting in the sense of total or complete obliteration of the memory image is not a fact. On the contrary, everything that once enters into consciousness leaves thereon, as it were, its trace; and this memory trace, in some inexplicable way, becomes ineradicable and, in ways more than one, voluntarily or involuntarily recoverable.

Memory, in other words, is never lost, as nothing in the universe is ever really lost. For if it were so, the absence of memories relating to a given period, say during the first few years of our lives, would force us to conclude that we were unconscious during that period simply because we have no memories whatsoever of those days. Forgotten, it is not really destroyed or obliterated, it merely sinks into the subconscious or unconscious, as the psychoanalyst or depth psychologist would say.

Physicists speak of energy as kinetic or potential, the active and the latent. So consciousness may be active and latent, kinetic and potential. We "remember" and we "forget," but what is forgotten has not really passed out of consciousness; it has merely become latent, and it can be actualized again into active memory.

No force, says the first law of thermodynamics, can be annihilated on the physical plane. As in the physical, so in the mental, the law of energy-conservation obtains. No experience on the mental plane, no thought, no idea can be destroyed. It can only sink into subconsciousness or unconsciousness; and it can be resuscitated and remembered again. There are many recorded cases of forgetting, partial or incomplete, and subsequent memory-revival.

Dr. Winslow, in his book *Diseases of the Brain and Mind,* tells of the case of the celebrated Danish traveler Niebuhr. When old, blind, and so infirm that he had to be carried from his bed to his chair, he used to describe to his friends with wonderful minuteness and vivacity the scenes which he had visited in his early days. When they expressed their astonishment at the vividness of his memory, he explained that as he lay in bed, all visible objects shut out, the pictures of what he had seen in the East continually floated before his mind's eye, so that it was no wonder that he could speak of them as if he had seen them yesterday.[8]

Even stranger than the revival of memory in old age are the cases of complete memory-reconstitution in the dying. What follows is a selection from Du Prel's *Philosophy of Mysticism,* quoted by Besant in her book, *Psychology*.[9]

> At the approach of death, also the extraordinary exaltation of memory, connected with a change in the measure of time, has been frequently observed. Fechner relates the case of a lady who fell into the water and was nearly drowned. From the moment when all bodily movement ceased till she was drawn out of the water, about two minutes elapsed, during which, according to her own account, she lived again through her whole past, the most insignificant details of it being represented in her imagination. Another instance of the same mental action in which the events of whole years were crowded together is described by Admiral Beaufort from his own experience. He had fallen into the water, and had lost his (normal) consciousness. In this condition "thought rose after thought, with a rapidity of succession that is not only indescribable, but probably inconceivable by anyone who has not himself been in a similar situation." At first the immediate consequences of his death to his family were presented to him; then, his regards turned to the past; he repeated his last cruise, an earlier one in which he was shipwrecked, his schooldays, the progress he then made, and the time he had wasted, even all his childish journeys and adventures. "Thus travelling backwards, every incident of my past life seemed to me to glance across my recollection in retrograde succession, not, *however in mere outline,* as

here stated, but the picture filled up with every minute and collateral feature; in short, the whole period of my existence seemed to be placed before me in a kind of panoramic review, and every act of it seemed to be accompanied by a consciousness of right and wrong, or by some reflection on its causes or its consequences. Indeed, many trifling events, which had long been forgotten, then crowded into my imagination, and with the character of recent familiarity." In this case, also, but two minutes at the most had passed before Beaufort was taken out of the water.[10]

So far we have brought forward three representative cases of memory-recovery, one accompanying extreme old age and the two others produced by the apparent approach of death.

Passing attacks of illness may also bring about the alteration of memory content in a manner so remarkable as to force us to conclude that the mind never loses its memory impressions, but retains all of them, some above the threshold of consciousness, hence *remembered,* and some below the threshold of consciousness, thus *forgotten.*

Forgetting and remembering, therefore, are both aspects of memory. The first we would call *unconscious memory* as distinguished from the second called *conscious memory.*

To remember is but to focus attention on what is temporarily on the screen of waking consciousness; to forget is but to lose focus of what temporarily sinks below the level of waking consciousness.

Now, what is remembered can be forgotten and what is forgotten can be remembered. There can be, in other words, a shifting up and down, of the contents of memory. In the language of psychoanalysis, the contents of consciousness can be repressed down into the subconscious and the contents of the subconscious can be released into the conscious.

That we forget what we remember is a common enough occurrence for everyone to accept as fact; that we sometimes remember what we forget is still common enough for us to regard as true; but to remember everything we have completely forgotten is something that strikes us as altogether wonderful.

But this is exactly what happens under certain circumstances.

The approach of death, extreme old age, sleep, dream, sickness, strong shock, the use of drugs, psychoanalytic abreaction, dianetic reverie, psychedelic stimulation, yoga practice, and hypnotism are some of the means whereby complete recovery of memory content may be made possible.

Here are three illustrative cases of memory revival through illness from Dr. Winslow's work, *Diseases of the Brain and Mind*:

> Dr. Hutchinson refers to the case of a physician who had in early life renounced the principles of the Roman Catholic Church. During an attack of delirium, he prayed only in the forms of the Church of Rome, while all recollection of the prescribed formula of the Protestant religion was effaced and obliterated from the mind by the cerebral affection.
>
> A gentleman was thrown from his horse while hunting. He was taken from the field to a neighboring cottage in a state of unconsciousness, and was subsequently removed to his residence. For the period of a week, his life was considered in imminent danger. When he was sufficiently restored to enable him to articulate, he began to talk in German, a language he had acquired in early life, but had not spoken for nearly twenty-five years.
>
> A gentleman had a serious attack of illness. When restored, it was found that he had lost all recollection of recent circumstances, but had a lucid memory as to events that had occurred in *early life*; in fact, impressions that had long been forgotten were again revived. As this patient recovered his bodily health, a singular alteration was observed in the character of his memory. He again recollected *recent* ideas, but entirely forgot all the events of the past years.[11]

Exaltation Of Memory

More astonishing than simple memory revival due to various causes is the exaltation of memory that may occur under certain specific conditions. By exaltation of memory we mean the unusual intensification of the power of memory that puts its possessor completely above the ordinary.

It may be induced either by natural or artificial means. Sickness, insanity, and shock are among the natural causes. Drugs and hypnotism are examples of the artificial means. In the East, as among the yogis of India, yoga is employed to develop it in a systematic and scientific manner.

Du Prel, in his *Philosophy of Mysticism,* gives the following instances of exaltation of memory:

> Coleridge mentions a maid-servant who, in the delirium of fever, recited long passages in Hebrew which she did not understand, and could not repeat when in health, but which formerly, when in the service of a priest, she had heard him deliver aloud. She also quoted passages from theological works, in Latin and Greek, which she only half understood, when the priest, as was his custom, read aloud his favorite authors when going to and from church.
>
> A Rostock peasant, in a fever, suddenly recited the Greek words commencing the Gospel of St. John, which he had accidentally heard sixty years before; and Benecke mentions a peasant woman who, in a fever uttered Syriac, Chaldean, and Hebrew words which, when a girl, she had accidentally heard in the house of a scholar.
>
> A deranged person, who was cured by Dr. Willis, said that in his attacks his memory attained extraordinary power, so that long passages from Latin authors occurred to him.
>
> A girl of seven, employed as neatherd, occupied a room divided only by a thin partition from that of a violin player, who often gave himself up to his favorite pursuit during half the night. Some months later, the girl got another place, in which she had already been for two years, when frequently in the night tones exactly like those of the violin were heard coming from her room, but which were produced by the sleeping girl herself. This often went on for hours, sometimes with interruptions, after which she would continue the song where she had left off. With regular intervals, this lasted for two years. Then she also produced the tones of a piano which was played in the family, and after-

wards she began to speak, and held forth with remarkable acuteness on political and religious subjects, often in a very accomplished and sarcastic way; she also conjugated Latin, or spoke like a tutor to a pupil. In all which cases this entirely ignorant girl merely reproduced what had been said by members of the family, or by visitors.[12]

An Explanation?

With this rough survey of illustrative cases of memory phenomena before us, we now ask for explanation and interpretation.

How shall we explain the relative permanence of memory, its complete revival under certain circumstances, its exaltation under specific conditions, its entire restoration under hypnosis, its voluntary reinstatement by yoga discipline?

Are these cases explicable in terms of the materialistic brain-theory which declares that memory is a function of matter in motion? Or are they better explained, more consistently, more comprehensively, and more coherently interpreted, by the non-physicalistic soul-theory which regards memory as a function of consciousness, or self, or soul, functioning *through* the brain, but not a resultant or consequence of it?

The Brain-Theory Of Memory

The generally accepted, that is the so-called scientific, theory of memory is the brain-theory. This theory regards memory as primarily and essentially a physiological process. Like all other so-called brain functions, it is supposed to be the result of vibrations of the nerve cells of the brain. As such, it is expressible in terms of matter and motion. Explained in accordance with this theory, the evolution of memory seems to be a very simple process. Let us trace this apparently simple process on the basis of the cerebrocentric hypothesis.

Memory, according to this theory, is a cortical process. Its materials, therefore, are sensations. Psychologists, in consequence, sometimes call the elementary components of memory centrally aroused sensations.

A stimulus sets up a vibration in some sense organ, the eye, for example. This vibration, now called a nerve impulse, or neurokyme, travels from cell to cell until it reaches the appropriate area or center in the brain. It arouses this cortical center in a given way, thus producing in it a predisposition to act in a similar way in the future. This predisposition is technically called the perseveration tendency. With repetition, this tendency becomes stronger, until finally, it may recur even in the absence of external stimulus. The original sensation has now become an idea. In other words, the memory-image has been formed. Now, whenever this particular cortical center vibrates as it has vibrated under the first stimulus, this memory image, now called an idea, recurs, and this recurrence is called memory.

Memory, thus, may be defined simply as "the rearousal of the cortical structures originally active";[13] or, as Herbert Spencer very aptly put it, "the re-excitation of the vesicles of the brain (groups of cortical cells).[14]

In brief, memory is cerebral vibration. This theory seems further strengthened by the fact that "extensive pathological changes or injury of the brain, including the frontal lobes, cause both in man and beast many psychical disturbances,"[15] usually, according to Pillsbury, "loss or disturbances of memories, as well as the loss of the capacity for sensations."[16]

Difficulties Of The Brain-Theory Of Memory

Peter Hogarth, a physiologist, advances the following reasons why most theories of memory have severe drawbacks: "First, he says, "there is simply not a great deal of reliable, unambiguous fact known about brain function, and secondly, because studies on individual neurons can reveal a limited amount about the functions of the brain as a whole, and to theorize on the basis of cell activity is futile without an understanding of what masses of neurons do together."[17]

Other limitations and difficulties spring from the fact that the cerebrocentric theory of memory ignores the primacy of consciousness in the first place. This attitude, as explained in previous chapters, leads to illogical conclusions. The brain cannot be conscious of itself, as the eye cannot see itself. Only consciousness is self-conscious, that is, conscious of itself. Now, since memory is a conscious process, and in man even a self-conscious one, therefore it cannot be a function of the brain which is both unsensing and unconscious in itself. The utmost one can say of the brain is that it is the physical instrument of consciousness.

In the second place, recognizing the causal priority of brain over consciousness makes psychology completely dependent on physiology. Now, as we said, this is a false orientation. It commits the fallacy of reduction. To say that there can be no consciousness without the brain is like saying that there can be no psychology without physiology. And to say that there can be no psychology without physiology is like saying that there can be no biology without chemistry. To be sure, the sciences are interdependent. Would the scientists themselves, however, agree that because all sciences are based on metaphysics, therefore, there can be no science without metaphysics?

The existence of special sciences recognizes the independence of fields of study. Biology studies life, chemistry the elements. It would, however, be wrong to say that life is completely chemical, just for the reason that so far we find life associated with chemical elements. In the same manner, it would be fallacious to say that the reality of water consists solely in its electronic structure, just for the reason that it is composed of electrons. Water is water, and the peculiar quality of *waterness* that it possesses is certainly absent in the electrons of which it is physically composed. A piece of paper, too, is composed of electrons, but can it quench thirst like water?

Brightman calls this error the fallacy of primitivism,[18] otherwise called the fallacy of reduction. It may, perhaps, be regarded as a special form of the fallacy of idealization. It consists in the supposition that the first stage of the development of any process reveals what the process really is.

Thus, to suppose that astronomy is nothing but astrology, just because astronomy began from astrology is to commit this fallacy. Or to interpret Kantian philosophy in terms of the earliest babblings of the little boy Immanuel is to fall into this error. Hence, to say that consciousness or memory is nothing but cerebration, just for the reason that they seem to be associated with each other, or that in the newborn infant there is evidence of brain but not of consciousness or memory, is to commit this fallacy.

The truth, however, is that we do not know the nature of this association between the consciousness and the brain. *In fact, we are not even sure if they are necessarily associated with each other.* We do not know whether or not consciousness started with the brain, since we have already said that there can be consciousness even without the brain, as in the amoeba, for example.

Furthermore, as there is no direct evidence of consciousness or memory in the child, so is there absolutely none even in the normal adult. *There is none we repeat.* There is only inference by analogy. I know I am conscious. I do not really know if you are, unless you tell me, or I infer by your actions that you are.

In other words, consciousness does not start with the brain. *Rather, it starts with the appearance of personality or the "I am."* This is important to note, since it proves very clearly that consciousness, and consequently also the memory, is a function not of the brain but of the personality, the self, the ego, the soul. The brain cannot say, "I am," or "I am conscious"; only "I" can.

Inadequacy Of The Brain Theory

In the third place, the brain-theory cannot adequately explain the indestructibility of memory and the fact that it can be totally revived under certain conditions.

That memory can be completely restored is theoretically and empirically true. Theoretically, it is in accord with the law of conservation of energy. Empirically, it is supported by the various phenomena of memory exemplified in the preceding sections of this chapter.

Where is memory stored up in its completeness before it is restored to waking consciousness? Depth psychology answers: In the unconscious.

But what is the unconscious? Is it the brain itself or some mysterious hidden part of it? Or is it the soul or personality in its infraliminal, or, as Myers calls it, subliminal level? If the unconscious be the brain itself, or any part thereof, how is memory stored in it?

The vexing question is: How can metaphysical ideas be contained in a physical container? If ideas, as materialistic psychologists declare, are vibrations, we may still ask what kinds of vibrations they are. And if they are physical vibrations, how then do we perceive them not as physical vibrations, but rather as metaphysical facts? And if they are metaphysical facts, how can they be generated by a physical organ like the brain? In other words, the utter incompatibility between the physicality of the brain, on the one hand, and the non-physicality of memory-ideas, on the other, makes the brain-theory of memory completely incoherent.

We are, thus, almost constrained to accept the existence of a nonphysical reality in man, such as the soul, in order to account for the storage as well as restoration of nonphysical ideas. In brief, soul-existence is the only explanation of the nature and behavior of memory. The psychoanalyst and the depth psychologist call it the unconscious.

I call it simply soul.

Theory Of Perseveration Tendency Unscientific

On the other hand, it may be said that what are preserved in the cerebral cells are not memory ideas, but only predispositions to them, in other words, tendencies to vibrate as in the past. This — the perseveration tendency theory — however, is unscientific.

If memory is a brain function, then it must behave in accordance with the laws of matter in motion. But it does not. Consider, for example, the Law of Interference in physics.

In general, according to this law, if a certain piece of matter is vibrating in a given way, and another rate of vibration is made to bear upon it, it loses its original vibratory rate and assumes a rate which is the resultant of both the original and the interfering rates.

In music, the operation of this law results in the production of silence, that is, obliteration of both rates. Applied to memory, it should mean total forgetting, that is, obliteration of memory.

Now, the brain, because it is physical, is expected to operate according to this law. Memory, however, operates as if there were no such law. It is never obliterated. It is, in a sense, not only indestructible, but even nontransformable.

It cannot be destroyed. It cannot be transformed.

Since this is so, the energy of the mind is not physical energy which, while non-destructible, is nevertheless transformable.

If it is not physical energy, therefore, it can be neither the brain nor an epiphenomenon of the brain.

Therefore, mind, memory, and consciousness are not physical; they can be co-extensive only with a non-physical reality. Call it whatever you will.

I call it simply soul.

Du Prel's Argument Against The Brain-Theory

Du Prel, in his *Philosophy of Mysticism,* gives substantially the same argument against the brain-theory of mind and memory. He said:

> On this hypothesis (brain-theory) memory would depend on material brain traces, left behind by impressions; by the act of memory such traces are continually renewed, rechiselled as it were, so there arise well-worn tracks in which the coach of memory is conducted with special facility.
>
> The deductions from this view had already been drawn by the materialists of the last century. Hook and others recognized that, since one-third of a second sufficed for the producing of an impression, in 100 years a man must have collected in his brain 9,467,280,000 traces or copies of impressions, or reduced by one-third for the period of sleep, 3,155,760,000; thus, in fifty years, 1,577,880,000; further that, allowing a weight of four pounds to the brain, and subtracting one pound for the blood and vessels and another for the external integument, a single grain of brain substance must contain 205,542 traces.
>
> Moreover, our intellectual life does not consist in mere impressions; these form only the material of our

judgement. These brain-atoms do not help us to judgement, notwithstanding their magical properties, so that we must suppose that whenever we form a sentence or a judgement the impressions are combined, like the letters in the compositor's box, these atoms, however, being at the same time compositor and box.[19]

If we should continue the argument of Du Prel, and reduce the materialistic brain-theory to absurdity, we would have something like this:

Each grain of brain substance is vibrating in 205,542 different ways, and is producing 205,542 different clear and completely individual ideas. How will the physicist react to such a statement?

Each grain of brain substance has, photographically speaking, 205,542 exposures, and is giving 205,542 different clear and well-defined pictures. How will any ordinary photographer regard such a statement?

Memory A Soul-Function

It is clear, therefore, that any materialistic interpretation of the non-physically conforming phenomena of mind and memory leads to illogical and irresponsible conclusions.

One other curious phenomenon of memory that points logically to its noncerebral origin is the exaltation or intensification of memory under both voluntary and involuntary conditions. Examples of exalted memory are plentiful in the field of hypnotism. We shall discuss them in the chapter on hypnotism. Two good cases of memory exaltation under involuntary circumstances, already quoted in a previous section of this chapter are given by Du Prel.

The first case is that of a lady who, according to Fechner, nearly died of drowning. She recounted her unusual experience of reliving her past life in only two minutes, just before she lost consciousness.

The second is that of Beaufort who, in his testimony, declared that he experienced all the events of his past life just immediately before he passed out of his normal consciousness to revive into remembrance a whole life-time of experience in only two minutes.

Memory, in this case, has almost become emancipated from time. This fact shows very clearly that it cannot be a function of the brain, but of the spaceless and timeless personality which is man himself, the self, the ego, the soul.

References

[1] Henri Bergson, *Mind-Energy*, translated by H. Wildon Carr, (Copyright, 1920, by Henry Holt and Company, Inc., New York. Copyright, 1948, by H. Wildon Carr) p. 11.

[2] Margaret Floy Washburn, *The Animal Mind, A Textbook of Comparative Psychology*, (New York: The Macmillan Company 1936) p. 41.

[3] W. B. Pillsbury, *The Essentials of Psychology*, (New York: The Macmillan Company, 1930) p. 437.

[4] H. W. B. Joseph, *Introduction to Logic*, (Oxford: Clarendon Press, 1906) p. 403.

[5] *Ibid.*, p. 404.

[6] Bergson, *op. cit.*

[7] Will Durant, *The Story of Philosophy*, (New York: Garden City Publishing Co., Inc., 1943) p. 339.

[8] From Dr. Winslow's *Diseases of the Brain and Mind*, quoted by Annie Besant in her book, *Psychology*, Second Edition, Los Angeles, California, Theosophical Publishing House, 1919.

[9] From Du Prel's *Philosophy of Mysticism*, quoted by Annie Besant, *op. cit.*, pp. 237-238.

[10] Haddock, *Somnolism and Psychism*, p. 213, as quoted by Annie Besant, *op. cit.*, p. 238.

[11] Winslow, *Diseases of the Brain and Mind*, quoted by Annie Besant, *op. cit.*, pp. 239-240.

[12] From Du Prel, *Philosophy of Mysticism*, as quoted in Annie Besant, *op. cit.*, pp. 240-241.

[13] W. B. Pillsbury, *Essentials of Psychology*, (New York: The Macmillan Company, 1930) p. 158.

[14] Herbert Spencer, *Principles of Psychology*, 1945, p. 258.

[15] Carl W. Wiggers, *Physiology in Health and Disease* (Philadelphia: Lea and Febiger).

[16] Pillsbury, *op. cit.*, p. 159.

[17] Peter J. Hogarth, "The Physiological Basis of Memory," *Advancement of Science*, 22, 696-700, April, 1966.

[18] Edgar S. Brightman, *A Philosophy of Religion*, (New York: Prentice Hall, Inc., 1946) pp. 37-38.

[19] Besant, *op. cit.*, pp. 247-248.

Chapter 15
EVIDENCES FROM THE PHENOMENA OF SLEEP
The Mystery Of Sleep

Sleep is one of the most common phenomena of life, but it is also one of the least understood. What it is or why it comes is, both to psychology and to physiology, still a matter of disagreement. There is no certain knowledge. There are only claims of knowledge.

Pavlov regards generalized internal inhibition due to the monotonous repetition of stimuli as the cause of sleep.

The cerebral ischemia theory, of which Howell is an ardent advocate, states that fatigue of the vasomotor center with consequent vasodilation of the peripheral vessels, especially of the skin, and reduction in cerebral blood flow were the primary changes responsible for the onset of sleep.[1]

Shepard demolished the cerebral ischemia theory of sleep and instead proposed an inhibitory theory which states, "as we go to sleep we become absorbed in a mass or complex of fatigue sensations. These tend strongly to inhibit other processes, especially motor activity and consciousness of strain sensation from the muscles."[2]

A more recent theory is that of Kleitman who has done exhaustive studies on sleep and wakefulness. According to him, sleep is due to the inactivity of the cerebral cortex resulting from a reduction in the number of afferent impulses, especially from the muscles, reaching the sensorium.

The chemical theory of sleep, on the other hand, attributes it to the accumulation of sleep-producing substances in the brain. Pieron, for instance, believes that hypnotoxin, a substance liberated by the brain during cerebration reduces the irritability of the brain, thus causing somnolence.

The neurodynamic theories consider sleep as due to severance of neuronic connections by a dynamic mechanism.

Exner and Cajal[3] suggest that sleep is produced by the breaking of synaptic connections brought about by the cortical ganglion cells drawing in their dendrites. Lepine[4] and Duval[5] theorize that histological changes in the neurones of the cerebral cortex are the cause of sleep.

Invalid Assumptions

In all these theories there is involved an invalid assumption that makes all of them incomplete and ineffective. This is the materialistic assumption that man is the body, so that, therefore, sleep must be due to something that happens in the body, as for example, the loss of blood in the brain (cerebral ischemia theory), or the accumulation of cerebral toxins (chemical theory), or the inhibition of cerebration (inhibitory theory), or the severance of neuronic connections in the brain (neuro-dynamic theory).

In other words, all these theories of sleep are body theories. They completely ignore the fact that man, in truth, is primarily and essentially consciousness and only secondarily and incidentally body. The result is that, because man is regarded as body and consciousness as only the epiphenomenon of its brain, both psychologists and physiologists define sleep as the loss of consciousness due to something that happens in the body. There is implicit in this usual definition of sleep the unwarranted and empirically false assumption that the body is conscious.

What sleeps? The body. What is sleep? The loss, whether total or partial, of consciousness. What loses consciousness, then? The body. Ergo, the body is conscious. For how can it lose consciousness unless first it is conscious?

But we have already shown in previous chapters that there is absolutely no empirical basis for assuming that the body, or even the brain, is at all conscious.

Thus, we realize that it is illogical and empirically unwarranted to regard sleep from the standpoint of the body, inasmuch as such procedure leads to the incorrect conclusion that the body is conscious.

It is more empirically justifiable to regard sleep from the standpoint of consciousness, and hence to define it, not as the loss of consciousness by the body (the body cannot lose what, in the first place, it does not have), but rather as simply an *altered state of consciousness* resulting from the temporary withdrawal of that consciousness or personality (some writers call the process transfocalization) from the body.

Valid Definition

This definition of sleep is valid for several reasons.

In the first place, it recognizes the primacy of consciousness. It takes cognizance of the fundamental priority of self or consciousness over the body. It is, therefore, empirically correct.

In the second place, it does not, when analyzed critically, lead to the same illogical conclusion to which the definition of sleep as loss of consciousness inevitably leads, namely, that consciousness can be unconscious.

The dilemma is something like this: Man is either the body or the conscious personality. Now, if sleep is loss of consciousness, therefore, either the body loses consciousness or the conscious personality loses consciousness. In either case we have illogicality. How can the body lose consciousness since it never has it? How can the conscious personality lose consciousness, since that would mean consciousness losing consciousness? In other words, how can the unconscious (that is, the body) be further unconscious (that is, asleep)? And how can consciousness (that is, the personality) be unconscious (that is, asleep)?

In the third place, this definition accords completely with the various phenomena attendant on sleep or concomitant to it, such as hypnagogy, hypnopompy, somnambulism, somniloquism, and dreams.

These phenomena are inexplicable in terms of the definition of sleep as a state of relative or absolute unconsciousness. They are, however, fully understandable in terms of the definition of sleep as the altered state of consciousness resulting from the temporary withdrawal of consciousness from the body; what follows, therefore, is a state of consciousness different from our normal waking consciousness.

The Sleep-Consciousness

All empirical data are in favor of the idea that sleep is a state of consciousness rather than unconsciousness. The whole weight of Eastern psychology, particularly the yoga psychology of India, supports it.

In Eastern psychology, there are four well-recognized states of consciousness, namely: the *jagrat* or waking consciousness, the *svapna* or dream consciousness, the *sushupti* or deep sleep consciousness, and the *turiya,* or cosmic consciousness, sometimes called *samadhi.*

Of these four states, sleep-consciousness consists of two stages, the dream-consciousness called *svapna* and the deep-sleep called *sushupti.* Both are sharply distinguished from the waking consciousness or *jagrat.*

In the West, the stages and depth of sleep have been classified according to the activity of brain waves during sleep as measured by an electro-encephalogram (EEG).

Loomis, Harvey, and Hobart described five stages in the transition from quiet wakefulness to deep sleep. This classification has been gradually accepted by subsequent workers and may be described as follows:[6]

> Stage A. Interrupted alpha. The normal 10/sec alpha rhythm dominates the record.
>
> Stage B. Low voltage. The alpha rhythm is lost and the record is quite straight with only small changes of potential.
>
> Stage C. Spindles. The line is slightly irregular with spindles of 14/sec waves occurring every few seconds.
>
> Stage D. Spindles plus random. The spindles continue together with large random delta waves, these latter being characterized by a duration of greater than 0.2 sec.
>
> Stage E. Random. The delta waves increase in voltage and duration, whilst the 14/sec spindle becomes inconspicuous.

The EEG record is thus a valuable index to the state of consciousness, the prominence of delta waves being proportional to the depth of sleep. If the alpha rhythm was prominent in the waking state it often showed depression or disappearance just as the subject became drowsy. When spindling at 14/sec (Stage C) occurred, this was a sure sign of real sleep.

Both Eastern and Western psychology recognize that man's consciousness is regarded as a continuum of several stages passing from waking or quiet wakefulness to deep sleep. Sleep, therefore, is consciousness of a sort different from our ordinary waking consciousness.

Now, if it is a state of consciousness, it cannot belong to the body, which is, empirically, never really conscious. We are, therefore, led to conclude that it belongs to the self or ego, the "I am." In other words, it is a state of the self, of the "I am". Furthermore, since the state or condition of the self in conjunction with the body is our normal waking consciousness, its state or condition in sleep cannot be in conjunction with the body. It must, therefore, be outside of it. And this is what we call sleep, or what the Hindus call either *svapna,* if we are dreaming through it, or *sushupti,* if it is a condition of profound dreamless slumber.

Sleep, therefore, is a condition of consciousness not within the body. It cannot be a state of consciousness in nothing. We are, thus, forced to conclude either that consciousness can exist apart from the body or that it exists in a higher dimensional body or vehicle. In either case, we are no longer constrained to regard consciousness as an epiphenomenon of the body or its brain. Rather, we are led to realize that consciousness is an independent reality, completely different from the body or its brain. Philosophers may call it self, ego, or personality.

I prefer to call it soul.

Evidences

That sleep is consciousness in a higher dimension, or as Hindu psychology technically calls it *svapna* or *sushupti,* is evinced by a number of curious phenomena attendant upon it.

Why, for example, does a sleeping man hear when we call him? If he is asleep, and sleep is unconsciousness, why, then, does he wake up? Evidently he hears; and if he hears, how could he be *unconscious*? Evidently, he is conscious. If he is conscious, what is conscious? It cannot be his body, since empirically, the body is never conscious. Therefore, there is in him something that is always conscious even in sleep. That something the psychoanalyst would call the subconscious or the unconscious. That consciousness which, empirically, can never be shown as becoming unconscious, whether in the waking, dreaming, or dreamless sleep state, I call the soul, no matter what others may call it.

Furthermore, suppose a man sleeps a profound dreamless sleep in the night. When he wakes up in the morning, he says, "I had a sound sleep last night." Now, if sleep is a state of unconsciousness, it constitutes a break or a gap in consciousness between the falling asleep at night and the waking up the following morning. The question is, who bridges that gulf when the man says in the morning, "I had a sound sleep"? In other words, who is conscious of the unconsciousness of a man in his sleep and thus is able to say in the morning, "I had a sound sleep last night"?

Here again, the unbreakable continuity of consciousness, even in sleep, is clearly evident. For if consciousness is broken between the sleeping and the waking, how explain its continuity or remembrance? Or, if we should say that memory is responsible for such continuity, then we are led to conclude that memory is a function of the soul and not of the brain, as explained in the preceding chapter. Therefore, we conclude that something in man does not sleep even during sleep. This I call the soul.

Somnambulism And Somniloquism

The two most interesting phenomena of sleep, however, are somnambulism and somniloquism. Popularly they are known respectively as sleep-walking and sleep-talking. They constitute the two most cogent evidences of the continuity of consciousness in sleep and, therefore, of the existence of the soul as an autonomous reality quite independent of the body or its nervous system.

Psychologists usually regard somnambulism and somniloquism as abnormal, even pathological states. At this juncture, it should be stressed that the difference between the normal and abnormal is purely a matter of degree and largely a matter of relative standards of observation and measurement.

"The knowledge and experience of modern psychiatry," says Dr. Frieda Fromm-Reichmann, one-time director of psychotherapy at Chestnut Lodge Sanitorium in Washington, D.C., "shows that there is, in essence, a difference only in degree and not in kind between the emotional and mental experiences and modes of expression of people who suffer from severe mental disorders (psychoses), persons who suffer from milder forms of difficulties in living (neuroses), and people who enjoy emotional stability (the so-called healthy)."[7]

This is the reason why specialists in abnormal psychology are very emphatic in warning that "abnormal psychology should not be viewed as a field of psychopathology, extreme deviation, or bizarre phenomena isolated from the rest of psychology and other sciences."[8]

Psychopathology is only an aspect of abnormal psychology. Furthermore, abnormality implies both subnormality, such as idiocy and moronism, and supernormality, as genius and prodigy. Abnormality means any deviation, big or small, from the normal, and the dividing line between the two, like that between night and day, is not easy to fix.

Anger is not a usual behavior of human beings. It is, however, not accurate to call an angry man necessarily abnormal. The most we can say is that he is temporarily deviating from the normal. When, however, this deviation becomes relatively permanent, we begin to suspect that there is something the matter with him. Then we say he is abnormal.

Moreover, abnormality is not necessarily a handicap. On the contrary, it may become a specific asset. Such, for example, is the case with the inarticulate or mute and detached creative personality who suffers from a schizophrenic mental disorder that incapacitates him in maintaining a proper relationship with society. His very aloofness, his muteness, may motivate him to express himself without articulation, through literary or artistic creativeness. Two good examples are the German composer Schumann and the Russian dancer Nijinski.

Other examples of people whose creative assets developed as a result of, or in connection with their abnormalities are the Scandinavian authors Hamsun and Strindberg, the British poet Oscar Wilde, the American writer Edgar Allan Poe, the Dutch painter Van Gogh, and the German philosopher Schopenhauer.

The Nature Of Somnambulism

Somnambulism need not be considered as an abnormality except when it is associated with or when it occurs in parasomniacs. In the first place, we do not know exactly its nature and cause. In the second place, it is a rather common occurrence. Many people manifest it early in life, then lose it afterward. In the third place, it is one of those psychological conditions or phenomena that throw into bold relief, against the background of so-called normality, the true nature of human personality.

It points, in other words, to the existence in man of a nonphysical element that completely overthrows the cerebrocentric philosophy of materialistic scientists.

That these scientists are too quick to judge somnambulism as abnormal merely shows that they have simply created for themselves a dogmatic yardstick that throws aside as abnormal all forms of behavior which do not conform to their physicalistic and corpocentric standards.

What is a somnambulist? Janet succinctly gives us the answer: "It is an individual who thinks and acts while asleep. Without a doubt that answer is not very clear, *for we do not know very well what sleep is.* That answer means only that the person spoken of *thinks* and *acts* in an odd way, different from that of other people, and that at the same time that person is in some way *like a person asleep.*"[9] In brief, repeating for emphasis the words underlined in Janet's definition, a somnambulist is a sleep-thinker and actor. He thinks asleep. He acts asleep.

If, in addition, he also talks, then he is not only a somnambulist. He is also a somniloquist. *He thinks asleep. He talks asleep. He acts asleep.*

Hence, we regard him as abnormal because in our judgment and according to our standard, it is normal to think, to talk, and to act only when one is awake. But when people do think, talk, and act while asleep, as in somnambulism and somniloquism, we naturally begin to wonder who is thinking, talking, and acting.

Science Tries To Explain

Morton Prince, in his theory of dissociation and amnesia, tried to give an indirect or implied explanation of somnambulism and somniloquism in terms of dissociation of personality and in turn, dissociation in terms of amnesia.[10] The somnambulist is, according to him, in a state of personality dissociation. His normal personality sinks into the unconscious, and another personality, during the somnambulic state, arises to take charge of him. In this state, he remembers nothing of his normal personality. When he awakens, he forgets absolutely his somnambulic personality. Now, when the somnambulic personality supervenes for a long time, it may even continue operating during waking hours. Such a case is no longer somnambulism simply. It becomes what Prince calls a dissociation of personality. It is better called technically a *fugue*.[11]

This interpretation assumes the alternation of personalities. What are these personalities? The only logical answer is that they are aspects of the total consciousness of the individual. When one aspect is in abeyance, the other is active. Thus, when the somnambulic personality is active, the normal waking personality is in a state of inactivity.

What is this somnambulic personality? Evidently, it is not a cerebrocentric entity, for, if it were, it would merge with the conscious personality which is generally regarded, though erroneously, as cerebrally motivated. Furthermore, asleep though the man is, this somnambulic personality can see, or, as Wiggers very naively said, can miraculously avoid all obstacles.[12] If seeing is a cerebral non-function; what then, "sees" in the somnambulic state, which is a state of sleep? The depth psychologists would answer, "The subconscious." Janet would say, "The somnambulic personality." I would simply answer: "The soul."

Interpretation

In the light of Eastern psychology, which is certainly more coherent, the conscious personality and the somnambulic personality are simply states of the total consciousness or soul or, better still, the self.

When the soul is focused on the external world through the brain, it manifests as the conscious personality. When it transfocalizes its consciousness and focuses it on the higher dimensional or inner world, certainly *not* through the brain but through higher nonphysical centers, it manifests as the somnambulic personality. The first is called *jagrat;* the second is called *svapna.*

That the second condition is really *svapna* or dream consciousness is shown by the fact that both dreams and somnambulic phenomena are accompaniments of the sleep condition. Dream and somnambulism sometimes accompany each other.

Somnambulism, therefore, is a state of consciousness, not a condition of the brain. If sleep is an altered state of consciousness and if, further, somnambulism is a phenomenon of sleep, then we have a right to say that somnambulism is a state of consciousness not obtaining through the brain, though it does affect the motor centers of the brain and thus enables them to act.

Two Cases

Two very interesting cases, one of somnambulism, the other of somniloquism, are within the personal knowledge of the author. A friend of mine, a doctor, had the striking experience of seeing his brother, a somnambulist, rise from his bed, sit down at his writing table, and write continuously on a piece of paper until it was half filled. This the doctor took away and put in its place a new blank piece of paper. The somnambulist then continued writing but in a most extraordinary manner. Instead of beginning at the top of the paper, he continued writing at the center of the paper where he had left off on the first sheet. Why? How? Evidently, he could see.

Question: Is somnambulic sight the same as clairvoyance? Evidently, it is. If it is, then we have here another valid reason for considering it as a non-cerebral condition of consciousness because, as Dr. J.B. Rhine convincingly proves in his ESP experiments, clairvoyance is due to a nonphysical element in man.

The case of somniloquism is that of a sister of mine, then seventeen years old. She frequently talked in her sleep.

One night she was saying fearfully, "I am afraid, I am afraid." Instead of awakening her, I asked, "What are you afraid of?" Strangely enough, she answered, "That man, that man!" "Who"? I insisted. Then she mentioned the name of a man who was then courting her, but whom she apparently did not favor. "Why?" I asked. She answered, "He is running after me, he is running after me!"

I woke her up, fearing she might develop a nightmare. Awake, she could remember nothing, until we told her. The important question is how she was able to answer me coherently. That she was dreaming is clear enough. That she was talking in her sleep is also clear enough. But how she was able to answer my questions is puzzling. She heard my questions. With what did she hear if she was asleep? She answered them coherently. Therefore, not only did she hear, she *understood*. With what did she understand?

How can a person understand, that is, *think* unconsciously? Here, then, is a most cogent proof of the existence of the soul.

Thinking presupposes not only consciousness, but *someone conscious*. In other words, a *thinker*. "Cogito, ergo sum," said Descartes.

Since my sister, though asleep, was able to answer me coherently, that is, to understand me, since the act of thinking presupposes, necessitates the existence of a thinker; and since, further, this thinker could not have been her body, for the reason that unconscious thinking is logically and empirically a contradiction; therefore, we can conclude that the real thinker in her, that something that did not sleep even if her body was unconscious, cannot but be the soul.

Let Freud call it the subconscious. Let Hartman call it the unconscious. Let psychologists call it the mind. Let whoever call it whatever. But I will call it — insist on calling it — the soul, because by the use of that word I am able to emphasize its autonomy from the brain as well as its inherent moral, religious, and aesthetic nature.

References

[1] Best, Charles Herbert and Norman Bucke Taylor, *The Physiological Basis of Medical Practice, A Text in Applied Physiology*, (Baltimore: The Williams and Wilkins Company, 1961) p. 1271.

[2] Nathaniel Kleitman, *Sleep and Wakefulness*, (Chicago and London: The University of Chicago Press, 1963,) p. 342.

[3] Cited in Kleitman, *op. cit.*, p. 343.

[4] Lepine, R., "Theorie mecanique de la paralysie hysterique du somnambulisme, du somneil natural et de la distraction." *C.R. Soc. Biol.*, 47: 85-86, 1895.

[5] Duval, M., "Hypothese sur la physiologie des centres nerveux. Theorie histologique du somneil." *C.R. Soc. Biology*, 47: 74-76, 86-87, 1895.

[6] Starling and Lovatt Evans, *Principles of Human Physiology*, 13th Edition, Edited by Hugh Davson and M. Grace Eggleton, (Philadelphia: Lea and Febiger, 1962) pp. 1180-1181.

[7] Carney Landis and M. Marjorie Bolles, *Textbook of Abnormal Psychology* (New York: The Macmillan Company, 1947) p. 4.

[8] Late Inmate of the Glasgow Royal Asylum for Lunatics at Gartnaval. *The Philosophy of Insanity*, with an Introduction by Frieda Fromn-Reichmann, (New York: Greenberg Publisher, 1947) p. 111.

[9] P. Janet, *The Major Systems of Hysteria* (New York: The Macmillan Company, 1907).

[10] Morton Prince, *The Unconscious* (New York: The Macmillan Company, 1929).

[11] Landis and Bolles, *op. cit.*, p. 348.

[12] Carl J. Wiggers, *Physiology in Health and Disease*, (Philadelphia: Lea and Febiger, 1949) p. 209.

Chapter 16
EVIDENCES FROM THE PHENOMENA OF DREAMS
Why Do We Dream?

The question, "Why do we dream"? is not difficult to answer, if we are asking not the nature of dreams but only their immediate causation; in other words, how they are produced. The causative factors of dreams are many, and many of them are scientifically and empirically valid, too. Furthermore, most of them are experimentable, so that they can be put to pragmatic verification.

Fundamentally, according to Pillsbury, dreams are an expression of the same laws as the processes of waking life.[1] This statement does not in any way explain the nature of dream-consciousness, but it gives, nevertheless, a broad idea of the generation and development of dreams. Thus, at times, dreams may be initiated by external stimulation; at other times, they may be traced to the influence of some striking events of the preceding day.

An interesting case of the first type consists of a series of experiments mentioned by Professor Harry L. Hollingsworth of Columbia University. The experiments were performed primarily to determine the degrees to which external impressions are woven into one's dreams and become their starting point.

> As the subject fell asleep in a convenient chair, the experimenter without prewarning stimulated him in some particular way, then awoke him shortly and listened to the dream, if one had occurred. Such results as the following were obtained:

The lips and nose were tickled with a feather: he dreamt of undergoing some severe torture in which the skin was torn from his face. Two pieces of iron were struck together a short distance from his ear; in his dreams he heard bells and revolution. He was made to breathe perfume: in his dreams he entered a perfumer's shop in Cairo. Pinched lightly on the cheek, he dreamed of a blister there, and later in the dream there appeared the figure of a physician who cared for him in childhood illness.[2]

Other theories of dream causation vary little from this external stimulation hypothesis. Dreams, according to David Hartley, Oxford neurologist, in his book *Observations in Man*, are due to cerebral and abdominal vibrations. J. Leonard Corning, American neurologist, in his *Treatise on Headaches and Neuralgia*, attributes dreams to respiratory difficulties. Wundt, the founder of experimental psychology, regards all dreams as having physiological origin. Ladd, prominent American psychologist and philosopher, localizes the physiological origin of dreams in the eyes. He considers dreams as retinal images excited by intra-organic stimulation.

Dreams may also be produced by drugs, by anaesthesia, by sickness, and by hypnotism. Freud would regard all dreams as expressions of suppressed desires, largely sexual in nature. Camille Flammarion, famous French astronomer, suggests that dreams are "reflected impressions" of waking problems.

Similar to this theory of Flammarion are those of W.H. Rivers, psychologist and anthropologist, who looks upon dreams as attempts to solve conflicts of waking life, and of Joshua Rosett, neurology professor of Columbia University, who considers dreams as subjective reproductions of past experiences.

Carl Gustav Jung, famous psychologist and psychoanalyst and author of voluminous books and articles on dreams, their nature, symbology, and interpretation, states that dreams are the voice and the gateway to the unconscious. He further states that through dreams, all phases of man's nature are revealed for the express purpose of directing and re-establishing, in a subtle way, the individual's total psychic equilibrium, thus enabling him to attain more balanced accomplishments in his physical, mental, and spiritual life. Edgar Cayce, America's foremost sleeping clairvoyant, also held the same view as Jung on the origin and function of dreams.

What Is Dream Consciousness?

All these theories of dream causation are, as we have previously stated, to a great extent, valid, both empirically and experimentally. All of them however, fail to make one thing clear, that is, the nature of the dream-consciousness itself, And this, as far as we are concerned, is the main problem.

I know, for example, that external stimuli affect my consciousness. That, indeed, is interesting information. More interesting, however, is *how* they affect my consciousness. But it would be most interesting to find out what consciousness itself is; in other words, to know who I am who is conscious.

So with dreams. It is interesting, indeed, to know that external stimulation, previous experiences, drugs, and hypnosis, for example, can induce dreams. But it is more crucially interesting to know what dream-consciousness itself is. Is it a brain-state? Is it a state of consciousness? Is it a higher dimensional consciousness? Or is it only hallucination?

Furthermore, what dreams? Is it the brain, or is it I? Am I the same in dreaming and in waking? Or does a new personality, a new "I" arise when I dream? What causes the sensation of reality in dreams? How about double dreams, or the dream within a dream? And how account for the apparent annihilation of space and time in the dream state?

All these questions may be summed up in the problem proposed by the greatest of China's metaphysicians, Chuang Tsu, in his parable of the "Transformation of Things."

> Once upon a time, I, Chuang Tsu, dreamed I was a butterfly hovering here and there, to all intents and purposes a butterfly. I did not know that it was Chuang Tsu. Suddenly I woke up and was myself again the veritable Chuang Tsu. Now I do not know whether I was then a man dreaming I was a butterfly, or now a butterfly dreaming I am a man.[3]

Nature Of Dream Consciousness

If dreams are an expression of the same laws as those which govern the process of waking life, it follows, in accordance with our analysis of man's conscious waking life, that the dream state is a state of consciousness. If it is a state of consciousness, therefore, it is a state of the self, of the personality. It cannot be a brain-state, since, as we have previously shown, the brain from a strict empirical point of view, is really never conscious. It is only an organ of consciousness. Therefore, it is not the brain that dreams, as it is not the brain that thinks.

The utmost I may say is that I think through my brain. Empirically, however, I do not even have direct proof of this. Hence, strictly, all I can really say is, I think.

Even so, I cannot say my brain dreams. It is empirically not possible to prove such a statement. But I can say, as can anyone else, I dream. To say I dream, therefore, is just the same as to say, I think. Both presuppose consciousness, the self, the experient, the ego.

The difference is not in the indispensable experiencing self; it constitutes the *sine qua non* of both. The difference lies only in the states of consciousness involved.

Thinking is an activity of the self in its waking state, or *jagrat*, as the Vedantin calls it. Dreaming, on the other hand, is an activity of the self in a different state of consciousness. It is called *svapna* in the East. Therefore, to dismiss dream-life as a form of hallucination, that is, as unreal, is equally to dismiss thought-life as unreal.

Both are, in the first place, under normal conditions, private to the self. They are completely inaccessible to anyone except to the dreamer or to the thinker himself. I do not know what you think unless you tell me. You do not know what I think unless I tell you. Your thought-life is yours alone. My thought-life is mine alone. Each monad, as Leibnitz correctly intimated, is windowless. The same thing can be said of my dream-life, of your dream life. Yours is real to you, mine is real to me.

We do not, however, dismiss thought-life as unreal, only because of its inaccessible privacy. Even so, we cannot simply dismiss the dream-life as hallucinatory, for the reason of its inaccessibility to any except the dreamer himself. Dismiss one, dismiss the other.

In the second place, dream-life, like thought-life, is rooted in an indubitable reality, consciousness itself. In fact, its inaccessible privacy is due precisely to the inaccessibility of the consciousness itself. And this proves clearly that it is a state of consciousness, since it possesses the most important characteristics of consciousness, namely, self-experience and privacy.[4]

Dream-life, therefore, like consciousness itself, as well as the various other phenomena of consciousness, points to the existence of a self, a personality, or, as I prefer to call it, a soul.

Just as we cannot regard consciousness, memory and sleep as functions or states of the brain, so we cannot consider dream as a cerebral state or function. It is a state of consciousness. Therefore, it is a state of the self, of I-am-ness, of the soul. I dream — not my body, nor my brain, nor my nervous system, nor any of its parts.

That external environmental influences, or internal body conditions, can cause me to dream is true. But it does not prove that my dream-life is a bodily or a cerebral state. On the contrary, it shows one of the important characteristics of the self, namely, what Brightman calls "response to environment."

The same thing can be said of thought-life. External environmental influences, or internal body conditions, can cause me to think. But this does not prove that my thought-life is a bodily or a cerebral state. It does not prove that my body or my brain thinks. On the contrary, it shows that I am aware of my environment, both external and internal. Now, since cerebral vibrations can influence me, can, in fact, elicit response from me, then it follows that they belong to my environment. Therefore, my brain is part of my environment, as Brightman correctly concluded. It incessantly affects my consciousness: in fact, I can even say that without it the physical world will cease to exist for me; just the same, it is still only one of my environing causes and no more.

I am not the brain, even if I use it as a switchboard for thought; as I am not the eyes, even if I use them as my optical instruments. I am the self. That I know indubitably, I am I. I am the ego, or, as I prefer to say, I am the soul.

The Brain And Dream-Consciousness

As in thought-life, so in dream-life, the brain is only an environing cause. The brain may affect the dream-life, limit it, even cause some of its phenomena, but it is not it. Dream-life is not brain-state, because dream-life is conscious life, and the brain is not conscious.

Electricity may cause heat, may produce cold, may induce light, may bring about death. But electricity is not heat, is not cold, is not life, is not death. These are only its effects.

So also cerebral conditions may bring about many dreams but only dreams or the dream-contents, not the dream-consciousness itself.

There are indeed many dreams, and their causes may, likewise, be many. But who dreams them? The dreamer dreams them. In other words, the dreamer is conscious of them. The dreamer, therefore, is a consciousness. Hence, dreaming is a state of consciousness of the dreamer. Dreaming, therefore, like thinking, is a function of consciousness, not of the brain.

Empirically, it is not possible to prove that it is the brain that thinks, since the act of thinking presupposes an "I-am" that thinks. The brain cannot say, "I am." So also, empirically, it is impossible to prove that it is the brain that dreams, since the act of dreaming presupposes an "I am" that dreams. The brain cannot say, "I dream." Only I, the personality, the self, the ego, can say, "I dream," as only I, the personality, the self, the ego, can say, "I think." This I, this personality, this self, this ego, I call the soul.

Dream-Consciousness Is Soul-Consciousness

That the dream-state is not a brain-state, but rather a soul-state, gains greater credibility by the discovery in many instances that dreams during anesthesia imply dreams in a condition of unconsciousness. These unconscious dreams

Evidence from the Phenomena of Dreams

are presumably non-cerebral, hence non-physical. In one way, they prove dreams are a new state of consciousness — the Eastern *svapna*; in another way, they point to the existence of a new state of consciousness, the soul.

That the dream-state is a state of consciousness in a higher dimension, hence freer and sometimes more exalted, may be further inferred from the nature of a number of dream phenomena, namely:
 1. Lucid dreams
 2. Prophetic dreams
 3. Exaltation of mental phenomena in the dream-state
 4. Annihilation of time and space in the dream-state

Phenomena Of Lucid Dreams

The greater number of scientific observers of dreams generally start their investigation of dream-phenomena on the basis of a prejudice. This is in the form of an unwarranted supposition that all dreams are more or less hallucinatory phenomena produced by certain bodily conditions and sensations. The result is that most dream experiments are directed toward the production of dreams by artificial bodily stimulations.

It must be granted with the materialistic hypothesis that bodily conditions and sensations do initiate dreams. This is fact, not assumption. To say, however, that all dreams are so generated and that, therefore, all dreams are brain-states is to make an illegitimate assumption based on insufficient evidence.

In the first place, the dream-consciousness, or *svapna*, is *sui generis*. Bodily conditions may produce dreams. *But they do not produce the dream-consciousness itself.*

In the second place, bodily conditions initiate dreams, but they do not determine, as Frederick van Eeden, the Dutch neurologist, correctly said, the character of our dreams. Thus, the ticking of a clock may be dramatized in the dream into the din of battle; or water dropped on the cheek into a storm at sea. But who or what does the transforming? Who transforms a pin prick into a stabbing affray, the ringing of a bell into a wedding ceremony, or a whisper in the ear into a whole process of quarrel?

Freud attributes all dream transformations to the dramatic powers of the subconscious. But what, in reality, is the subconscious? What is the difference between the self active in the dream-state transforming ordinary stimulations into dramatic self-experience and the self of a poet or a dramatist absorbed in the creation of some stirring work of art, a poem, for example, or a climactic scene? Do not both situations presuppose consciousness? Do not both involve self or personality or the I-am? The difference, of course, is in the state of consciousness. One we would call dream-consciousness, the other, waking consciousness. But both are, therefore, real, each in its own peculiar way. Both are activities of the experiencing self.

In the third place, there are certain dream experiences which are completely free from bodily stimulations and conditions. This, for example is the testimony of Dr. Frederick van Eeden, in the report he submitted to the Society for Psychical Research:

> As the outcome of careful observations, I maintain my conviction that the bodily conditions of the sleeper have, as a rule, no influence on the character of dreams, with the exception of a few rare and abnormal cases, near the moment of waking up, or in those dreams which I have classified as *pathological,* or some poison, plays a role, and which form a small minority. For myself as the observer, I may state that I have been in good health all the time of observation. I had no important complaints of any nervous or visceral kind. My sleep and digestion both are usually good. Yet I have had the most terrible nightmares, while my body was as fresh and healthy as usual . . . .[5]
>
> I wish, therefore, to define the true dream as *that state wherein bodily sensations, be they visceral, internal, or peripheral, cannot penetrate to the mind directly, but only in the psychical, non-spatial form of a symbol or an image* . . . .[6]

Here is the nearest approach, in Western investigation of dreams, to the Eastern idea of dream as a state of consciousness, or *svapna,* a conscious state of the self in a higher dimension, quite distinct from its conscious state in the physical world.

Evidence from the Phenomena of Dreams 137

Dr. van Eeden continues:

> I quite agree with Mr. Havelock Ellis, that during sleep the psychical functions enter into a state of *dissociation*. My contention, however, is that it is not dissociation, but, on the contrary, *reintegration,* after the dissociation of sleep; that is the essential feature of dreams. *The dream is a more or less complete reintegration of the psyche, a reintegration in a different sphere, in a psychical, non-spatial mode of existence. This reintegration may go so far as to effect full recollection of day-life, reflection, and voluntary action on reflection* . . . .[7]

Here now is the Eastern theory of *svapna* clothed in the technical language of Western psychology. If we were to paraphrase Dr. van Eeden's paragraph in ordinary non-technical language, it would be something like this: The soul separates from the physical body at sleep, and it enters into a temporary condition of unconsciousness (dissociation of sleep). Then it awakens (process of reintegration) into a *different sphere* of consciousness, *a non-spatial mode of existence,* and becomes conscious there. This new state of consciousness is the dream. In that state of existence, it can even remember its physical, spatial, temporal life in earth. It can think. It can exercise volition.

It can, as in my personal experience, even see, as distinct and apart from itself, its own physical body.

Such dream which, in the East, is simply called *svapna,* Dr. van Eeden calls "lucid dream."

It is defined as a dream in which "the reintegration of the psychic functions is so complete that the sleeper remembers day-life and his own condition, reaches a state of perfect awareness, and is able to direct his attention, and to attempt different acts of volition."[8]

Dr. van Eeden collected and analyzed about five-hundred of his dreams. Of these 353 were all lucid dreams.[9]

In the East, the Yogi would simply say that Dr. van Eeden entered into *svapna* 353 times. In other words, he separated from his body consciously 353 times.

Sleep, therefore, is the transfocalization of consciousness from the physical to a superphysical state. Dr. van Eeden calls this superphysical state a "different sphere," a "nonspatial mode of existence." In the East, it is called *kamaloka,* the locus of desire, a four-dimensional world of consciousness.

To dream, in the lucid form, is to become conscious in this superphysical state, in this nonspatial mode of existence, in the four-dimensional *kamaloka.*

Dr. van Eeden, in his investigations, was even led by the fact that he could clearly distinguish himself from his physical body to the unavoidable conclusion that he was using a *dream-body* in the lucid dream state.[10]

This is the *kamarupa* of the Vedantins, the *linga sharira* or *temporal body* of Ouspensky, the *astral body* of the theosophists.

Conclusions

From the foregoing discussion of lucid dreams, with an incidental comparative study of Dr. van Eeden's analysis of dreams and the Eastern concepts of *svapna, kamaloka,* and *kamarupa,* we draw the following conclusions:

1. That dreams, especially the lucid type, are completely inexplicable in terms of bodily states, but are quite explicable in terms of a conscious personality or soul, operating in a superphysical, nonspatial mode or sphere of existence.

2. That this state of consciousness is quite distinct from the physical waking state of consciousness.

3. That the personality or self, in the lucid dream state of consciousness, thinks deliberately, distinguishes itself from the physical body which it can even see, performs acts of free volition, and reaches a condition of self-awareness.

Further Evidence

That the dream-consciousness is soul-consciousness is further confirmed by its nonspatiality. Its nonspatiality is proved, on the other hand, by the existence of prophetic dreams.

A well-known example of a prophetic dream is that of the famous writer Maurice Maeterlinck who, "when arriving at the commencement of an event that he had previous-

Evidence from the Phenomena of Dreams

ly dreamed, was able to tell a companion exactly what was going to happen next."[11]

A very interesting and intriguing case is that of a seventeen year old girl who saw her own death in a dream. This was reported in the *Manila Bulletin* of July 28, 1967. The news item reads:

> A religious girl, Patricia Adriano, 17, had a bad dream while taking her siesta yesterday afternoon.
>
> Immediately after she woke up, she told her Lola (grandmother) Maria about her dream. She said she dreamt of a coffin lying beside her with a "dark shadow moving about in the coffin."
>
> Patricia then gathered her mother, her brothers and sisters around her and told them she had a premonition of death. She begged her mother, Consalacion, to "prepare everything."
>
> Her mother decided to take Patricia to the city hospital as she was not feeling well. She was reported suffering from an enlargement of the heart.
>
> But before leaving for the hospital, Patricia asked her mother to continue going to church every Friday for nine weeks on her behalf. She said she had promised God she would do this "before I breathe my last."
>
> At the hospital, Patricia's condition worsened and she asked her mother to take her back home as she wanted to die at home.
>
> Patricia died at home at around 5 p.m. barely three hours after her dream.

Can the unthinking body thus prophesy? Can the physical, spatial, temporal, three-dimensional brain prophesy? As P.D. Ouspensky correctly intimated, only a four-dimensional consciousness can escape the bonds of time, and thus be able to prophesy.

That prophecy is possible in dreams shows that dream-consciousness is four-dimensional consciousness. If it is four-dimensional consciousness, it cannot be a brain-state. It must, therefore, be soul-consciousness.

In fact, Dr. J.B. Rhine's experiments on precognition point unerringly to the existence of a non-physical reality in man.

Moreover, the exaltation of mental powers in the dream-state shows that dream-consciousness is the activity or the condition of a personality in full possession of its faculties.

I wrote a full poem of eleven stanzas in a dream. I was able to recollect it completely when I woke up. It is a Christmas poem entitled "Stranger Child." It was published in a nationwide weekly, the *Philippine Free Press,* on December 14, 1935.[12]

The most remarkable historical example, however, of a poem written in a dream is "Kubla Khan" of Samuel Taylor Coleridge. The full account of how Coleridge dreamed this poem is given in his "Literary Reminiscences," written in the third person.[13]

That we can study in sleep is acknowledged by a number of psychologists. Pillsbury is one of them. How? Who studies? The brain? The answer should be obvious. An unsleeping entity. The entity that dreams lucid dreams. The entity that composes poems even when the body is asleep and the brain is not cerebrating, that is, not thinking. The entity that, in dreams, sees its own physical body sleeping. The entity that, in the sleep of its body, "remembers day-life and his own condition, reaches a state of perfect awareness, is able to direct his attention, and performs acts of free volition."[14]

References

[1] W. B. Pillsbury, *The Essentials of Psychology,* (New York: The Macmillan Company, 1930) p. 393.

[2] Ralph Woods (Editor) *The World of Dreams — An Anthology,* (New York: Random House, 1947) pp. 781-782.

[3] Adams L. Beck, *The Story of Oriental Philosophy,* (New York: Farrar and Rhinehart, Inc., 1928) p. 366.

[4] Edgar S. Brightman, *A Philosophy of Religion,* (New York: Prentice Hall, Inc., 1946) pp. 351-353.

[5] Woods, *op. cit.,* p. 311.
[6] *Ibid.,* p. 312.
[7] *Ibid.,* pp. 313-314.
[8] *Ibid.,* p. 314.
[9] *Ibid.,* pp. 309-310.
[10] *Ibid.,* pp. 314-315.
[11] *Ibid.,* p. 330.
[12] See Appendix A.
[13] See Appendix B.
[14] F. van Eeden, quoted in Woods, *op. cit.,* p. 314.

Chapter 17

EVIDENCE FROM THE PHENOMENA OF HYPNOTISM

The Meaning Of Hypnotism

Warren defines hypnotism as "the scientific investigation of hypnosis and hypnotic phenomena."[1]

It should not be confused with hypnosis, the hypnotic condition itself. Warren defines hypnosis as "an artificially induced state, usually (though not always) resembling sleep, but physiologically distinct from it, which is characterized by heightened suggestibility, as a result of which certain sensory, motor, and memory abnormalities may be induced more readily than in the normal state."[2]

From the first definition we gather that hypnotism has a recognized scientific status; from the second, that hypnotic phenomena are accepted scientific data. No scientific conclusion, however, has so far been made as to how the hypnotic trance comes about; and there is no scientific explanation until now of the various hypnotic phenomena. Science, in other words, does not know exactly the nature of hypnosis. It accepts as facts the different phenomena of the hypnotic state, but is altogether incapable of giving them any adequate explanation or interpretation.

"Today," write Landis and Bolles "hypnotism still . . . . is believed to be something mysterious. In spite of all of the experimental work which has been done on the subject during the past century, no one has yet been able to state explicitly just how the hypnotic trance comes about."[3]

The Mystery Of Hypnotism

True, no one has yet been able to explain the nature and operation of the hypnotic trance. But "no one" here includes only materialistic scientists who seek to explain all forms of human behavior, whether normal or abnormal, in terms of the activity of the brain and the nervous system. Naturally, from such a source no acceptable explanation can be forthcoming. It is utterly hopeless to explain thought, memory, and the other functions of the mind in terms of the brain alone.

It is utterly hopless to explain the *psi* functions in terms of physical motivation and reactions. It is equally utterly hopeless to explain the phenomena of hypnotism solely in terms of brain and nervous activity. Not even one century of experimentation, as Landis and Bolles said, has done that.

We cannot expect any explanation from a source where no explanation is available. We cannot find the black cat in the dark room when the cat is not there. We cannot expect any explanation from the materialistic, physicalistic, cerebrocentric hypothesis of human nature, because it is not there. Materialism is a bankrupt philosophy. It has lost its interpretative cash-value. If we must have an adequate explanation of hypnosis and hypnotic phenomena, we must look for it somewhere else. We must look for it in the nonmaterialistic theory that man is the soul, and the body only its physicalistic organ.

So that instead of regarding the brain and the nervous system as the causative sources of mental life, we shall henceforth consider them as limitations through which consciousness expresses itself partially in the physical world and from which sometimes, as in the state of hypnosis, it is able to liberate itself and thus express itself more fully, more completely, and more gloriously.

The result of such a release, such an emancipation, is the manifestation of astounding phenomena, and the exaltation of sensory as well as of mental capacities.

Types Of Hypnotic Phenomena

Among the different types of hypnotic phenomena which require for their explanation the assumption of a non-physical element in man, the following are the most significant:

1. The exaltation of the senses and the mental capacities.
2. The vision of physically nonexistent things.
3. The inhibition of physical vision.

Let us consider the various facts under each of them and determine which theory explains them better, the cerebrocentric or the psychocentric theory of human nature.

Exaltation Of The Senses

One of the most unusual phenomena of the hypnotic state is the exaltation of the senses as well as of the powers of the mind, particularly memory.

The condition of the hypnotized person, according to Binet and Fere, may vary from anesthesia to hyperesthesia, that is, from insensibility to acute sensitiveness.[4] The body may be rendered completely insensitive to pain, so that critical operations may be performed without the use of ordinary material anesthetic. On the other hand, hypnotization may produce extreme hyper-sensitiveness.

Binet and Fere say:

> The state of the senses in hypnotic subjects ranges from anaesthesia to hyperesthesia. During lethargy all the senses are suspended, with the occasional exception of the sense of hearing, which is sometimes retained, as it is in natural sleep.
>
> During catalepsy, the special senses are partially awake; the muscular sense, in particular, retains all its activity.
>
> Finally, in somnambulism (the lucid hypnotic state), the senses are not merely awake, but quickened to an extraordinary degree. Subjects feel the cold produced by breathing from the mouth at a distance of several yards (Braid). Weber's compasses, applied to the skin, produce a twofold sensation, with a deviation of 3 degrees, in regions where during the waking state, it

should be necessary to give the instrument a deviation of 18 degrees (Berger). The activity of the sense of sight is sometimes so great that the range of sight may be double, as well as the sharpness of vision. The sense of smell may be developed so that the subject is able to discover by its aid the fragments of a visiting card which had been given to them to smell before it was torn up (Targuet). The hearing is so acute that a conversation carried on the floor below may be overheard (Azam).[5]

Clairvoyance and telepathy, as will be noted in the succeeding chapter, may develop during hypnotic trance. For example, Professor Richet took a playing card from a deck at random, put it in an opaque envelope, and asked his somnambulistic subject, Leonie, to identify it. Leonie was able to identify the card not only once, but many times in a series of tests.[6]

Traveling clairvoyance of the more experimental type may also be induced during hypnosis. For instance, Sir William Barrett, an English physicist, Dr. Alfred Backman, a Swedish physician, and many others, reported that they were able to direct a hypnotized subject to project himself mentally to a distant scene and bring back a reliable account of specific happenings or other items of information that would tally with later verification. The information obtained was unknown to all present, so that the results obtained were attributed to traveling clairvoyance and not to telepathy.[7]

In several books like *Isis Revelata,* Du Prel's *The Philosophy of Mysticism* and Dr. Haddock's *Somnolism and Psychism,* the case of Madam Lagandre, a somnambule, is given. She used her somnambulic or hypnotic clairvoyance to diagnose the sickness of her mother shortly before the latter's death. She described the state of the right lung and heart, the stomach and the liver, declaring that the right lung had shriveled up and that there was water in the cavity of the heart. A post-mortem examination of the body in the presence of Dr. Brousart M. Moreau, secretary to the surgical section of the Royal Academy of Medicine, Paris, and Dr. Chapelain, by Cloquet and Pailloux showed that the organs were exactly as the somnambule described them.[8]

Exaltation Of The Mind

It is in the intellectual realm, however, that hypnosis produces some of its more extraordinary phenomena.

Memory, for example, becomes unbelievably retentive and vivid during hypnotic trance. A poem read to a hypnotized person was repeated by her correctly; awakened, she forgot it; on being hypnotized again, she was able to recall and repeat it.[9] At the Salpetriere, a hypnotized subject gave the menu of dinners she had eaten a week previously.[10]

Charcot, leader of the Salpetriere school of hypnotism, used to hypnotize patients and have them recall childhood memories. At present, in fact, hypnotic recall of forgotten memories is a common and useful method among psychoanalysts for purposes of reconstructing the past life of a patient and thus unearthing possible causes of his mental illness.

Then general mental capacity of a person may also be quickened under hypnosis. In *Isis Revelata,* the case of Jane Rider is mentioned. Hypnotized and then blindfolded carefully, she was asked to play backgammon. She consented, knowing nothing of the game, learned it rapidly, and won the sixth game from an experienced player. Awakened, she was asked to play, but said she had never seen the game, and she could not even see the men.[11]

Dr. Abercrombie, in his *On the Intellectual Powers,* gives a long account of a girl who, according to him,

> when awake, was dull, awkward, and very slow in receiving instruction, though much care was bestowed on her, but who when in the lucid hypnotic condition could "descant with the utmost fluency and correctness on a variety of topics, both political and religious, the news of the day, the historical parts of the Scripture, public characters, and particularly the characters of members of the family and their visitors. In these discussions, she showed the most wonderful discrimination, often combined with sarcasm, and astonishing powers of mimicry. Her language through the whole was fluent and correct, and her illustrations often forcible and even eloquent. She was fond of illustrating her subjects

by what she called a fable, and in these her imagery was both appropriate and elegant.¹²

Seeing Non-Physical Things

The most unusual phenomena, however, of the hypnotic state are the seeing of what does not exist physically and the not seeing of what actually exists physically; in other words, the vision of physically non-existent things and the inhibition of physical vision. The manifestation of these two types of hypnotic phenomena is within the power of any amateur hypnotist to produce in a given subject.

There are some interesting examples of the first type:

> 1. On a piece of white paper a white card was placed, and an imaginary line was drawn round this card, with a blunt pointer, *without touching the card,* the patient being told that the line was being drawn. When she awakened, she was given the blank piece of paper, and she saw on it the rectangle which had not been traced; asked to fold the paper along the line she saw, she folded it exactly so that it was just covered by the card when the latter was placed on it. (Richer)¹³
>
> 2. A patient was told that she saw a black circle; on waking she looked about, rubbed her eyes, and on being questioned, complained that she saw a black-circle everywhere she looked, and that it was extremely annoying. (Richer)¹⁴
>
> 3. A patient was told that Dr. Charcot was present when he was absent, and on waking she addressed him.¹⁵

The Blocking Of Vision

Equally interesting are the examples of the other type, namely, the blocking of vision, or the failure to see what normally should be seen. Here are some cases:

> 1. Ten cards were shown to a hypnotized subject, and she was told that she could not see one of them. When she was awakened, that card remained invisible. Similar results were obtained with keys, thermometers, and other objects. (Richer)¹⁶
>
> 2. A hypnotized subject was told, "You will not see Mr. X." On waking Mr. X was invisible to her. (Binet and Fere)¹⁷

Evidence from the Phenomena of Hypnotism

3. A hypnotized subject was told she would cease to see Mr. F., but would continue to hear his voice. On waking she heard the voice of an invisible person, and looked about the room to discover the cause of this singular phenomenon, asking about it with some uneasiness. (Binet and Fere)[18]

4. A hypnotized subject was told that she would not be able to see Mr. F. On being awakened, she could not see Mr. F. who was right in front of her. She was then told that she might retire, and she went towards the door against which Mr. F. had placed himself. Unable to see him, she bumped against him, and on a second attempt to pass through the door, became alarmed at the incomprehensible resistance. She refused again to go near it. A hat was placed on his head, and "words cannot express" the subject's surprise, since it appeared to her that the hat was suspended in the air. Her surprise increased when Mr. F. took off the hat and saluted her with it several times; she saw the unsupported hat describing curves in the air. Mr. F. then put on a cloak, and she saw the cloak moving and assuming the form of a person. "It is," she cried, "like a hollow puppet." A number of other experiments were tried with her, all of them showing that she was completely unconscious of Mr. F.'s presence. (Binet and Fere)[19]

Analysis And Interpretation

Just as it is not possible to explain the *psi* process of Dr. Rhine in terms of the materialistic theory that man is purely a physical organism, so also is it impossible to find in this theory an explanation of the various hypnotic phenomena we have just described.

As long as students of the phenomena of hypnosis insist on explaining them in terms of materialism, so long will hypnotism remain a mystery to science, despite the undeniable reality of its various manifestations.

How, for example, can we explain the complete revival of memory under hypnotic trance? If memory, like thought, is nothing but motion of brain-substance, as the cerebrocentric theory of human nature insists, how and by what law of matter can we explain the total preservation of memory images and their complete restoration under hypnosis?

It is well known in physics that if a body be set vibrating, and new forces be successively brought to act upon it and set up new vibrations, there will not be in that body the co-existence of each separate set of vibrations successively impressed upon it, but it will vibrate in a way differing from each single set and compounded of all.

Memory, therefore, if regarded from the cerebrocentric point of view, being a mode of matter in motion, would not give a record of the past, but would present us with a new story, the resultant of all those past vibrations, and this would constantly be changing, inasmuch as new impressions, causing new vibrations, would continuously be coming in to modify the resultant of the old.

Memory, then, in the actual acceptation of the term as the preservation, recall, and recognition of past experiences, would be impossible from the materialistic interpretation of man's mental life.

The fact, however, that complete revival of individual memories is possible under conditions of hypnosis shows that neither the mind nor the memory is physicochemical in nature, although they may have relationships with the physicochemical behavior of the brain.

The mind is not a physical organ. It is a non-physical function of consciousness. It is a function of the soul. No other hypothesis can explain memory except that of the soul.

A man under hypnosis can reconstitute his memories. But since memory cannot be a brain function, it follows that man is not by nature cerebrocentric. He is psychocentric. He is essentially a psyche, a conscious self, a soul.

Seeing The Physically Non-existent

From the materialistic point of view, it is impossible to explain how hypnotized subjects see what does not exist physically. To call the vision of nonexisting things hallucination does not really explain it, because we also do not know the nature and *modus operandi* of hallucination.

To call a mystery by another name is not to explain it; it does not cease to be mysterious.

Evidence from the Phenomena of Hypnotism 149

This hypnotic phenomenon, whether hallucination or not, actually occurs. How explain this? After all, even hallucinations should be explained.

How will the brain-theory of human nature explain this hallucination?

It seems that the materialistic hypothesis is completely belied by experience.

It is highly unempirical.

Let us consider the physiological basis of visual perception. These are the conditions, as every properly informed man knows: rays reflected from the object, their impingement on the retina, the vibration of nerve cells, the nervous stimulus, its journey through the optic nerve, the activity of the optic lobe; then, finally, the vision.

With regard to the phenomenon we are considering, only the last step in the visual process is present; namely, the vision or the perception. All the preceding steps are absent. Only the suggestion of the hypnotist awakens the perception. Yet, this suggestion, completely non-physical, is sufficient to produce the sensation of sight.

This nonphysical suggestion from the hypnotist is an idea or a series of ideas. That it can start perception in the subject shows that what it is stimulating in him is not the physical visual apparatus, but the mind itself as a distinct entity from the brain: the mind, in other words, can create its own images regardless of the absence of sensory stimulation.

What is this mind that can create its own images apart from the brain? Depth psychologists choose to call it the unconscious. I prefer to call it the soul.

Tangentially, it should be pointed out here that this hypnotic phenomenon of seeing what actually and physically does not exist tends to destroy the long standing psychological law stated by Locke: There is nothing in the mind which was not first in the sense. This seems no longer true inasmuch as telepathically and clairvoyantly one can see without using the eyes. The mind can perceive directly, and, therefore, can develop its ideas or images independently of the ordinary sense organs.

The Blocking Of Vision

This, too, is completely inexplicable in terms of the materialistic theory of vision in orthodox cerebrocentric physiology and psychology.

If visual perception be only the result of vibrating cells, how can it happen that in spite of all its elements being present, the vision itself is absent? This phenomenon is the exact opposite of the preceding one. In the preceding one, all the steps of visual perception are absent, but vision is present. In this case, all the steps of visual perception are present, but the vision itself is absent. The object is there sending off light waves, the retina is there being stimulated by light waves, the nerve impulse is there, too; so also the optic nerve, and the optic center in the occipital lobe.

But the vision is absent. The hypnotized subject cannot see the object.

Inexplicable in terms of the cerebrocentric theory, it becomes clear from the psychocentric point of view. Assume the mind as independent of the brain; assume it as the real seat of perception; then we can understand why, even if the entire physical visual mechanism is active, the subject cannot see. The reason is that he is *mentally blind,* though *physically,* he is not. The inhibition is not of the nerve; it is of the mind. The hypnotist has entered the subjective world of the patient and controlled his visual faculty itself, and not its instrument, the physical mechanism of vision. The result is mental blindness.

This, also, is the only explanation that can be given to all psychological cases, of paralysis of sensation, like the case, for example, mentioned by Eder, of "the Australian soldier at Gallipoli who was firing through an embrasure when bullets struck several times near his head. He could no longer see with his right eye, although the tissues were perfectly normal."[20]

Now, if the mind could be so paralyzed as to inhibit perception, even if the physical apparatus of perception be intact and operative, it follows, as an inevitable conclusion, that the mind and its physical apparatus, the body and its brain, are not the same. They are distinct from each other.

Evidence from the Phenomena of Hypnotism 151

What, then, is this nonphysical mind which can function independently of the brain? The depth psychologists call it the subconscious. Dr. Rhine calls it, with the usual scientific reservation characteristic of all scientists, the "psychological soul." I call it unreservedly the soul.

The Clincher Proof

An experiment may be performed whereby it can be proved conclusively that in the hypnotic state it is the nonphysical mind or soul, not the physical mechanism, that is active in the hypnotized subject.

Furthermore, it will show that the brain is a limitation of our consciousness, an important instrument, instead of the creator of thought.

Let a man be put under hypnotic trance. In this condition as can be experimentally demonstrated, cerebration, or brain activity, is at its lowest ebb. No blood, or very little blood, flows through the brain cells.

How can this be proved to be a fact?

Scientists have invented an apparatus which tests the physical condition of the beating of the heart, as well as of other organs, while the subject is in the hypnotic trance. It consists generally of a revolving cylinder, covered with black lead paper, upon which is set a pencil. This pencil is attached to a lever, and the lever in turn is attached to the region of the heart so that any motion of the heart is registered by the pencil's pressing against the cylinder. As the cylinder revolves the pencil would draw a straight line, if there were no motion of the heart; but with any motion it would draw a curve.

Now, it has been shown, by the use of this apparatus, that when a person is in the hypnotic state, the beating of the heart is entirely changed; it reaches a point so slight that although the movement is still shown on the revolving cylinder, no instrument less delicate would show that it is beating at all. So also with the lungs, the apparatus shows that the movement of the lungs is so slight that no breath seems to be coming from the lips at all.

Now, what is the condition of the brain, when the body, as revealed by the low metabolism of the heart and the lungs, is in such a state, in other words, when the subject is in the hypnotic trance?

In the first place, the blood supply is checked because the blood pump, the heart, is not beating properly. Probably there is no beating at all; there is perhaps only fibrillation. As a result, the blood moves very sluggishly through the vessels of the brain, and in the tiny vessels, the capillary vessels, its movement is stopped.

In the second place, the blood in this state is not properly aired in the lungs. Consequently, it is highly charged with the products of decomposition.

What happens with the subject under these conditions? He enters into a state resembling coma in certain ways. Now, coma, as doctors know, is a condition in which "the brain is totally refractory to excitation."[21] In other words, the brain is to a great extent inactive. It is in a state of unresponsiveness. No cerebration occurs that can in any way be considered to resemble the usual normal physiological brain processes.

At this juncture, we set forth the crucial problem:

If the cerebrocentric theory of human nature is true; if it is true that thought is the product of brain activity, so that there can be no thought without brain action, it should follow that in this state of hypnotic trance, which resembles the comatose state, or cerebral inactivity, thought must completely disappear.

But it does not.

On the contrary, it becomes intensified; it becomes hyperactive. Not only does it not disappear; rather, it enters into a condition of exaltation quite unattainable during the normal waking state of the subject.

In this state of cerebral refractoriness to stimulus, when the mental life of the subject should be expected to vanish completely, in accordance with the cerebrocentric theory of the mind, the subject becomes, *tout au contraire,* hypersensitive and mentally hyperactive.

What normally, in his waking consciousness, he cannot do, now he can accomplish with marvelous efficiency and ease. Let him recall every little event of the preceding day, of the preceding week, of the preceding month, of the preceding year, and he will recapture it with astounding celerity and accuracy. Let him repeat word for word a poem of twenty stanzas that you have read to him only once, and he will repeat it without difficulty. Let him repeat verbatim a page from a book in Greek that you have read to him only once, and he will repeat it even if he does not know a single word in that language.

He may even become temporarily clairvoyant, or clairaudient, or precognitive.

Exaltation of sensation? Exaltation of the mind? Yes, but not of the brain, not of the physical nervous system, since all the time that these processes or functions are in operation, the subject is in a state resembling coma, and the brain, therefore, is inactive and, as far as thought is concerned, completely non-functional.

Who, or what, then, thinks in this condition? Who remembers? Who sees? Who hears? Who creates thought?

The brain, being inactive, should not be expected to produce thought. Furthermore, since the various sensory lobes of the brain are non-functional, all sensations should be expected to stop. Nevertheless, in this state of cerebral torpor and inactivity, the subject thinks, remembers, sees, hears, imagines; he even becomes mentally more alert and sensorially more acute than he actually is in his normal waking consciousness.

We are, thus, forcibly led to conclude that the mind is not the epiphenomenon of the brain; that thought and sensation are not the mere outcome of material motion; that the brain is only the organ of the mind in the physical world and not the mind itself; that the mind can operate in spite of the brain and, as a matter of fact, can operate more effectively without it than with it or through it; and that, therefore, there is something in man that is non-physical, that is the real creator of thought, that is the real source of all mental life, all will, all memory, all life, and all action. Dr. Rhine calls it the psychological soul. I call it simply the soul.

References

[1] Howard C. Warren, *Dictionary of Philosophy*, (Cambridge: Houghton Mifflin Co., The Riverside Press, 1934) p. 128.

[2] *Ibid.*, p. 128.

[3] Carney Landis and Marjorie Bolles, *Textbook of Abnormal Psychology*, (New York: The Macmillan Company, 1947) p. 518.

[4] Binet and Fere, *Le Magnitisme Animal* (Animal Magnetism) quoted in Annie Besant's *Psychology*, 2nd Edition, (Los Angeles, California: Theosophical Publishing House, 1919) pp. 210-211.

[5] *Ibid.*

[6] J. B. Rhine, *The Reach of the Mind*, (New York: William Sloane Associates, Inc., 1947) p. 30.

[7] *Ibid.*, pp. 29-30.

[8] Annie Besant, *Psychology, supra.*, pp. 212-213.

[9] *Ibid.*, p. 168.

[10] *Ibid.*, p. 213.

[11] *Ibid.*, p. 214.

[12] *Ibid.*, pp. 214-215.

[13] *Ibid.*, pp. 172-173.

[14] *Ibid.*, p. 173.

[15] *Ibid.*, p. 217.

[16] *Ibid.*, p. 174.

[17] *Ibid.*, p. 174.

[18] *Ibid.*, pp. 174-175.

[19] *Ibid.*, pp. 175-176.

[20] W.B. Pillsbury, *The Essentials of Psychology*, (New York: The Macmillan Company, 1930) pp. 335-336.

[21] Carl J. Wiggers, *Physiology in Health and Disease*, (Philadelphia: Lea and Febiger) p. 212.

Chapter 18

EVIDENCES FROM THE PHENOMENA OF PSYCHICAL RESEARCH

Meaning Of Psychical Research

Psychical Research is a relatively new science, although the phenomena it investigates are all old as man himself. Warren defines this new science as "the systematic investigation of various borderline or debatable phenomena of body and mind," and distinguishes it from ordinary psychological research in that "its typical phenomena are attributed to unknown causes of supernormal or occult nature."[1] It is also known under various other names, such as crytopsychism, parapsychology, psychic science, and metapsychism. Parapsychology is one of its most popular names now.

Charles Richet, in his book, *Thirty Years of Psychical Research,* calls it metapsychics and defines it as "the study of physical or psychical phenomena apparently dependent upon (a) an undetermined intelligence, (b) unknown but intelligent forces, (c) unknown powers in the human mind, or (d) subconscious or unconscious processes."[2]

Richet groups metapsychic phenomena under two main branches, namely, *objective metapsychics,* which deals with mechanical, physical, or chemical effects, such as raps, levitation, and apparitions; and *subjective metapsychics,* which deals with psychical or subjective phenomena, such as telepathy, clairvoyance, and presentiments.[3]

Dr. D.H. Prins, in his article, "Psychical Research,"[4] uses an almost similar classification, grouping all parapsychological phenomena in two main categories, namely, the *mental* and the *physical*.

156   Evidence of the Existence of the Soul

Under the mental type he puts thought transference from brain to brain without any physical contact; extra-sensory perception of past or distant events, or so-called clairvoyance; dreams and hallucinations of a prophetic nature; and the communications from mediums which are said to be due to incorporeal agencies and which are often claimed to contain evidence of the survival of the human personality after the death of the body. The common characteristic of all mental types of parapsychological phenomena, according to Dr. Prins, is the reception of knowledge by a recipient without any sensory stimulation of the well-known kind.

The physical types of parapsychological phenomena, all of which are apparent exceptions of accepted physical law, include "the enigmatical materializations, the spontaneous coming into existence of new physical forms and the equally enigmatical dematerializations, the dissolution of those forms into nothingness; telekinesis, the moving of physical objects without anyone touching them; levitation, a special form of telekinesis in vertical direction. . . . hauntings; raps and psychic lights, sounds or lights without a known physical cause."

A more detailed outline of parapsychology is given in *The Theosophical World*.[5] It includes the following:

   1. *Parapsychical*: telepathy and clairvoyance, both experimental and spontaneous; dowsing; previsionary and monitory dreams and hallucinations; psychometry; veridical "spirit" communications; etc.

   2. *Parapsychophysical*: telekinesis, levitation, "psychic light," "apports," temperature changes, etc.

   3. *Parapsychophysiological*: materializations, dematerializations, ectoplasmic extrusions and elongations, blood stigmata, etc.

   4. *Parapsychopathological*: "possession pathology," "psychic healing" of organic disease, beyond effect of suggestion.

   5. *Parapsycholiterary*: and other *paraphychoartistic*: creative writing or other art, clearly impossible as a result of natural training, like xenoglossia, for example.

Evidence from the Phenomena of Psychical Research

There are two important questions pertinent to the problem of psychical research or metapsychics:

1. Are parapsychological phenomena true? Do they actually occur? For example, is clairvoyance a fact? Can we communicate with the dead? Is prophecy true? How about mental telepathy, ghosts, telekinesis, levitation?

2. If they are true, how do they occur? What is their *modus operandi*? By what process, or processes, are they effected? How shall we explain them, how interpret?

These are our two questions. The first is the question of factuality; the second is the question of interpretation. They may be answered in either of two ways, materialistically in terms of the physicalistic theory which declares that man is the body and all the phenomena of his being — life, consciousness, thought, memory, volition, desire, morality — are epiphenomenal manifestations of the brain and the nervous system; or idealistically in terms of the nonphysicalistic theory which declares that man is not only body but also soul; and the rich phenomena of his life are expressions of his multi-dimensional consciousness. Which of these two theories can explain better the various phenomena of psychical research or parapsychology?

Are Parapsychological Phenomena True?

The mere fact of the existence of an officially recognized science for the study of parapsychological phenomena is a proof that scientists have now at least accepted the validity of certain facts which their colleagues in the past have condemned unilaterally as claptrap or bunkum.

Hitherto, it has been the custom to deride psychic phenomena either as inconsequential superstition or as downright imposture. Even now, in fact, very few people realize that the great majority of the world's intelligentsia accept them as real.

It is strange but true that, whereas formerly it was the uneducated who believed in the reality of metapsychical phenomena, it is now the educated class who give them validity. Consider, for example, the number of world-famous names included among those who regard psychic phenomena as real. Vincent Gaddis, in his introduction to Sylvan Muldoon's *Psychic Experiences of Famous People* enumerated at least 100 well-known scientists in his list.[6]

Among the Americans, the following names are outstanding: Dr. Joseph Banks Rhine, professor of psychology at Duke University, Durham, North Carolina, top-ranking researcher in extrasensory perception; Dr. William McDougall, famous for his sponsorship of the soul-idea in modern psychology; Dr. Charles B. Stuart and Dr. Hornell Hart, both of Duke University; Dr. Nicholas Murray Butler, Columbia University; Prof. W.J. Lengworthy-Taylor, Nebraska University; Dr. Alexis Carrel, late officer of the Rockefeller Foundation; Walter Franklin Prince, late officer of the Boston Society for Psychical Research; Dr. William B. Johnson and R.A. Watters, Reno Nevada; John J. O'Neil, science editor of the *New York Herald-Tribune*; Dr. Morton Prince, expert on dissociation phenomena; Dr. Daniel F. Comstock; Austin C. Lescarboura; Dr. Neville Whymant; Dr. W.H. Bates; J. Gilbert; Dr. Edwin Bowers; Claude Bragdon, architect and exponent of yoga and fourth dimensional philosophy; Dr. Titus Bull; Cecil Stokes, discoverer of the auroratone process of music in color; and Sir Hubert Wilkins, the explorer, who reported a remarkable series of telepathic experiments with Harold Sherman, in his *Thoughts through Space*.

Among early American exponents of parapsychology, we have the following: Professor William James of Harvard University, one of the greatest psychologists of all time; Prof. William Brown, Yale University; Prof. Edgar Lucien Larkin, director of Mt. Lowe Observatory; Prof. Robert Hare of the University of Pennsylvania, famous for his oxygen hydrogen blowpipe; Dr. James H. Hyslop, Columbia University; T.W. Stanford, founder of the California University that bears his name; Dr. Richard Hodgson, director of the American Society for Psychical Research for many years; Dr. George Wyld; Dr. Robert S. Wyld; Dr. Duncan McDougall; and Dr. Hereward Carrington whose untiring research in metapsychics made Muldoon call him "the greatest of them all."

Evidence from the Phenomena of Psychical Research 159

Great Britain offers a number of great names of contemporary and relatively recent students of psychic phenomena. Some are: Dr. Whately Carington, English psychologist; Dr. Frederick H. Wood; S.G. Soal; C.E.M. Joad; Lieut. Com. Rupert T. Gould; Harry Price; Dr. Nandor Fodor; Prof. Gardner Murphy; Sir Ernest Fiske, director of the Amalgamated Wireless of Australia; J.W. Dunne, whose theories on the nature of time added much to our understanding; F.W. Warrick; and Dr. Alexander Cannon, the London psychiatrist.

In earlier years, the name of Sir Oliver Lodge, the distinguished physicist, was outstanding. Equally outstanding was that of Sir William Crookes, president of the Royal Scientific Society, who invented the world-famous Crookes tube which made the X-ray possible. He was the first researcher to weigh a materialized entity. Other great names are Dr. Alfred Russell Wallace, co-discoverer with Charles Darwin of the principle of natural selection; Prof. Elliot Coues; Prof. Herbert Mayo; Prof. James Challis; Dr. J.W. Crawford; Dr. Robert Chambers; Dr. Ellis Powell; Prof. Henry Sidgwick, founder of the English Society for Psychical Research in 1882; Sir William Barrett; Dr. J.W. Kilner; Dr. J.M. Gully; F.W.H. Myers; Frederick Bligh Bond; Stanley de Brath; Dr. Paul Gibier; Prof. N.S. Shaler; Dr. F.L. Nicholls; Hudson Tuttle; Havelock Ellis; Edmund Gurney; E.E. Fournier d' Albe; Sir Arthur J. Balfour; William Harvey; Frank Podmore; Sir Humphrey Davy; Prof. A.O. Rankine; Lord Rayleigh; Prof. C.W. Surya; Sir Lockhart Robertson; Prof. A. DeMorgan; and Prof. William Denton.

In France we have Dr. Gustave Geley; Dr. Paul Feire; Dr. Eugene Osty; Dr. Charles Lancelin; Prof. Edouard Grinard; Col. Albert de Rochas; Charcot; Commandant Darget; Prof. Pierre and Mme. Curie; Prof. Charles Richet; Hector Durville; Dr. Baraduc; Allan Kardec; Henri Bergson; L. Figuer; Charles Fauventy; Louis Farigoule; Prof. Charles Henry; Dr. Jean Labadie; Prof. G. Geresa; and the outstanding Camille Flammarion, world famous astronomer.

Holland gives us the names of Dr. J.L. Matta; Dr. Van Zelst; Dr. Frederick van Eeden; Tenhaeff; and Dr. P.W. Koning.

Other eminent European names in the field of psychical research are: Herr Max Seiling, Finland; Th. Flournoy, Switzerland; Alexander N. Aksakof and P.D. Ouspensky, Russia; Dr. Ochorowicz, Poland; and Prof. Miguel San Benito, Spain.

Italian psychical research is graced by the names of Prof. Ernest Bozzano; Paul Pictet; Prof. G. Schiaparelli; Prof. A. Brofferio; Prof. Cesare Lobroso; Prof. Chiapelli; Prof. Vazzani; Prof. F. Bottazzi; Dr. Mucchi; and Prof. Moselli.

German psychical research is enriched by the works of Prof. J.C.F. Zollner; Baron Von Schrenck-Notzing; Dr. Emil Mattieson; I.H. Fichte; Baron Von Reichenbach; Dr. Constantin Oesterreich; Dr. Carl du Prel; Dr. F. Schwab; Prof. Hans Dreisch; Dr. William Haas, psychologist and author of *The World of Psychical Things;* and Prof. Fritz Hommel.

The long list already given will not be complete without including the names of Prof. H. Nielson; Prof. C. Hannessor; Adolf D' Assier; Dr. Dellane; Dr. Macario; Prof. Bouilland; Prof. Fukurai; Prof. James Coates; Dr. T. Glen Hamilton; Henry M. Stanley; and Prof. J. Tillyard.

No doubt, in the future, as methods of research improve and the minds of men become more and more free from prejudice and dogmatism, knowledge of parapsychology will increase and spread among all mankind.

Are parapsychological phenomena true? Let us answer in the words of Dr. Alfred Russell Wallace, "No other science (psychical research) rests upon a larger body of ascertained facts."[7] It takes a great man to say something against the prejudice of time and place, but Dr. Wallace was both a great man and a great scientist.

Phenomena Of Clairvoyance

We cannot consider all the phenomena of parapsychology in this book. They are too many and too complex. We shall limit ourselves to the discussion of the more typical or representative ones. Of these, one of the most interesting and illuminating is the phenomenon of clairvoyance.

What is clairvoyance? In its simplest form, it is the "ability to see without the use of the eyes."[8] In its more complex forms, it includes the "awareness of the past, present, and future events without the use of the special senses."[9]

Because it enables a person to see without the use of the eyes, modern investigators sometimes call clairvoyance "eyeless sight." It is also called "X-ray sight" or "roentgen ray eyes," because it gives its possessor power to see through opaque bodies.

The phenomenon of clairvoyance is neither recent nor rare. It has presented itself continuously throughout the whole range of human history and the ESP experiments of Dr. J.B. Rhine seem to indicate its presence in varying degrees in all human beings.

Spontaneous cases of clairvoyance are frequent and have been reported.

One case reported in the *Phantasms of the Living* and cited by J.B. Rhine in his book, *The Reach of the Mind*,[10] tells of a little girl of ten who, while walking along a country lane reading a geometry book, suddenly saw her surroundings fade away and her mother lying apparently dead on the floor of an unused room at home. Disturbed by the phenomenon, she called a doctor instead of going to school. "When the doctor and the girl arrived at home, they met the father going into the house. Seeing the doctor, the father immediately asked, 'Who is ill'? The child told him that her mother was ill and at once led them to the unused room. There on the floor lay the mother exactly as she had been seen in the vision. The mother was found to be suffering from a heart attack. It was only when the episode was over that the father discovered that his wife had been taken ill after the child had left the house. None of the servants knew of the sudden illness." The girl's vision of the scene is a good case of spontaneous clairvoyance.

Clairvoyance can be inborn, as in the case of the Spanish boy, Benito Paz, whose extraordinary clairvoyance was reported in *The Medical World* of May 10, 1929. Geoffrey Hodson gives an account of this in his book, *The Science of Seership*.[11]

Benito Paz was five when his father noticed his clairvoyance. He could read the letters in a closed alphabet book.

He could see objects inside closed boxes. The father took him to Madrid to be examined by the well-known eye surgeon, Dr. Pedro Niel. D. Niel found nothing abnormal or pathological about the boy. His eyes were normal. But he found out that the boy could see clearly and describe objects enclosed in a metal case. He could easily read letters enclosed in three or four coverings. He could without difficulty describe what you had in your various pockets. He could even indicate the colors of the objects. His powerful vision could pierce through metal, cloth and paper.

There are two cases of clairvoyance within my personal experience which I should like to include, one in which I tested the alleged clairvoyance of a certain person and the other in which I myself underwent the experience of spontaneous clairvoyance. In both cases the experience happened in public.

The first case involved a man by the name of Vicente Salumbides, a Filipino, who was a well-known sleight-of-hand performer. I had known him as such for some time until in a program held in the hall of a school in Pasay City, during which there were about two hundred people present, he demonstrated what should be regarded as a remarkable case of clairvoyance or clairaudience, or both.

He offered to have himself blindfolded and to perform, during that time, acts which normally could be done only with open eyes. I was then a third year student of philosophy and psychology at the University of the Philippines (1937), skeptical but eager to discover whether he could really prove that he had the faculty he claimed. I volunteered to blindfold him.

I borrowed a black *tapis* (a large native Filipino kerchief about one and a half yards long and one yard wide), doubled it neatly into a blindfold, and wrapped it twice around his head and eyes. It was impossible for him to see in any manner.

Then the test began. Every single performance was done in daylight in the presence of about two hundred witnesses. I walked around in different directions. He followed about two yards behind me everywhere I went. Never did he hesitate at any instant; it was as though he could actually see me as I walked. He was either clairvoyant, or clairaudient, or both. To reduce, if not to eliminate completely the use of his ears, I gave him a piece of chalk and told him to write on the wall everything that I wrote on it. He did. Finally, to isolate clairvoyance completely, I told him to imitate the movement of my hand as I formed figures in the air. He never made a single mistake.

Without doubt he could see. But his eyes were completely blindfolded. Decidedly he was clairvoyant.

The second case was my own personal experience of spontaneous clairvoyance which happened during a lecture on "The Seven Last Words of Christ on the Cross" in the hall of the Theosophical Society of the Philippines, in Quezon City. In the Philippines an address on the seven last words of Christ on the cross is customarily presented on Good Friday from high noon till three o'clock. Usually the sermon is given by a Catholic priest.

I was invited to deliver one such lecture which started at exactly high noon on Good Friday of 1953. The hall was packed and there were people outside listening through a loud-speaker system. There were musical numbers generally lasting from ten to twenty minutes between each two interpretations. During each musical intermission I sat facing a window on the side of the hall through which I could see a tall guava tree.

I was looking at the guava tree while listening to the strains of Gounod's "Ave Maria" preparatory to delivering the lecture on "Woman, behold thy son," when something made me look at the guava tree more intently. It was *burning!* But not actually so in terms of ordinary combustion. It was burning probably in the way the bush of Moses burned. Every leaf was aglow with a golden flame around it and through it, as though it was translucent with yellow fire. The whole tree was surrounded by a beautiful, golden glow extending in some places about two or three inches beyond it. Of course I thought it was all hallucination.

Then, as from a distance, I heard the voice of the master of ceremonies announcing that I would talk on the next word. Without removing my eyes from the glowing guava tree, I stood and walked toward the center of the stage and slowly turned my eyes to the waiting audience.

I saw the entire hall suffused with a golden glow which penetrated through the window and surrounded everyone present with a translucent yellow light of very delicate beauty. And I saw each man, woman and child, both the young and the old, aglow with the same golden aura. And they were all young and beautiful! Even the old seemed young; they were all wondrous and lovely to behold.

I began talking about Mary and John, and Jesus on the cross; but I was talking almost mechanically because my whole attention was concentrated on what I was seeing: each man, each woman, each child, all beautiful and young, as though I were seeing them all as souls, shining with a golden glow around them, as though they were all burning with soft yellow fire. Then, somehow, I began describing them and everything I was seeing. I even called some of the people by their names, and I was telling them how beautiful they all were. I even heard somebody say, "Dr. Reyes is in a trance." The hall was very quiet, and I continued talking of the light and fire that both penetrated and surrounded them.

Suddenly I saw a priest in a pulpit delivering a sermon. I could not hear what he was saying. But I could see him clearly. I began describing him to the audience. I said, "I am seeing a priest and he is giving a sermon on the Seven Words. But something seems to be happening to him. Yes, he seems to be in pain, because he is clutching at his heart and holding on to the pulpit railing. Yes, he is falling. I think he is dying. Yes, he has fallen."

Then I stopped talking and there was some movement in the hall as though some people were moving toward me. I still saw the golden glow in the hall. I sat down and the guava tree was still aglow but not quite as radiantly as before. Then I closed my eyes and somebody came to me to give me water. I drank. When I opened my eyes the golden fire was gone, both from the guava tree as well as from the hall.

I continued the lecture until three and the people were careful not to tell me about the vision. I felt that they thought they should not talk about it.

The next day, Holy Saturday, all the metropolitan papers of Manila announced the death of a priest of San Sebastian Church in the pulpit, between two and three o'clock in the afternoon of Good Friday, while delivering a sermon on the Seven Words.

The hall of the Theosophical Society in the Philippines is in Quezon City near Mayon Street. The San Sebastian Church is in the district of Quiapo in the City of Manila, about two kilometers away. I saw the priest and his death across two kilometers.

Clairvoyance may accompany hypnosis, though it need not be a result of it. Mesmer himself testified to the reality of clairvoyant experiences in his entranced subjects. He wrote, referring to what we would call now a hypnotized subject: "Sometimes through his inner sensibilities the somnambulist can distinctly see the past and future."[12] Professor Richet, experimenting on a somnambulistic subject, Leonie, discovered also that hypnotism can induce clairvoyance.

Dr. Louise Farigoule tested before a large crowd the clairvoyance of M. Ouvrien, a Frenchman. A doll was hidden in a drawer in the dark room of Dr. Farigoule's laboratory. Blindfolded, Ouvrien at once went to the drawer and picked it out. Blindfolded, he drove his motorcar through the heavy traffic of Paris, dodging other cars and even stopping when the traffic lights required it.[13]

While it is true that clairvoyance manifests as an accompaniment of hypnotic trance, it can be developed normally in a man who is willing to undertake the training necessary for its awakening. Such is the declaration of a scientifically trained clairvoyant, Mr. Geoffrey Hodson, author of that highly illuminating book, *The Science of Seership*.

Mr. Hodson demonstrated his clairvoyant powers by actually working with scientists, *under test conditions,* in various fields, such as astronomy, bacteriology, physics, psychology, and medical diagnosis. I have personally met the man and have, in fact, been his student for quite a time.

Evidence of the Existence of the Soul

His clairvoyant experiments on the electron and the nature of the electric current, for example, fulfilled all the rigid test conditions which, later, Dr. Rhine required in his ESP tests on telepathy and clairvoyance. Mr. Hodson was able to indicate the direction of deflection of the magnetic needle, not by observing the position of the magnet, but rather the actual direction of the stream of electrons as changed every now and then by varying the position of the magnet.

That he actually saw the electrons is proved by the fact that in Test A, consisting of five changes of the position of the magnet, he made four correct observations. In Test B, also consisting of five items, he again gave four correct answers.

Here are the results of the two tests as reported by E.W. Preston, M. Sc., in a pamphlet entitled, *The Occult Study of the Electron*:[14]

No.	Position of Magnet	Observed Deflection (Clairvoyant)	If Correct According to Science
Series A			
1	N.S.	Left	Correct
2	S.N.	Right	Correct
3	N.S.	Left	Correct
4	N.S.	Left	Correct
5	N.S.	Right	Wrong
Series B			
1	S.N.	Right	Correct
2	N.S.	Left	Correct
3	N.S.	Left	Correct
4	N.S.	Right	Wrong
5	S.N.	Right	Correct

In the language of mathematics, it can be said that there exists a rather high preponderance of probability that Mr. Hodson actually saw the electrons in motion. Four correct answers out of five, in each of two successive series, cannot, in any language and from the standpoint of the scientific law of probability, be attributed purely to chance. It was a case of *actual* sight; in other words, clairvoyance.

References
[1] Howard Warren, *Dictionary of Psychology*, (Cambridge: Houghton Mifflin Co., The Riverside Press, 1934) p. 216.
[2] *Ibid.*, p. 167.
[3] *Ibid.*, p. 167.
[4] D. H. Prins, "Psychical Research" in D. D. Kanga's *Where Theosophy and Science Meet, A Stimulus to Modern Thought*, Four volumes. Madras, India: The Adyar Library Association, 1949, Fourth Vol., pp. 13-14.
[5] *The Theosophical World*, Vol. 2, no. 7 (July, 1937).
[6] Sylvan Muldoon, *Psychic Experiences of Famous People*, With Introduction by Vincent H. Gaddis. (Chicago: Aries Press, 1947).
[7] Quoted in "The Cloud of Witnesses," by Meade Layne, *Round Robin*, Vol. IV, No. 4, (April-May, 1948) p. 14.
[8] Warren, *op. cit.*, p. 45
[9] *Ibid.*, p. 45.
[10] J. B. Rhine, *The Reach of the Mind*, (New York: William Sloane Associates, Inc., 1947) p. 27-28.
[11] Geoffrey Hodson, *The Science of Seership*, (London: Rider and Co.)
[12] Rhine, *op. cit.*, p. 29.
[13] Mary K. Neff, "The World's Awakening to the Powers Latent in Man," in *Theosophy in Australia*.
[14] Geoffrey Hodson, *The Science of Seership*, (London: Rider and Co.. Paternoster E.C. 4) pp. 35-38.

Chapter 19
EVIDENCES FROM THE PHENOMENA OF PSYCHICAL RESEARCH
THE PHENOMENA OF EXTRASENSORY PERCEPTION AND PSYCHOKINESIS

ESP And PK Experiments

The ESP and the PK experiments of Dr. J.B. Rhine at Duke University constitute probably the most thought-provoking of modern laboratory researches into the unknown powers of the human mind.

ESP stands for "extrasensory perception" and it refers to those powers of the mind which man exercises, voluntarily or involuntarily, without the use of the normal sense organs.

PK, on the other hand, stands for "psychokinesis" and it refers to the action of the mind upon a physical system."[1] It is more popularly known as the power of "mind over matter."

Aside from PK, the principal parapsychological phenomena subjected by Dr. Rhine to repeated mathematically computed and rigorously conducted laboratory experiments include the ESP powers of:

1. *Clairvoyance,* or "the awareness of objects or objective events without the use of the senses."[2]

2. *Telepathy,* otherwise called thought-transference, or the "communication of feelings, impulses, ideas, or more complex experiences, from one mind to another, effected without sense organs".[3]

3. *Precognition,* better known as prophecy, or "the ability to predict events that have as yet no existence."[4]

The procedure and the results of these experiments, as well as valid conclusions from them, are contained in four books by Dr. Rhine and his associates.

The first two, both by Dr. Rhine, *Extra-Sensory Perception* and *New Frontiers of the Mind,* contain the record of thousands of clinical experiments which prove the existence of supersensory powers. The third book, *Extrasensory Perception After Six Years* was written by Dr. Rhine with the help of J. G. Pratt, B.M. Smith, C.E. Stuart, and J.A. Greenwood.

A highly stimulating book, *The Reach of the Mind,* was published in 1947.

The Experiments

The utter trustworthiness of the Rhine experiments cannot be better judged than by the statement of a noted American scientist, Dr. Waldemar Kaempffert, who said: "Fraud is ruled out. Incompetence and deception are also ruled out, in view of the constant criticism to which Dr. Rhine was subjected by his colleagues (scientists) . . . . It is the most important single step along the scientific path toward the explanation of many valid occurrences heretofore considered fakes, stunts, and mysteries."[5]

The Rhine experiments consist mainly of two types, the ESP experiments for testing the reality of clairvoyance, telepathy, and precognition or prophecy and the PK experiments for testing the reality of psychokinesis or whether the mind can directly influence the motion of material objects.

Clairvoyance Experiments

A typical experiment in clairvoyance is simple. Subjects are asked to identify concealed cards. A 25-card deck, now known as the ESP cards, is used. It contains five designs — a star, a rectangle, a cross, a circle, and wavy lines.

First, the subject is shown the cards. Then the deck is shuffled, cut, and placed face down before him. No one, therefore, knows the order of the cards. The procedure thus precludes telepathy, and tests only clairvoyance. The subject is then made to identify the top card, after which it is removed but not looked at; then the next similarly, and so on until the whole deck is finished.

The run is repeated as many times as the experimenter wants. Dr. Rhine made as many as 700 runs in his experiments.

Results Of Clairvoyance Experiments

From chance alone, the average score mathematically expected is 5 hits per 25 cards. But if a performer runs through the deck of cards 700 times and averages about 8 hits per 25 cards, the results can no longer be attributed to chance, because the odds against averaging a score of eight or better for 700 or more runs would require a paragraph of figures to record.

In other words, such a performance rules out the element of chance completely, and permits the assumption of an extra-chance element to explain the phenomenon.

That extra-chance element is clairvoyance. In plain language, the performer actually "sees" the inverted cards.

The most notable results were obtained in the following experiments:

1. *University of Colorado Experiment.* Conductors, psychologist Dorothy Martin and mathematician Frances P. Stribic. Number of runs, 12,000. Average hits per run for more than 3,500 runs, 6.85. Average hits per run for 12,000 runs, 5.83. The odds against such scores being attainable by chance is astronomical.

2. *Hunter College Experiment.* Conductor, Prof. B. Reiss. The conductor in one building, the subject in another. The subject, a girl who had acquired a local reputation as a nonprofessional "psychic," scored an average of more than 18 hits per 25 through a series of 74 runs through the deck. One of these runs gave a perfect score of 25, and several of them ran above 20.

3. Dr. Rhine's experiment with a student named Pearce who made a perfect score of 25 hits several times. Another was the case of Lillian who made a perfect score of 25.[6]

Telepathy Experiments

In telepathy experiments, no cards are used. The experimenter simply thinks of any of the five ESP cards and the subject, who may be far away in another room, is supposed to receive the thought.

In the Turner-Ownbey telepathy test, Miss Turner, the subject, averaged less than eight hits per run when she was in the same room with the experimenter, but she averaged ten hits per run in eight runs when she was 250 miles away. Distance, therefore, does not diminish telepathic power.

Precognition Experiments

In the precognition or prophecy test, the subject is made to predict the card as it would appear after the cards are shuffled. Machine-shuffling, not hand-shuffling, is used. The number of successful predictions obtained through more than 4,500 runs, in experiments conducted by Dr. Rhine, raised the odds to 400,000 to 1 against chance alone.

Precognition, or the power of the mind to predict future events, is now established as a datum for further scientific investigation. But could not the mind of the subject directly influence the shuffling machine itself? In other words, might not psychokinesis be responsible for the results of the precognition tests?

PK Experiments

In these experiments dice throwing is used. A typical PK experiment proceeds as follows: Let us say the target chosen for the runs is sevens. The subject is asked to shake the dice in a cup and throw them onto a padded table top. The upper faces are observed, called aloud, and recorded by the experimenter. All the combinations making seven (6 and 1, 5 and 2, 4 and 3) are circled on the record sheet and after each run of 12 throws, the hits are counted. Two sevens are, on the average, to be expected from pure chance in a run of 12 throws.

Hundreds of thousands of experimental trials enabled Dr. Rhine and his colleagues to conclude that the mind has a force that can act on matter.

Other PK experiments by other investigators gave conclusive results as to the actual existence of psychokinetic energy. Notable were those of Frank Smith, graduate student of Yale; E.P. Gibson, a city engineer in East Grand Rapids; Professor MacDougall in England, on leave from Duke University; and H. L. Frick, psychologist at Wayne University.

Estimate Of The Rhine Experiments

Does official science accept the Rhine findings? Not yet, though many individual scientists do. It can be said, however, that eventual acceptance is inevitable because, according to Dr. Rhine himself, "There is simply no alternative to acceptance. Every conceivable counterexplanation has been considered and found inapplicable to the findings."[7]

At this juncture, the corroborative statement of one of the world's leading scientists is worth quoting. Dr. Alexis Carrel, Nobel Prize winner in medicine and inventor with Lindberg of the perfusion pump, said in his book, *Man the Unknown*:

> Clairvoyance and telepathy are a primary datum of scientific observation. The existence of telepathic phenomena, as well as other metapsychic phenomena, is not accepted by most biologists and physicians. The attitude of these scientists should not be blamed. For these phenomena are exceptional and illusive. Besides, they are hidden in the enormous mass of the superstitions, lies, and illusions accumulated for centuries by mankind. Although they have been mentioned in every country and at every epoch, they have not been investigated scientifically. It is, nevertheless, a fact that they are abnormal, although rare, activities of the human being.[8]

From this statement by Dr. Carrel, we reach the conclusion that one undeniable service to truth which Dr. Rhine, together with his colleagues, has rendered is to salvage metapsychical phenomena from the enormous accumulation of mankind's superstitions and to give them scientific dignity by subjecting them to experimental investigation.

With regard to the mathematical basis of Dr. Rhine's experiments, the American Institute of Mathematical Statis-

Evidence from the Phenomena of Psychical Research 173

tics made public the following statement at its annual meeting:

> Dr. Rhine's investigations have two aspects, experimental and statistical. On the experimental side, mathematicians of course have nothing to say. On the statistical side, however, recent mathematical work has established the fact that, assuring that the experiments have been properly performed, the statistical analysis is essentially valid. If the Rhine investigation is to be fairly attacked, it must be on other than mathematical grounds.[9]

If it should be asked why many scientists still persist in ignoring the reality of parapsychological phenomena, the answer is that the human mind is highly resistant to change. The acceptance by science of the facts of parapsychology would mean a total revolution in the realm of human knowledge. It would mean a change of scientific foundation and philosophical attitude. It would mean the complete overthrow of many pet theories, such as the naturalistic theory that physical energies and forces are the only ultimately causal or determining agencies in the universe and the corpocentric theory that man is the body only and his conscious experience is the product of his brain. For many scientists, it would mean the unlearning of many false acceptations and the learning of new facts. It would mean, in fact, the total overhauling of the scientific mind and the rewriting of science as a whole in accordance with new knowledge. Such a change, such a revolution, such an over-hauling cannot happen in a short time.

The natural inertia of man's mind will prevent it, but not ultimately, and not for long, because ultimately truth will win out, and the majesty of fact cannot, in the end, be denied.

In the meantime, all truth-lovers should remember the words of Professor Thouless of Cambridge University regarding extrasensory perception:

> The reality of the phenomena must be regarded as proved as certainly as anything in scientific research can be proved. . . . Let us now give up the task of trying to prove again to the satisfaction of the skeptical that the psi effect really exists, and try instead to devote

ourselves to the task of finding out all we can about it. With fuller knowledge of its nature, the difficulties of believing in its existence may appear less formidable than they do now.[10]

Interpretation

In other words, *psi*[11] is an established fact; No further proof is needed. If the unbeliever remains unbelieving and the skeptic, skeptical, if the dogmatist remains dogmatic and the bigot, bigoted, let them perish in their blindness.

Now, if parapsychological phenomena are facts, how shall we explain them? What do they indicate? What do they point to? Of what are they signs?

Let Dr. Rhine himself answer:

> Our basic problem — the nature of man — was worded at the start in terms of the familiar soul theory, a nonphysical system. Individual theologians, of course, have many added meanings for the terms. But our concern is merely: Is there anything extraphysical or spiritual in human personality?
>
> The experimental answer is "yes." There now is evidence that such an extraphysical factor exists in man. The soul hypothesis has been established, although its religious aspects have been ignored in this inquiry — nothing has been dealt with so far but the soul's elemental reality.[12]

Clairvoyance, both in time and space, is completely inexplicable in terms of the body-theory of man, so is telepathy, so is prophecy or precognition, so is psychokinesis. If inexplicable in terms of the corpocentric theory of man, then can the cerebrocentric theory explain it? In other words, can mental states cause bodily events? Most emphatically, yes! Ducasse puts this into proper perspective when he said:

> It is said, of course, that to suppose something nonphysical, such as thought, to be capable of causing motion of a physical object, such as the body, is absurd. But I submit that if the heterogeneity of mind and matter makes this absurd, then it makes equally absurd the causation of mental states by stimulation of the body. Yet no absurdity is commonly found in the assertion that cutting the skin causes a feeling of pain, or that alcohol,

caffein, bromides, and other drugs cause characteristic states of consciousness. As David Hume made clear long ago, no kind of causal connection is intrinsically absurd. Anything might cause anything; and only observation can tell us what in fact can cause what.[13]

No kind of causal connection is intrinsically absurd; there is only one explanation of the entire *psi* phenomena, and that is the soul-theory which regards man as a spiritual entity and not as a body mechanism.

Both ESP and PK phenomena completely escape the laws of physical motion. Physicochemical laws cannot explain them. In fact, parenthetically, we may state here that physicochemical laws can hardly explain themselves.

Keeton and others have pointed out in their article, "Some Ambiguities in the Theory of the Conservation of Energy," that the conservation of energy is not something observation has revealed or could reveal, but only a postulate — a defining postulate for the notion of an "isolated physical system."[14]

How, for example, does a somnambulist "see"? Assume that he is in a state of temporary clairvoyance, and it is no longer difficult to understand why he "sees" without using his normal visual sense organ.

With what does he "see," then, if he is not using his normal visual sense organ? That he "sees" without using his eyes shows that he is not the eyes, nor the brain, for the brain cannot see without the eyes, nor is he the body, for the body is equally sightless without the eyes. Therefore, if he is not the eyes, nor the body, he is nonphysical consciousness, immaterial self, spiritual I-am.

This alternative is inescapable, because the primacy of consciousness cannot be denied even in the state of somnambulism, and clairvoyance implies consciousness, selfhood, I-am-ness. This egoic consciousness, this I-am, I call the soul.

The same logical analysis can be applied to the other *psi functions,* such as telepathy, precognition, and psychokinesis, and the same conclusion will be arrived at: namely, the existence of the soul or a nonphysical factor in man is inescapable, if we must have a logical and coherent explanation of parapsychological phenomena.

PSI Functions Are Nonphysical

Dr. Rhine gives several important reasons why all the *psi* functions must be regarded as nonphysical.

1. *They are not affected by space or distance, and distance is a major element in all laws of physics governing energy transfer.*

"In comparing the results obtained at different zones of distance, ranging from a few miles to several thousand," said Dr. Rhine, "one gets the impression that distance is of no importance to ESP success. The only factor that seemed to make any difference in the scoring was the individual subject's own capacity for extrasensory perception. . . . Those nearest the target were not consistently the most successful, nor those farthest away the least."[15]

Among the successful ESP tests involving long distances were the following:

a. The Usher-Burt Experiment, in which experimenter and subject were from 120 to 960 miles apart.

b. The Pearce-Pratt Experiment, in which experimenter and subject were at varying distances of 1 yard, 100 yards, and 250 yards from each other.

c. The Turner-Ownbey Experiment, in which the subject, Miss Turner, made the better score of 10 hits per run at a distance of 250 miles over the 8 hits per run she made when she was in the same room with the experimenter.

2. *Physical barriers do not obstruct the operation of any psi function.*

Clairvoyance and telepathy, for example, can operate even when the experimenter and the subject are in different rooms, or the eyes of the subject are blindfolded, or barriers are interposed between them, such as mountains, for instance.

3. *There is no known physical wave length or radiation that can emanate from the ESP cards to affect the brain of the subject.*

4. *The position of the ESP cards, or even the position of the experimenter or the subject, does not affect at all the results of the experiments.*

5. *This is probably the most formidable difficulty in giving a physical explanation of the psi functions; there is absolutely no known physical law that can give an adequate*

Evidence from the Phenomena of Psychical Research 177

analysis of the pure telepathy test in which no card, no drawing, nothing physical at all, is used in the experiment.

The brain certainly generates energy of an electrical nature. This is the Berger Rhythm or the EEG (electro-encephalogram), discovered by the German psychiatrist, Hans Berger, in 1929.[16] It is usually called "brain waves."

To assume, however, that it is these "brain waves" which are operative in the pure telepathy test is to make the more gratuitous assumptions *that the subject can see these waves with his eyes and read the ideas of the sender in them.*

Conclusion

"Therefore," concludes Dr. Rhine, "as things stand today, extrasensory perception must admittedly transcend the laws of physics . . . and hence be essentially extraphysical."[17]

The same can be said of precognition or prophecy. There is no possible *physical explanation* of how the mind can predict the happenings of an event that has not yet happened. In fact, the only explanation of prophecy worth any logical acceptance is the fourth-dimensional theory of consciousness given by P.D. Ouspensky in his *Tertium Organum*. If prophecy is a fourth-dimensional function, it certainly is not physical.

Now, if all the *psi* functions are not physical, therefore, they are not functions of the brain, of the nervous system, nor of the physical body.

The question, then, is: Of what are they functions? One thing is admittedly true; they are functions of the mind. If they are functions of the mind, but are not functions of the brain, it therefore follows that the mind is not physical at all. In other words, the mind is not a function of the brain. It is something *sui-generis*. It is something unique. It is not an epiphenomenon of the brain, although it can interact with the brain and even affect matter, as in psychokinesis.

Experimentally, therefore, the *psi* functions and the various studies on them prove that the mind exists as an autonomous reality capable of self-determination and volition.

Dr. Rhine calls this nonphysical mind the psychological soul, but because I want to give it also a religious and moral significance, I call it simply soul. The soul exists. It is a fact.

The consequences of this experimental discovery are tremendous:

It strikes a mortal blow at materialism.

It solves an age-old problem which has baffled the minds of men for hundreds, even thousands, of years — the existence of the soul.

It re-creates the science of psychology by liberating it from the limitations of physiology and restoring to it its original meaning and function, the science of the soul.

It points out a way of bringing about a closer cooperation between science and religion.

It vindicates the moral code of the spiritual life of humanity.

It opens a path to a better understanding of death which may lead man to the conquest of his mortality.

References

[1] J. B. Rhine, *The Reach of the Mind*, (New York: William Sloane Associates, Inc., 1947) p. 87.

[2] *Ibid.*, p. 27.

[3] Howard C. Warren, *Dictionary of Psychology*, (Cambridge: Houghton Mifflin Co., The Riverside Press, 1934) p. 216.

[4] Rhine, *op. cit.*, p. 65.

[5] From the *Theosophical World*, Vol. 2, No. 7, (July, 1937).

[6] All experiments mentioned are recorded in Dr. Rhine's book, *The Reach of the Mind*, (William Sloane's Associates, Inc., New York).

[7] *Ibid.*, p. 154.

[8] Alexis Carrel, *Man the Unknown*, (New York: Harper and Brothers, 1939) p. 124.

[9] Rhine, *op. cit.*, pp. 161-162.

[10] *Ibid.*, p. 172.

[11] The Greek Letter "psi" is now the accepted symbol for all psychic and parapsychic phenomena. It stands for the entire ESP-PK process. It was originated by two British scientists, Dr. Thouless and Dr. Weisner.

[12] J. B. Rhine, "The Reach of the Mind," *The Readers Digest Condensation,* (February, 1948, Vol. 52, No. 310) p. 141.

[13] C. J. Ducasse, "The Empirical Case for Personal Survival " quoted in *Body, Mind, and Death,* edited by Antony Flew, (New York: The MacMillan Company, 1946) p. 229.

[14] M. T. Keeton, "Some Ambiguities in the Theory of the Conservation of Energy," *Philosophy of Science*, Vol. 8, No. 3, July, 1941.

[15] Rhine, *op. cit.*, pp. 57-58.

[16] John Fulton (Editor) *Howell's Textbook of Physiology*, (Philadelphia and London, W. B. Saunders Co., 1946) p. 525.

[17] Rhine, *op. cit.*

Chapter 20
EVIDENCES FROM THE PHENOMENA OF PSYCHICAL RESEARCH
THE PHENOMENA OF TRAVELING CLAIRVOYANCE

The Problem Of Survival

One important fact with tremendous scientific and philosophical significance is the discovery that the *psi* processes operate without the limitations of time and space.

If the *psi* processes operate independently of time and space, there is therefore sufficient reason to presume that they are functions of a nonphysical factor or element in human personality which is likewise nonspatial and nontemporal. I call it soul.

Such nonspatial, nontemporal, nonphysical factor or element in man can also be presumed to be exempt from the law of death. In fact it cannot die, since death, being a spatiotemporal halt or stoppage, can affect only spatiotemporal objects. The soul, therefore, is deathless. If deathless, then endless. If endless, may we not say that it is, therefore, also beginningless?

But this, as well as similar other questions, interesting and important though they may be, is quite beyond the scope of this book.

The empirically important question is this: Is there any known parapsychological phenomenon which may serve as a basis, or a point of departure, for the investigation or study of the problem of survival?

In terms of the *psi* functions, the question would be whether there exists any factual parapsychological phenomenon which shows or tends to show that the *psi* functions are really nonspatial and nontemporal. The answer is that there is.

There is an interesting phenomenon of parapsychology which indicates the following points very clearly:

1. That the *psi* functions are nonspatial and nontemporal.
2. That the soul or the "I-am" is nonphysical.
3. That the soul and the body are two distinctly different things.
4. That, in fact, the soul is separable from the body, and it can separate from the body temporarily, even before the permanent separation known as death.
5. That the soul is naturally clairvoyant and telepathic, and possibly psychokinetic when apart from the body.
6. That the *psi* functions are, therefore, inherent and natural powers of the soul, and that the body or the nervous system or the brain can and does in fact, when not suitably developed, or fully unfolded, act as limitation or an obstruction to the full manifestation of these natural soul-powers.

This rarely recorded but, nevertheless, real parapsychological phenomenon is called technically "traveling clairvoyance."

What Is Traveling Clairvoyance?

Traveling clairvoyance is a rather clumsy term. Which travels, one might ask, clairvoyance or the clairvoyant himself; the power of the soul or the soul itself? But does anything travel at all? Traveling implies time and space. It is, thus, inapplicable to the spacelessness and timelessness both of the *psi* powers and the possessor of those powers.

Tenhaeff, well-known lecturer on Psychical Research in a Netherlands university, calls traveling clairvoyance by the term "excursion-phenomena."[1] F. van Eeden calls it "lucid dream," though it is not really a dream in the ordinary acceptance of the term. Muldoon, in his book, *The Projection of the Astral Body,* calls it "projection of consciousness."[2]

There are two well-known recorded cases of traveling clairvoyance, one given in the fourth volume of Sir Arthur

Thomson's four volume *The Outline of Science*; the other, reported in *The Scotsman* of February 27, 1937. The latter is headed "On edge of death: record of out of the body experience: brought back to life," and is a paper read to members of the Royal Medical Society by the late Lord Geddes[3] (then Sir Auckland Geddes) on the occasion of the bicentenary of the Society.

It should not be supposed that there have been no cases of traveling clairvoyance other than these two. There must have been many, but almost all of them unrecorded. Two reasons for the *apparent* rarity of this phenomenon are, first, that it happens generally only to persons who seem to be dying, but who ultimately survive, and second, that it is often dismissed, after its occurrence, as either a form of hallucination or as a case of delirium.

We may suppose that it happens to all dying persons, either remotely or immediately, or sometimes throughout the entire period prior to death. This has been the universal testimony of men who have almost died, for example, of drowning, or of poisoning, or of asphyxiation.[4]

We have every reason to suppose that what happened to men who almost died must have happened also to men who actually died.

Let us consider the case reported by Lord Auckland Geddes.

"Record Of Out Of The Body Experience"

What follows is a most interesting case of traveling clairvoyance or "out of the body experience" reported by Sir Auckland Geddes before the Royal Medical Society of Edinburgh on February 26, 1937. It records the experience of a man who passed through the portals of death and was brought back to life by medical treatment. The record was taken down in shorthand by a skilled secretary as life was re-establishing itself. Here is an excerpt of the recorded experience:

> On Saturday, November 9th, a few minutes after midnight, I began to feel very ill, and by 2 o'clock was definitely suffering from acute gastro-enteritis, which

kept me vomiting and purging until about 8 o'clock. . . . By 10 o'clock I had developed all the symptoms of very acute poisoning; intense gastro-intestinal pain, diarrhoea; pulse and respirations becoming quite impossible to count. I wanted to ring for assistance, but found I could not, and so quite placidly gave up the attempt. I realized I was very ill, and very quickly reviewed my whole financial position: thereafter at no time did my consciousness appear to me to be in any way dimmed, but I suddenly realized that *my* consciousness was separating from another consciousness, which was also me. These for purposes of description we could call the A and B consciousness, and throughout what follows the ego attached itself to the A consciousness. The B personality I recognized as belonging to the body, and as my physical condition grew worse and the heart was fibrillating rather than beating, I realized that the B consciousness belonging to the body was beginning to show signs of being composite, that is, built up of "consciousness" from the head, the heart, and viscera, etc. These components became more individual and the B consciousness began to disintegrate, while the A consciousness which was now me, seemed to be altogether outside my body, which it could see. Gradually I realized that I could see not only my body and the bed in which it was, but everything in the whole house and garden, and then I realized that I was seeing not only "things" at home, but in London and in Scotland, in fact wherever my attention was directed it seemed to me; . . . . I next realized that my vision included not only "things" in the ordinary three dimensional world, but also "things" in these four or more dimensional places that I was in.

Just as I began to grasp all these I saw "A" enter my bedroom; I realized she got a terrible shock, and I saw her hurry to the telephone; I saw my doctor leave his patients and come very quickly; and heard him say or saw him think "He is nearly gone." I heard him quite clearly speaking to me on the bed, but I was not in touch with the body and could not answer him. I was really cross when he took a syringe and rapidly injected my body with something which I afterwards learned was camphor. As the heart began to beat more strongly,

I was drawn back, and I was intensely annoyed, because I was so interested and just beginning to understand where I was and what I was "seeing." I came back into the body really angry at being pulled back, and once I was back all the clarity of vision of anything and everything disappeared, and I was just possessed of a glimmer of consciousness which was suffused with pain.[5]

Analysis

A careful analysis of the Geddes report yields us the following pertinent facts:

1. The heart of the patient was no longer beating; it was only fibrillating.

Fibrillation, whether auricular or ventricular, is an arrhythmic condition of the heart. It is characterized by "ceaseless, but incoordinate and aimless spread of ineffective waves of contraction."[6] It is a condition in which "the movement (of the heart) as a whole is more or less incoordinate, and therefore ineffectual."[7]

In the state of fibrillation, therefore, the heart, being *incoordinate* and *ineffectual,* cannot be expected to maintain the normal circulation of blood throughout the body. Under such a condition, brain anemia naturally develops since the cerebral capillaries do not receive enough blood supply. The brain ceases to function normally. Cerebration either stops or is at its lowest ebb.

2. The patient experienced a main consciousness with which he felt identified and little or minor consciousness belonging to each of the various sense organs. The latter were all absorbed into the former.

3. The patient found himself outside the body. He saw his body as distinct from his own self.

4. Outside the body, he saw not only "things" at home, but in London and in Scotland, miles away, and wherever his attention was directed.

5. Outside the body, he *saw* "A" hurry to the telephone; he *saw* his doctor leave his patients; he *heard* him say or *saw* him *think,* "He is nearly gone."

6. Once sucked back into his body, the clarity of his vision dimmed and a glimmer of consciousness suffused with pain remained with him.

Conclusion And Interpretation

The phenomena of traveling clairvoyance tend to show or prove the following:

1. *That consciousness can function outside the body.* Therefore, it is not a function of the brain. Epiphenomenalism, then, is entirely false. In fact, the converse theory, which Ducasse calls hypophenomenalism, is probably truer. He attributes the term to Schopenhauer, but it is also a possible theoretical development of Lamarckian thought. The theory states that "the instruments which the various mechanisms of the body constitute are the objective products of obscure cravings for the corresponding powers; and, in particular, that the organization of the nervous system is the effect and material isomorph of the variety of mental functions exercised at a given level of animal existence."[8]

2. *That consciousness can think, see, hear, and will outside the body.* Thought, perception, and volition, therefore, are not brain functions. That thought is noncerebral is shown by the fact that the patient was continuously thinking while he was outside the body. That perception is noncerebral is proved by the fact that he could see and hear in his extraphysical state. That volition is noncerebral is evinced by the fact that he resisted return to his body when he felt a strong force sucking him in as shown by the fact that he went "back into the body really angry at being pulled back."

3. *That consciousness is inherently multidimensional,* using Ouspensky's terminology; *or innately extrasensorially perceptive,* using Dr. Rhine's nomenclature. In other words, consciousness is, by original nature, clairvoyant and clairaudient; in general, cryptaesthetic.[9] This is shown by the fact that once outside the body the patient immediately became clairvoyant. He could see things and places miles away or wherever his attention was directed.

4. *That consciousness not only is completely independent of the brain in all its functions, but is even limited by it*

when it has to function through it. This is proved by two facts: first, that the patient was clairvoyant only outside the body; and second, that once sucked back into his body, the clarity of his vision disappeared, and the range of his consciousness became greatly diminished.

At this juncture, the objection might be raised that all the phenomena experienced by the patient outside the body were hallucinations; in other words, that he was not really outside the body.

This objection is invalidated by the following points:

First, the patient recognizes himself outside the body; in fact, he became clairvoyant in that condition. Empirically, no suppositional objection can nullify this. Experience, in other words, is primal. Nothing, save an opposite experience, can render it invalid.

Second, the brain of the patient was physiologically inactive, since cerebration either had stopped or had gone down to its lowest ebb. Yet, it was precisely in this state or condition that he became mentally supernormal, that is, clairvoyant. How can we explain this incompatible relation of lowest cerebration and highest mentation?

Traveling Clairvoyance Proves The Soul

From the foregoing analysis and interpretation, only one conclusion seems logically possible, and it is this: That man is not the body. Rather, he is the soul, capable of perception, thought, and volition apart from the body he uses for physical expression and action.

No other conclusion is possible, because, other than the soul-interpretation, no other hypothesis can explain adequately, consistently, and coherently the nature and operation of traveling clairvoyance. In fact, it can be said that where *psi* experiments prove the soul by inference, traveling clairvoyance is an empirical demonstration of its reality. What we need, of course, is a sufficent number of well attested cases.

Traveling Clairvoyance Not Infrequent

Despite the lack of recorded cases, it cannot be said that the occurrence of traveling clairvoyance is rare. On the contrary, it is quite common. Frequently, however, it passes under other names because it happens under varying conditions.

Under abnormal conditions of the body, such as high fever or strong emotional shock, the consciousness may separate temporarily from its physical habitation. The man may actually see his body; in fact, he may become clairvoyant. Usually, however, we call this delirium. It is characterized by "illusions and hallucinations, and clouding of consciousness."[10]

So it must be, inasmuch as it is really only a sort of prelude to the condition of traveling clairvoyance, its threshold, as it were. Its accompanying phenomena, however, need not be regarded as illusory or hallucinatory. But for the fact that clairvoyance is now regarded as a scientific datum, we would be calling it a form of hallucination.

If traveling clairvoyance or projection of consciousness be hallucinatory, then all the yogis of India who testify to the reality of all soul-excursion phenomena are under hallucination.

Yogananda Paramahansa's book, *An Autobiography of a Yogi*, gives a number of cases of projection of consciousness.

There is a difference, of course, between the way most Western students understand traveling clairvoyance and the way the yogis of India understand it. To the Western student of psychology and physiology, traveling clairvoyance is an abnormal state of consciousness that occurs only under extraordinary, usually pathological, conditions. To the Hindu yogi, however, it is quite a normal thing. It is a power that lies dormant in the undeveloped soul. It can be awakened under proper guidance. That guidance is supplied by the Eastern science of yoga.

My Experience

I have personally undertaken the practice necessary for the awakening of this consciousness. And I have not failed. I cannot say I am an expert. In fact, after years of practice, I still regard myself as a tyro.

But one thing is certain. I have had experiences that prove the reality of the Eastern claim.

I have been a vegetarian for the last thirty-eight years at least and for almost the same number of years I have been practising concentration and meditation.

My first experience of separation from my body occurred when I was nineteen. I was not sick, as Sir Geddes' patient was, nor abnormal, unless vegetarianism be considered a form of abnormality.

It was ten o'clock in the evening, and I had just finished studying my lessons. I was still studying then at the University of the Philippines. I went to bed, not to sleep, but only to rest. I was intending to read until midnight.

The moment my head touched the pillow, I immediately felt an unusual sensation of motor inability. I could not move, although I was wide awake. I was alertly conscious of myself as well as of my surroundings. At the same time, I heard a peculiar buzzing sound in the region of my head. This went on for several minutes. Suddenly, against my will, and without any clear idea of what was to happen, I felt that I rushed out of my body, through my head, through the ceiling, through the roof, and up.

Panic seized me. I shouted, "Master! Master;" As suddenly as I went out, I plunged back into my body with the utterance of that word. I did not wake up, because I did not sleep. I was awake all the time. But I recovered the use of my body. I was again able to move.

I regretted my sudden panic. Because the sensation was so startlingly new, I could not control my sudden fear. I, therefore, decided to be mindful of myself the next time, should the phenomenon happen again. And it happened again the following night.

This time I was ready. The same preliminary circumstances occurred: the physical rigidity, the buzzing sound, the lightness on the shoulder regions. When I felt I was slipping out of my body, I steadied myself, so that instead of suddenly rushing out, I was able to go out gradually.

Then I felt and knew myself outside the body. I was hovering over my body, but I could not see it. *I seemed to be blind.* I was moving all around the house with a unique kind of undulating motion, but I did not really exert any effort in moving. In fact, I just willed to be in any given place and I was there.

The same thing happened many times thereafter, usually at night, but also at other times, even at noontime, during my siesta.

But I still could not see my body. Then one night it happened: I saw my body. I saw it lying in bed, and I was not it. The realization that I was not the body suddenly made me think I was dead, but only for a time. The next realization was one of peace. To know you are not the body but the soul; to know that even if the body dies, you do not die; to know that you are something spiritual and, therefore, essentially indestructible; to know yourself apart from the pains of the body, its illness, its death; to know these things, and to know them not through reading or hearing, but through actual experience — this was the realization that gave me peace.

Since then, it has become customary for me to slip out nightly from my physical encasement and to live not as soul imprisoned in body, but as soul in the plenitude of understanding and self-realization.

Hallucination Or Dream?

I, myself, have asked that question.

If it has been all hallucination, then I have been in a consistent state of hallucination for over thirty-five years. If it has been all a continuous dream, then I have been dreaming all along.

Would hallucination that has been consistent and voluntary for over thirty-five years be still hallucinatory? Is it possible for a man to dream every night the same dream for all these years and to dream it voluntarily? Would it still be a dream, even if he were awake, consciously, and with his will in full operation?

During these years many corroborative experiences of soul existence have happened to me — sometimes with other people involved. To write them all down would require another volume of many hundreds of pages. I include in this book two such experiences involving other people.

One time, in a meeting, I felt faint and was made to lie down. A doctor whom I met then for the first time, Dr. Garcia-Ageo, a Filipino physician, a graduate of the College of Medicine of the University of Santo Tomas, Manila, Philippines, relieved me by simply pointing his fingers toward my heart and releasing what I felt were like icy pin pricks hitting my breast. He told me after I was relieved that he would visit me the following night. About eleven o'clock that night I lay down to rest when suddenly I felt the hypnagogic state of loss of motor control, although I retained full awareness of everything.

I saw Dr. Garcia-Ageo come through the window. His sudden appearance disconcerted me somewhat, but I did not feel any fear at all. He stood by the bed and told me he would help me. Before leaving, he said, "I know you will not believe this at all after I leave. So I would like to give you a possible proof that I have indeed come. I will recite a little prayer which I want you to remember. Tomorrow, at ten in the morning, please come to my clinic, and when we meet, do not tell me anything. I will recite this little prayer again to remind you of my visit." Then he went through the window and disappeared. I regained full control of myself and he was gone. I even called my mother to ask if she had seen any man enter my room. She said she had not. Obviously Dr. Ageo did not visit me in his physical body. How did he come through the window?

The following morning, I went to his clinic. The doctor met me at the door and smiled. Then he recited the little prayer and asked, "Are you convinced now"? I just looked at him wondering whether to say yes or simply to thank him.

The other experience is quite similar but it involved a man still living in New York, Dr. Robert T. Brown, who taught me Sanskrit and who wrote a formidable little book entitled *The Mystery of Space*. I used to visit him regularly for a year or so while he was living in Manila about forty years ago. I learned from him the rudiments of Sanskrit and quite a great deal of Indian philosophy. One night, in a hypnagogic situation similar to my experience with Dr. Garcia-Ageo, Dr. Brown came to me and began showing me a notebook containing Sanskrit words such as *sat, chit,* and *ananda.* He began explaining them to me and with a smile, he said, "It is easier to teach and learn in the inner plane. But I know you will consider all of this a dream after I leave. But I want to prevent that. Tomorrow, when we meet again, I will show you this same notebook together with the Sanskrit words we are discussing now."

When he left, I looked for him, although because of my previous similar experience with Dr. Garcia-Ageo, I expected somehow that he would not be there physically.

The following day, as I was wont, I visited him at his place at three in the afternoon. He admitted me into his study and immediately he showed me a notebook which he opened to the page where the previous night I had seen the three Sanskrit words.

It was the same notebook! It was the same page! And the Sanskrit words were there in the same succession: *sat, chit, ananda!*

Dr. Brown looked at me and with a twinkle in his eyes asked me, "Is this the notebook I showed you last night?"

I answered almost inaudibly, "Yes, I think so. I think it is."

These experiences cannot be submitted as proofs for other people. But they are enough for me.

No one can prove color to the congenitally blind. No one can prove sound to the congenitally deaf. Experience, after all, is the final proof of truth. The only thing one who has not had the experience can do is patiently to wait for the time when the experience will be his also.

In the meantime, if my reader should ask for corroborative experiences among other people, I should tell him:

Go, ask the mystics of mankind for their experiences; ask the clairvoyants; ask the yogis of India and China.

I should like, at this juncture, to recommend one book particularly, probably the only one of its kind in the world, Tibet's greatest contribution to humanity, the not too well-known *Bardo Thodol,* or, as it is usually translated, *The Tibetan Book of the Dead.*[11] It describes with almost scientific precision how the soul separates from the body.

References
[1] Tenhaeff, *Het Spiritisme,* in D. H. Prins, "Psychical Research," in D. D. Kanga's *Where Theosophy and Science Meet, A Stimulus to Modern Thought,* (Adyar, Madras, India: the Adyar Library Association, 1949) p. 30.
[2] *Ibid.,* p. 32.
[3] Dr. Geddes was knighted in 1917, being known from that time as *Sir* Auckland Geddes until his elevation to the peerage in January 1942 under the title of Baron Geddes of Rolvenden.
[4] See Chapter XIII of this book for examples.
[5] *The Scotsman,* February 26, 1937, p. 16, Columns 3-4.
[6] John F. Fulton, (Editor), *Howell's Textbook of Physiology,* (Philadelphia and London: W. B. Saunders Co., 1946) p. 776.
[7] *Ibid.,* p. 747.
[8] C. J. Ducasse, "The Empirical Case for Personal Survival," in *Body, Mind, and Death.* Introduction by Anthony Flew, (New York: The Cromwell Publishing Company, 1964) pp. 230.
[9] Cryptaesthesia is a generic term embracing telepathy, clairvoyance, prevision, etc. See Howard C. Warren, *Dictionary of Psychology,* (Cambridge: Houghton Mifflin Co., The Riverside Press, 1934) p. 66.
[10] Warren, *supra.,* p. 72.
[11] W. Y. Evans-Wentz, *The Tibetan Book of the Dead or the After-Death Experiences on the Bardo Plane, According to Lama Kazi Dawa-Samdup's English Rendering* (London: Goeffrey Cumberlege, Oxford University Press, 1951 Second Edition.)

Chapter 21

EVIDENCES FROM THE PHENOMENA OF PSYCHEDELICS

Our normal waking consciousness, rational consciousness as we call it, is but one special type of consciousness, whilst all about it, parted from it by the filmiest of screens, there lie potential forms of consciousness entirely different . . . . No account of the universe in its totality can be final which leaves these other forms of consciousness quite disregarded. How to regard them is the question . . . .

These statements were written more than half a century ago by William James, psychologist and educator. How to regard the "other forms of consciousness" is no longer a complete mystery at present inasmuch as the sciences of chemistry and pharmacology have opened the minds and imaginations of men and propelled them to strange and indescribable new dimensions of awareness, new spheres of consciousness, and vistas unknown.

Those "potential forms of consciousness entirely different" are now a reality with the use of such "consciousness-expanding" or "mind-manifesting" drugs as mescalin, psilocybin, d-lysergic acid diethylamide tartrate (LSD, for short), to name only a few.

In reality, the ancients discovered and made use of these drugs in their natural forms centuries ago. To the primitive peoples of South America, India, Africa, and the Middle East, "sacred" or "magic" mushrooms, peyote cactus, hashish, and other drugs were used extensively in religious rites and private ceremonies, and as a means of escape from a world of boredom and conflict to a new world of exciting visions.

Evidence from the Phenomena of Psychedelics 193

However, it was not until such men as Ludwig Lewin, Gordon Wasson, Havelock Ellis, William James, Aldous Huxley, Hofmann, and many others, took "mind-expanding" preparations, in their natural or compounded forms, and wrote about their experiences with the use of them that the scientific world woke up and took notice of their unimaginable propensities and powers in altering and expanding consciousness.

These preparations or drugs have since found their way in "hippy" and "jet-set" societies, in schools and campuses, in churches and religious organizations, and in many psychiatric clinics in the treatment of various mental disorders. Except in the latter cases, where the use of these drugs has been carefully controlled, the psychedelic drugs have unfortunately been taken indiscriminately, and this has led too often to serious biological and psychological damage.

The Nature Of Psychedelic Phenomena

Because of the variable ways in which LSD and other mind-expanding drugs act, the exact nature of the psychedelic phenomena cannot as yet be known in a definitive way.

In the first place, and in spite of many years of scientific experimentation and research, scientists have not adequately described or explained the exact nature of LSD and similar drugs and their action in the body. In the second place, the little knowledge we have about the brain, its structure and functions, has compounded the difficulty of understanding how these drugs expand and alter consciousness. Only theories, therefore, have been offered to explain the startling, exciting, indescribable, sometimes weird and horrifying, world of psychedelics.

It is thought by some authorities that LSD and other preparations act by disturbing the enzyme balance of man. Others theorize that LSD acts either directly or indirectly on serotonin, a substance found in the brain and considered important in the maintenance of mental stability; or it acts as antiserotonin, or by combining in some way with serotonin, produces "natural" hallucinogen with the body which in turn causes the startling mental transformations in the mind.[1]

Others suggest that these preparations may act as "triggers" releasing some unknown substance in the body which causes the various mental aberrations associated with hallucinogen.

Once inside the body, these preparations cause immense, startling, and dramatic changes in perception, mentation, and behavior, heretofore unknown and not usually experienced during our ordinary waking consciousness.

John Cashman, in his book *The LSD Story*, describes these changes as gleaned from the subjective reports of volunteers and patients who have taken LSD. He writes:

> Colors blaze and often have sound. Sounds throb with unbelievable beauty and intensity and often have color. Time seems to stand still or to move at a snail's pace. Thoughts race and tumble over each other. Insights of the unfathomable abound. The ego dissolves. Visions appear, disappear, and appear. Walls seem to breathe. Objects recede and approach. Memories race by the mind's eye with the clarity of film. Interest in the outside world diminishes.[2]

In discussing these experiences, it must be understood that they are given only as examples to illustrate the possible existence of the soul, but they do not indicate support of uncontrolled experimentation with drugs, which can be exceedingly dangerous in their psychological and physical effects.

Depending upon the expectation, the atmosphere, and the experient's mental balance, a world of beauty, may or may never become a reality. It can, instead, turn into a nightmare of horrifying experiences and indescribable misery.

Because of the diversity of experiences resulting from the intake of mind-expanding drugs, many new words have been coined to give them an appropriate generic description. The words *psychomimetic* and *mysticomimetic* have, for example, been coined to describe the power of these drugs to produce phenomena simulating or mimicking psychosis and the mystic experience, respectively.

Dr. Humphrey Osmond summarized his semantic search in an article he wrote for the *Annals of the New York Academy of Science*:

> I have tried to find an appropriate name for the (psychomimetic) agents under discussion: a name that will include concepts for enriching the mind and enlarging the vision. Some possibilities are: psychephoric, mind moving; psychehormic, mind rousing; and psycheplastic, mind molding. Psychezymic, mind fermenting, is indeed appropriate. Psycherhexic, mind bursting forth, though difficult, is memorable. Psychelytic, mind releasing is satisfactory. My choice, because it is clear, euphonious, and uncontaminated by other associations, is psychedelic, mind manifesting.[3]

Psychedelic phenomena as used in this book will, therefore, refer to those experiences which alter and expand consciousness as they are induced by certain drugs such as LSD, mescalin, hashish, and other related preparations.

Illustrative Examples Of Psychedelic Phenomena

A number of phenomena connected with psychedelics show clear indications involving a higher probability that man is not only a physical organism, pure and simple, but a highly complex process involving what in ancient times has been called a soul but which we shall call, in a scientific way, the nonphysical factor in human personality.

While the psychedelic movement has, in its way, given corroboration of one of humanity's most basic beliefs — the soul belief — it is unfortunate that it has taken the course it has. Most people have taken drugs without regard to the setting and without a clear understanding of the nature of the drugs being employed. For this reason the psychedelic movement has become greatly discredited.

There have, however, been some serious psychedelic experiments which have indicated scientific evidence in favor of soul-belief, among which the following deserve special mention:

1. Traveling clairvoyance as a common experience of those who have undergone psychedelic experiences.

Examples to illustrate this phenomenon are not wanting. In fact the voluminous articles on psychedelics clearly show projection of consciousness into a world that is physically and materially non-existent.

While considering the evidence of different experiments, which have been reported by various people, it cannot be too strongly repeated and emphasized that, without proper safeguards and conditions, and without medical supervision, the taking of drugs can be extremely dangerous. There is an increasing body of literature documenting the effects which can occur as the result of the indiscriminate use of drugs. These can produce permanent damage to the biological and psychological systems of man.

An experience resembling traveling clairvoyance is given by a subject of Dr. Beringer in Heidelberg whose researches and laboratory experimentations with mescaline are perhaps the most extensive to date. Dr. Beringer's subject generally took mescaline in the form of an injection, the dose employed being usually 400 milligrams. Dr. Beringer's subject relates his experience, thus:

> My ideas of space were strange beyond description. I could see myself from head to foot as well as the sofa on which I was lying. About me was nothingness, absolutely empty space. I was floating on a solitary island in the ether. No part of my body was subject to the laws of gravitation. On the other side of the vacuum — the room seemed to be limited in space — extremely fantastic figures appeared before my eyes. I was very excited, perspired and shivered, and was kept in a state of ceaseless wonder. I saw endless passages with beautiful arches, delightfully colored arabesques, grotesque decorations, divine, sublime and enchanting in their fantastic splendor. These visions changed in waves and billows, were built, destroyed, and appeared again in endless variations first on one plane and then in three dimensions, at last disappearing into infinity. The sofa island disappeared. I did not feel my physical self; an ever increasing sense of dissolution set in. I was seized with passionate curiosity; great things were about to be unveiled before me. I would perceive the essence

Evidence from the Phenomena of Psychedelics

of all things, the problem of creation would be unravelled. I was dematerialized.[4]

An equally fascinating experience was described by an amateur botanist named Gordon Wasson who, in 1953 in a trip to Mexico in search of new varieties of mushrooms, discovered the powerful properties of teonanacatl, the native Mexican name for the psychedelic mushroom. Wasson partook of the sacred mushroom and publicized its powers in a series of articles, one in *Life*. This short text describes his personal visions:

> They were vivid in color, always harmonious. They began with art motifs, such as might decorate carpets or textiles . . . then I saw a mythological beast drawing a regal chariot. Later it was as though the walls of our house had dissolved, and my spirit had flown forth, and I was suspended in mid-air viewing landscapes of mountains with camel caravans advancing slowly across the slopes . . . The visions were not blurred or uncertain. They were sharply focused, the lines and colors being so sharp that they seemed more real to me than anything I had seen with my own eyes. I felt that I was now seeing clearly, whereas ordinary vision gives us imperfect view; I was seeing the archetypes, the Platonic ideas, that underlie the imperfect images of everyday life. The thought crossed my mind: could the divine mushrooms be the secret that lay behind the ancient Mysteries?[5]

What is interesting in the two experiences which have just been related is the persistence of the awareness of the self as separate from the body which is perceived quite clearly as a thing apart. Whereas in ordinary consciousness, man's usual experience of the self is one of identity with the body, in psychedelic consciousness, he realizes the self as actualized apart and quite distinct from the physical organism.

2. Exaltation of both the senses and the mind during psychedelic experiments.

Perhaps the most outstanding and interesting characteristic of experiences of people who have taken mind-expanding drugs is the exaltation of the mind and the senses, especially the visual and auditory senses. Accounts of these experiences are replete with color and beauty, indescribable profusion of sights and sounds, and other extraordinary sensations.

Havelock Ellis, English psychologist famous for his pioneer studies in the field of human sexual behavior, experimented with mescal buttons and gives us the following interesting account of his exciting experience:

> The first symptom observed during the afternoon was a certain consciousness of energy and intellectual power. This passed off and about an hour after the final dose I felt faint and unsteady; the pulse was low, and I found it pleasanter to lie down. I was still able to read, and I noticed that a pale violet shadow floated over the page around the point at which my eyes were fixed. I had already noticed that objects not in the direct line of vision, such as my hands holding the book, showed a tendency to look obtrusive, heightened in color, almost monstrous, while, on closing my eyes, after-images were vivid and prolonged. The appearance of visions with closed eyes was very gradual. At first there was merely a vague play of light and shade which suggested pictures, but never made them. Then the pictures became more definite, but too confused and crowded to be described, beyond saying that they were of the same character as the image of the kaleidoscope, symmetrical groupings of spiked objects. Then, in the course of the evening, they became distinct, but still indescribable — mostly a vast field of golden jewels, studded with red and green stones, ever changing. This moment was, perhaps, the most delightful of the experience, for at the same time the air around me seemed to be flushed with vague perfume — producing with the visions a delicious effect — and all discomfort had vanished, except a slight faintness and tremor of the hands, which, later on, made it almost impossible to guide a pen as I made notes of the experiment: it was, however, with an effort, always possible to write with a pencil. The visions never resembled familiar objects; they were extremely definite, but yet always novel; they were constantly approaching, and yet

constantly eluding, the semblance of known things. I would see thick, glorious fields of jewels, solitary or clustered, sometimes brilliant and sparkling, sometimes with a dull rich glow. Then they would spring up into flower-like shapes beneath my gaze, and then seem to turn into gorgeous butterfly forms or endless folds of glistening, iridescent, fibrous wings of wonderful insects; while sometimes I seemed to be gazing into a vast hollow revolving vessel, on whose polished concave mother-of-pearl surface the hues were swiftly changing. I was surprised, not only by the enormous profusion of the imagery presented to my gaze, but still more by its variety. Perpetually some totally new kind of effect would appear in the field of vision; sometimes there was swift movement, sometimes dull, somber richness of color, sometimes glitter and sparkle, once a startling rain of gold, which seemed to approach me. Most usually there was a combination of rich, somber color, with jewel-like points of brilliant hue. Every color and tone conceivable to me appeared at some time or another. Sometimes all the different varieties of one color, as of red, with scarlets, crimsons, pinks, would spring up together, or in quick succession. But in spite of this immense profusion, there was always a certain parsimony and aesthetic value in the colors presented. They were usually associated with form, and never appeared in large masses, or if so, the tone was very delicate. I was further impressed, not only by the brilliance, delicacy, and variety of the colors, but even more by their lovely and various textures — fibrous, woven, polished, glowing, dull-veined, semi-transparent — the glowing effects, as of jewels, and the fibrous, as of insect's wings, being perhaps the most prevalent . . .

The visions continued with undiminished brilliance for many hours, and as I felt somewhat faint and muscularly weak, I went to bed, as I undressed being impressed by the red, scaly, bronzed, and pigmented appearance of my limbs whenever I was not directly gazing at them. I had not the faintest desire for sleep; there was a general hyperaesthesia of all the senses as well as muscular irritability, and every slightest sound seemed magnified to startling dimensions. I may also have been kept awake by a vague alarm at the novelty of my condition, and the possibility of further developments.

After watching the visions in the dark for some hours I became a little tired of them and turned on the gas. Then I found that I was able to study a new series of visual phenomena to which previous observers had made no reference. The gas jet (an ordinary flickering burner) seemed to burn with great brilliance, sending out waves of light, which expanded and contracted in an enormously exaggerated manner. I was even more impressed by the shadows, which were in all directions heightened by flushes of red, green, and especially violet. The whole room, with its whitewashed but not very white ceiling, thus became vivid and beautiful. The difference between the room as I saw it then and the appearance it usually presents to me was the difference one may often observe between the picture of a room and the actual room. The shadows I saw were the shadows which the artist puts in, but which are not visible in the actual scene under normal conditions of casual inspection . . . .[6]

3. Experiences resembling yoga in the East and mysticism in the West.

Whether psychedelic experiences have a religious import is still a controversy. It cannot be denied, however, that drug-induced expanded consciousness closely resembles that brought about by the practice of yoga and mysticism. Aldous Huxley, makes the claim that his experiences under the influence of mescaline are closely comparable to a genuine mystical experience. Dr. W. T. Stace, a leading authority on mysticism and Professor Emeritus at Princeton University, puts it more bluntly when asked about the similarities of drug-induced experience and mystical experience when he said, "It's not a matter of its being *similar* to mystical experience; it *is* mystical experience."[7]

A very interesting account of two religious experiences, one occurring under the influence of drugs and another without their influence, was given as a test by psychologist Dr. Huston Smith to a group of Princeton University students to test their power of discernment. The students were asked to determine which experience was drug induced and which was an account of an actual mystical experience. The accounts of these experiences are given below:[8]

I

Suddenly I burst into a vast, new, indescribably wonderful universe. Although I am writing this over a year later, the thrill of the surprise and amazement, the awesomeness of the revelation, the engulfment in an overwhelming feeling-wave of gratitude and blessed wonderment, are as fresh, and the memory of the experience is as vivid, as if it had happened five minutes ago. And yet to concoct anything by way of description that would even hint at the magnitude, the sense of ultimate reality . . . this seems such an impossible task. The knowledge which has infused and affected every aspect of my life came instantaneously and with such complete force of certainty that it was impossible, then or since, to doubt its validity.

II

All at once, without warning of any kind, I found myself wrapped in a flame-colored cloud. For an instant I thought of fire . . . the next, I knew that the fire was within myself. Directly afterward there came upon me a sense of exultation, of immense joyousness accompanied or immediately followed by an intellectual illumination impossible to describe. Among other things, I did not merely come to believe, but I saw that the universe is not composed of dead matter, but is, on the contrary, a living Presence; I saw that all men are immortal; that the cosmic order is such that without any preadventure all things work together for the good of each and all; that the foundation principle of the world . . . is what we call love, and that the happiness of each and all is in the long run absolutely certain.

The test result showed that twice the number of students (46) answered incorrectly as answered correctly (23). The first experience was drug-induced. This clearly shows that drug-induced experiences closely and strikingly resemble mystical experience, even if they may not be wholly and unquestionably mystical experiences in themselves.

Analysis And Interpretation

How does one explain the presence of the soul or the nonphysical factor in human personality on the basis of these phenomena?

In analyzing and interpreting the voluminous data available on psychedelics, we turn to Western science, especially psychology, and find it inadequate in explaining the vastness and richness of altered and expanded consciousness. Psychology, as has already been noted, has always avoided the study of this phenomenon, and has concentrated on the mensurable, controllable, and predictable, which consciousness and the nonphysical element in man are not.

In the interpretation of psychedelic phenomenon, as in hypnosis, memory, dreams, and psychical research, the usual approach, therefore, is to explain them on the cerebrocentric thesis that man is only a physical body, and that consciousness is a product of the brain or a resultant of brain activity. Neurophysiologists and materialistically-oriented scientists have, in fact, equated consciousness or mind with brain. On this basis, pharmacologists and chemists have, in essence, tried to explain the action of psychedelic preparations on the assumption that these substances disturb the enzyme system in man, or act as "triggers" in the brain to produce the startling transformations characteristic of many of these experiences.

Such assumption is untenable, unacceptable, and illogical for the reason that no scientifically proven data have shown where consciousness resides. That being the case, it cannot be regarded except as *sui generis,* that it is not an epiphenomenon of brain functions and bodily activities; in fact, it is itself an independent process, not dependent upon but, nevertheless, functioning in relation with the brain as an instrument of physical expression.

The brain and nervous system and the sense organs, in fact, limit the fullest expression of this consciousness. The late Aldous Huxley, master essayist and one of the most outspoken experients of psychedelic phenomena, upon reflecting on his experiences, found himself agreeing with the eminent Cambridge philosopher, Dr. C. D. Broad, that:

> ... we should do well to consider much more seriously than we have hitherto been inclined to do the type of theory which Bergson put forward in connection with memory and sense perception. The suggestion is that the functions of the brain and nervous system and sense organs are in the main *eliminative* and not productive. Each person is at each moment capable of remembering all that has ever happened to him and of perceiving everything that is happening everywhere in the universe. The function of the brain and the nervous system is to protect us from being overwhelmed and confused by this mass of largely useless and irrelevant knowledge, by shutting out most of what we should otherwise perceive or remember at any moment, and leaving only that very small and special selection which is likely to be practically useful.[9]

Huxley explains that according to such a theory, each one of us is potentially Mind-at-Large. But in so far as we are physical organisms, our business is, at all costs, to survive. To make biological survival possible, Mind-at-Large has to be funneled through the reducing valve of the brain and nervous system. What comes out at the other end is a measly trickle of the kind of consciousness which will help us to stay alive on the surface of this particular planet.[10]

Man is the soul. There can be no other more plausible explanation. The soul uses the body or the brain only as an instrument for expressing its functions and activities. Witness, for example, the multidimensional transformations that take place once outside the body, the seeing of physically nonexistent things, the exaltation of the mind and the senses of hearing, seeing, and smelling, as well as the timelessness and spacelessness of all these experiences under the influence of pychedelic preparations or other consciousness-expanding activities.

Fact or fantasy? Reality or hallucination? Both: hallucination from the standpoint of cerebrocentric philosophy, inasmuch as it regards everything as illusion or delusion which does not conform to the limited yardstick of materialistic science; but also reality, by a mere change of scale of observation from the standpoint of soul-psychology, which includes in its evaluation both the physical and spiritual dimensions of the universe. But even if hallucination, the experiences do happen. As such, they belong to a real world of happening, the world of experience, and in so belonging they require impartial interpretation and evaluation and not a dictatorial dismissal into the limbo of hallucination which, from the materialistic point of view, usually means "not real" and therefore meaningless.

Is there really a world "out there"? Who or what sees, feels, tastes, smells, and thinks once outside the body? Who separates? What separates? Does anything separate at all?

Physicalistic or materialistic scientists will readily say there is no other world aside from the physical world. Nothing separates; man is only a body; consequently, it is only the body that sees, feels, tastes, smells, and thinks.

But how tenable are these conclusions? Eastern thought has always, since time immemorial, recognized and believed in a spiritual, nonphysical entity in man and in the universe. In fact, as stated earlier, many of these consciousness-expanding experiences induced by drugs strongly resemble mystical experiences which in religious philosophy are regarded as spiritual, not material, in nature.

Such mystical experiences underlie some of the great religions of the world like Buddhism, Hinduism, Taoism, and Christianity. No mere speculative philosophy, belief in the existence of the soul, is grounded in the science and practice of a discipline called yoga. Through practice of intense concentration and meditation, fasting and bodily exercises, the body comes under the control of the mind; through yoga the mind dissociates from the body to unite with a higher form of consciousness — cosmic consciousness, the soul of the universe.

Western science is terribly late, many hundreds of years late; but it is now slowly picking up and learning the great teachings of the East. The presence of a physically non-existent world has merited not only speculation but study out of which learned men and scientists have given us an insight into their broad understanding and wisdom.

The late Georges I. Gurjieff, a leading theoretician and practitioner of the techniques of the expansion of consciousness, states that "normal consciousness is a form of sleepwalking and that somewhere there exists a form of awareness, of reality, from which one would not want to return."

William James, whose experiences with nitrous oxide are well known, presents to us in the opening quotation of this chapter a potential form of consciousness entirely different from our normal or rational consciousness.

Aldous Huxley finds the ordinary waking consciousness very useful and, on most occasions, an indispensable state of mind; "but it is by no means the only form of consciousness, nor in all circumstances the best. Insofar as he transcends his ordinary self and his ordinary mode of awareness, the mystic is able to enlarge his vision, to look more deeply into the unfathomable miracle of existence."

In a remarkable book entitled *The Soul of the Universe,* Dr. Gustaf Stromberg, internationally known astronomer of the Mount Wilson Observatory of the Carnegie Institute of Washington from 1917 to 1946, makes a very interesting attempt to explain, in as scientific a way as possible, the nature of the soul as well as its relation to the body.

In the introduction to the book Professor Albert Einstein said:

> Very few men . . . present the material as concisely as Dr. Stromberg succeeded in doing. What especially impressed me was his successful attempt to isolate the essential facts from the bewildering array of discovered data, and the presentation of them in such a way that the problem of unity of our knowledge becomes a rational one . . .[11]

A very able interpretation of the book was written by Vincent H. Gaddis in, *Mysterious Fires and Lights.* Rather than give my personal paraphrase of Dr. Stromberg's interesting idea about the soul, I quote in full Gaddis' very simple interpretation of it:

> Dr. Stromberg believed that modern science had failed to offer any comprehensive explanation of man's place

in the cosmos. He launched a long project of research and thought, and was assisted in his work by top scientists in other fields. Among these scholars were Dr. F. R. Moulton, Dr. Walter S. Adams, Sir Arthur Eddington, Dr. Thomas Hunt Morgan, Dr. John E. Boodin, Dr. Karel Hujer, and Dr. O. L. Sponsler. Not all of them, of course, agreed completely with Dr. Stromberg's final conclusions which entered the domain of philosophy, but each contributed his specialized knowledge to this composite fact and theory.

To understand Dr. Stromberg's theory we must first realize that modern science no longer regards solids as solids. All matter is composed of atoms. Atoms are made up of subatomic "particles" — electrons, protons, neutrinos, etc. But the word "particles" does not define their nature. They appear to be little more than congealed wave patterns — a complex of different frequencies that have particle-like characteristics in about the same manner that wave patterns in tones produce certain sounds. Thus they are cores or points of energy concentration rather than independent entities.

Dr. Stromberg conceived of a realm or dimension that exists beyond our senses and from which the world we see around us has emerged. This realm is of a nonphysical or quasi-physical nature. From it emerge fields of force or energy that are the pattern molds that form all living things — men, animals, and vegetation. These patterns are filled in by the "matter" of our world. They are the organizing principles of all life, and determine whether a fertilized ovum will produce a human being, or a horse, or a dog. He believed that the electromagnetic fields in all living things discovered by Dr. H. S. Burr and his associates were parts of these energy patterns.

To clarify this we must regard the universe as energy, and matter (as we know matter) as congealed energy. The patterns are independent of matter. The appearance of your body, all your physical characteristics, were determined at your birth by a pattern of organizing energy that came out of this other realm or dimension. Thus we — along with all life — are actually beings made up of energy from this other realm, and our physical bodies are only temporary "shells" — masses of congealed force composed of atoms and subatomic wave patterns.

Dr. Stromberg called these patterns "autonomous fields" of "emergent energy." They are responsible for the almost miraculous directive processes of cell division and growth. The non-physical realms from which they emerge is beyond the reach of our scientific instruments. It interpenetrates the world of our senses.

It was the doctor's opinion that the mind and consciousness of man actually exist in this energy pattern, and the physical brain is merely the instrument of the mind. Memory, then, must be carried in the pattern structure. We accumulate in our minds memories for periods of eighty years or more. How can memory last, he asked, when the cells in the brain are constantly changing, new atoms replacing old? There must be a "force field" in the brain, independent of the atoms, that never changes and may be indestructible.

Thought originates in this structure — "A combination of atoms cannot of itself give rise to human thought." And the mind may be a receiver of impressions from other thought structures (telepathy), or even from a greater cosmic mind (inspiration), which he called the "soul of the universe."

No actual loss of memory with age seems to occur. Its activation may be impaired, but consciously forgotten memories can be recovered under hypnosis. Electrical disturbances in the living brain are unable to destroy or damage the complex pattern structure. Thus it should be able to survive the brain's disintegration of physical death.

"Our nerve cells," he wrote, "seem to be the links which connect our physical brain with the world in which our consciousness is rooted. At death our "brain field" is not destroyed . . . (it) disappears at death, apparently falling back to the level of its origin." Since our memories are "engraved" in this force field, he believed that after death we can probably recall them all when our minds are no longer blocked by inert matter.

Man's electromagnetic being can be considered as a force intermediary between the physical world and this more refined, subtle realm, serving as a pattern and organizing field for the physical body and brain.

Through the brain, sensations pass to a directing consciousness and a memory repository in the emergent energy structure beyond. The "real man" therefore exists beyond our senses; our physical body and brain are its instruments.

If Dr. Stromberg's theories are true, the "electrical theory of life" — man's electrodynamic being and its relatively recent discovery — may be the first step toward eventual scientific proof that the consciousness of man may survive physical death. Personality may change, even within a lifetime, but individuality may go on.

That is the promise of the electrodynamic man. And in the long years to come, we should eventually know.[12]

In all of these expositions and illustrations, we see something we must perforce call a soul, something in man and in the universe which is impervious and undiscernible insofar as our ordinary waking consciousness and sense organs are concerned. From a cosmic point of view, we call it the realm of "superconsciousness," "mind at large," or the "other world." From the standpoint of my philosophy of man, I call it simply soul.

References

[1] John Cashman, *The LSD Story*, (A Fawcett Gold Medal Book, Greenwich, Connecticut, 1966), p. 37.
[2] *Ibid.*, pp. 6-7.
[3] *Ibid.*, p. 14.
[4] Robert S. DeRopp, *Drugs and the Mind*, (New York: An Evergreen Black Cat Book, Grove Press, Inc., 1957) pp. 51-52.
[5] Cashman, *op. cit.*, p. 24.
[6] DeRopp, *op. cit.*, pp. 36-40.
[7] Huston Smith "Do Drugs Have Religious Import?" in David Solomon, (Editor), *LSD—The Consciousness-Expanding Drug*. G. P. Putman's Sons, New York, 1964), p. 159.
[8] *Ibid.*, pp. 157-158.
[9] Aldous Huxley, "The Doors of Perception," *Collected Essays*, (New York: Bantam Books, Inc., 1966), p. 332.
[10] *Ibid.*
[11] Quoted in Vincent H. Gaddis, *Mysterious Fires and Lights*, (New York: David MacKay Company, Inc., 1967, p. 278.
[12] Gaddis, *supra*, pp. 277-280.

Chapter 22

EVIDENCES FROM THE PHENOMENA OF DEATH

Sleep And Death

May it not be really, as many writers and poets intimate, that sleep and death are kindred to each other, differing only in degree and not in kind? That sleep is temporary death, and death the sleep that knows no waking? That they differ from each other not in their essential psychological nature, but only in the relative temporariness of the one as compared to the relative permanency of the other? That the difference, as Bigelow puts it, is nothing more than this — "that in one case our carriage is left standing at the door to take us back again, while in the other we have no *animus revertendi* — that having reached home, we have no further use for our carriage and it is dismissed?"[1]

What, for example, is the psychological difference between a *dead* man and another in a state of suspended animation? Physiologically they are different, but psychologically both are *unconscious,* even if they may be in two different states of unconsciousness. Both are completely unconscious of their individual psychological lives as well as of the circumambient phenomenal world. Both are completely oblivious of the stirrings of passion as well as of the voluntary quickenings of thought and action. Both are, in fact, physiologically dead. One, however, will awaken again; the other is past resurrection.

The Indian yogi, for example, while in that state of consciousness known as *samadhi,* the eighth stage in yoga practice, is dead, as far as physiology is concerned. Sensation disappears; action ceases. A yogi in *samadhi* may not move for forty days. A good example is portrayed in the film "Black Narcissus." In fact, all metabolism seems to stop: no drinking, no eating, no breathing, apparently no blood circulation, hence, no bleeding when wounded, apparently no neurokymic or nervous circulation, hence, no sensation when stimulated.

Physiologically and psychologically, he is dead as far as the physical world goes, as far as materialistic science is concerned. That he is not officially declared dead is due merely to the fact that after a time, say ten or twenty or even forty days, he reawakens, asks for a glass of water to drink, and becomes normal as before.

Should such a thing happen in a place where very little is known about the phenomena of yoga, one of two things might happen. Either he would be officially declared dead and would be buried; or, if by some fluke of circumstance, he should reawaken before burial, then, by the people he would be immediately regarded as a miracle, and by the so-called intelligentsia, as a fake and a charlatan.

There is, in fact, nothing unnatural in the phenomenon of suspended animation. It occurs quite normally in the animal kingdom. The bear hibernates. The cicada lives seventeen years of its normal life underground. But the most striking example of suspended animation known to science is that of the *tardigrada*.

According to Dr. Alexis Carrel, these anthropodous animals "completely stop their metabolism when they are dried. A condition of latent life is thus induced. After a lapse of several weeks, if one moistens these desiccated animals, they revive, and the rhythm of life again becomes normal."[2]

What difference is there between the yogi in the state of *samadhi* and the *tardigrada* in the state of complete non-metabolism?

What would medical science call a bodily state characterized by total absence of metabolism for a period of forty days or several weeks? Evidently, death.

But neither the yogi in *samadhi* nor the *tardigrada* in non-metabolism can be regarded as dead. Both reawaken after some time and resume the normal rhythm of their individual lives.

The Meaning Of Death

It appears, therefore, that in a sense sleep and death are psychologically kindred phenomena; that, as Shakespeare so wisely and beautifully said, sleep is death's counterfeit.

If sleep is death's counterfeit, if these two phenomena are so akin that to understand one is to understand the other, what, then, it may be asked, is the nature of death?

In chapter fifteen we said that, for various reasons, the only valid psychological definition of sleep is the altered state of consciousness of the body. More accurately, it is the temporary transfocalization of consciousness from the physical plane to the next higher dimensional plane. It is, therefore, essentially a change from one state of consciousness to another.

Suppose this withdrawal should become permanent; suppose this transfocalization should become irreversible; suppose, as in the case of people who, like Plato died in their sleep, this change should become immutable, would it not, then, be death? Would not sleep, then, cease to be merely "death's counterfeit," and become in fact, its actual prefigurement, its psychological *avantcoureur*?

Death, therefore, cannot be regarded as annihilation. Annihilation of what? Of the body? Even that is scientifically untenable. Nothing can be annihilated, not even the body. It can only be transformed, so says the Law of Energy Conservation.

Even granting, however, that the body is destroyed at death, how about the consciousness? How about the self, the "I-am"? Is this, too, destroyed?

There is not only poetry but science as well in the words of Longfellow when he said:

> There is no death,
> What seems so is transition.

Logically, there is no way of proving that the consciousness is ever destroyed or extinguished, for the reason that it is the very first basis of proof.

How can I prove that I will ever end? How can consciousness prove its own extinction? To state that death extinguishes the mind and all its manifestations is to ignore altogether the considerable amount of evidence to the contrary.

The Society for Psychical Research, over many years, has gathered and carefully checked evidence to prove the illogicality of this contention.

The following are illustrative cases from C.J. Ducasse's "The Empirical Case for Personal Survival," quoted in *Body, Mind, and Death,* edited by Antony Flew:[3]

> This evidence which is a variety of kinds, has been reviewed by Professor Gardner Murphy "An Outline of Survival Evidence," *Journal of the American Society for Psychical Research* for January, 1945. He mentions first the numerous well-authenticated cases of the apparition of a dead person to others as yet unaware that he had died or been ill or in danger. The more strongly evidential cases of apparition are those in which the apparition conveys to the person who sees it, specific facts until then secret. An example would be that of the apparition of a girl to her brother nine years after her death, with a conspicuous scratch on her cheek. Their mother then revealed to him that she herself had made that scratch accidentally while preparing her daughter's body for burial, but that she had then at once covered it with powder and never mentioned it to anyone.
>
> Another famous case is that of a father whose apparition soon after death revealed to one of his sons the existence and location of an unsuspected second will, benefiting him, which was then found as indicated. Still another case would be the report by General Barter, then a subaltern in the British Army in India, of the apparition to him of a lieutenant he had not seen for two or three years. The lieutenant's apparition was riding a brown pony with black mane and tail. He was much stouter than at their last meeting, and, whereas formerly clean-shaven, he now wore a peculiar beard in the form of a fringe encircling his face. On inquiry the next day from a person who had known the lieutenant at the time he died, it turned out that he had indeed become very bloated before his death; that he had grown just such a beard while on the sick list; and

that he had some time before bought and eventually ridden to death a pony of that very description.

Other striking instances are those of an apparition seen simultaneously by several persons. It is on record that an apparition of a child was perceived first by a dog; that the animal's rushing at it, loudly barking, interrupted the conversation of the seven persons present in the room, thus drawing their attention to the apparition, and that the latter then moved through the room for some fifteen seconds, followed by the barking dog. (The documents obtained by the Society for Psychical Research concerning this case, that of the lieutenant's apparition, and that of the girl with the scratch, are reproduced in Sir Ernest Bennett's *Apparitions and Haunted Houses,* London, Faber & Faber, 1945, pp. 334-337, 28-25, and 445-450 respectively).

On the other hand, how can we prove that the consciousness of a dead man is already destroyed or annihilated? Only he can testify to that, and he cannot normally do it because he is physically dead.

Furthermore, is it logical to conclude that because a dead man manifests no sensorially obvious signs of consciousness, therefore his consciousness is already extinguished? How about the *tardigrada* in its state of total nonmetabolism? How about the yogi in the state of *samadhi*?

Is it not more logical to assume that a dead man displays no sensorily obvious signs of consciousness, not because his consciousness has been annihilated, but rather because it has already been withdrawn from the physical body; has, in other words, already vacated it and transfocalized itself into a higher dimension, thus leaving it as it were, tenantless, movementless, motiveless, that is, in fact, soul-less?

Suppose, by some circumstance, the consciousness should re-enter a body officially declared dead, what would science call the phenomenon? Would it, then, accept resurrection as a fact, as it is so accepted in the religions of the world?

Suppose further, that the discarnate consciousness should be able, in one way or another, to declare to us who are still incarnate its continued self-conscious existence on the other side; would science, then, accept the fact that the soul can, bodiless and brainless, go on living in a nonphysical world appropriate to its nonphysical condition? Would science thus recognize the reality of the after-death world, otherwise called *kamaloka* by the *Hindus*,[4] *astral world* by Theosophists,[5] the *objective world of the unconscious* by Jung,[6] the *world of psychical things* by Dr. Wilhelm Haas,[7] and *bardo*, by the Tibetans.[8]

And suppose further, that it is possible for a man so to train himself as to enable him to study clairvoyantly the after-death world and its condition; would science accept the testimony thus given?

That resurrection is a fact, as far as the Bible is concerned, is shown in several instances of raising from the dead in both Old and New Testaments. Elisha, in the Old Testament, resurrected the child of the Shunamite woman.[9] In the New Testament, Jesus resurrected Lazarus and also the daughter of Jairus.[10]

That the dead can and do communicate with the living is the universal testimony of the movement known as spiritualism. In the following chapter, we shall examine impartially, though briefly, the claim of the spiritualists, with special emphasis on the new science dedicated to the investigation and interpretation of psychic and spiritualistic phenomena, the science of psychical research, otherwise called metapsychics by Charles Richet.

That a man can be trained to become a clairvoyant and thus develop the power of voluntarily transfocalizing his consciousness to the after-death plane is the sincere attestation of a number of well-accredited clairvoyants such as Geoffrey Hodson in his books *The Science of Seership* and *The Mystery of Death* and C.W. Leadbeater in several of his books: *Clairvoyance, The Astral Plane,* and *Man Visible and Invisible*. This, too, is the declaration of the yogis of India and the mystics of Europe. This, likewise, seems to be the tendency of Dr. J.B. Rhine.

Modern cases of resurrection, although discredited by official science, are not wanting. A very interesting case is that of the Hawaiian kahuna resurrection of a dead child as related by Max Freedom Long in his gripping best-seller *The Secret Science Behind Miracles*.[11] Another case is that

Evidence from the Phenomena of Death

of Sotera Flandez, mother of Professor Delfin Batacan, Far Eastern University, Manila.

The Kahuna Resurrection

Max Freedom Long's *The Secret Science Behind Miracles* is the result of many years of research among the Hawaiian kahunas or witch-doctors regarding an ancient system of workable magic (literally, wisdom; *cf. magi*, wise men) practiced widely in Polynesia, India, and Africa.

Among other thing such as walking barefoot on burning lava, curing broken bones, causing death by incantation, and predicting and even changing future events, the *huna* or magic of the Polynesians enables its practitioner, called *kahuna*, to resurrect the dead.[12]

Mr. Long accumulated his information on *huna* both by direct investigation among the *kahunas* and by study of materials supplied to him by Dr. William Tafts Brigham, a deep student of the Polynesian secret wisdom, who was, in fact, regarded by the native *kahunas*, as a *kahuna* himself, the white *kahuna*, as he was called.

As a scientist, Dr. Brigham was naturally reticent about his huna knowledge. He was an authority on botany and his name appears in *Who's Who in America*, 1922-1923. When asked by Long about the *kahunas* with whom he had lived a long while and by whom he seemed to have been adopted, he proved rather evasive. Finally, however, he yielded, but exacted from him a promise to respect his confidence, stating that he had "a little scientific standing which I wish to preserve even in the vanity of my old age."

Here is Mr. Long's full account of the resurrection of a dead child by a Hawaiian *kahuna* as witnessed by Dr. Brigham:

> Dr. Brigham, during one of his field trips in search of rare indigenous plants in Hawaii, took refuge in a coastal village during a very severe storm. In the storm a native lad of about sixteen was drowned. All efforts to revive him failed, and a *kahuna* living some distance away was summoned.
>
> The *kahuna*, an old man, arrived and began work about eight hours after the accident. The boy's body was

cold, and, when examined by Dr. Brigham shortly before the arrival of the *kahuna,* seemed to have begun to stiffen in *rigor mortis.*

The *kahuna* sat down near the body and set to work to use his psychic powers to learn what had become of the lad's two spirits. In this work, as he later explained, he had the help of several spirit friends. (The shadowy body cord must still have connected the body to the lower self of the lad, although probably stretched to the breaking point .) The boy's selves were found wandering in a confused state and brought back to the body, being urged to remain there and make every possible effort to reenter it.

The body was warmed, and while the *kahuna* applied his hands to it, he gave of his own vital force. He also used verbal suggestion to cause the return into the body, using as a physical stimulus a stroking and squeezing, as if the spirits were reentering by way of one of the big toes, and was being squeezed up the leg into the body. The *kahuna* also invoked "the god" (High Self) asking for aid. After about an hour he announced that the spirits of the boy were entering the body. Gradually the flesh became warmer. The heart began to beat and the boy opened his eyes. The recovery was so rapid that in a short time he was asking for food.

Dr. Brigham, greatly impressed by the demonstration of *kahuna* magic, asked many questions of the *kahuna,* learning little beyond the fact that the "god" whose aid had been given was one of the *Aumakuas,* or parental and greatly trustworthy spirits who have formerly been men living in bodies on earth.

He kept track of the Hawaiian lad for a number of years and there seemed never to have been appreciable after effects from the "death by drowning."[13]

Analysis And Interpretation

Take it or leave it. But truth is really stranger than fiction. The strange things that happen in science itself are really even stranger than scientific fiction.

"To the man of science," said Kirtley F. Mather, Harvard geologist, "every event in the history of the universe is a miracle. It is both awe-inspiring and significant, a "sign

Evidence from the Phenomena of Death 217

and a wonder." The more we know about the world, the more mysterious and marvelous it becomes. The arrogance which characterized so many scientists of preceding generations has given place to a true humility, admirably displayed by most of the leaders in contemporary scientific progress. The expanding horizon of knowledge has simply lengthened the line of contact between man and the unknown elements of the cosmos."[14]

Call it a miracle, or simply strange, but it is strange how I hold my fountain pen, from the standpoint of the physical theory of atoms and electrons. It is strange how I see, how I hear, how I think. It is strange how radio waves are transformed into sound waves or light waves, but these things nevertheless occur.

Equally, the *kahuna* resurrection is strange. It is a *miracle,* so to speak. Shall we reject it simply because it is strange? Shall we ignore it simply because we do not understand it? Then we should reject the fact that we can hold an object, or that we can see and think, or that radio and television exist, because, scientifically, we do not know how we hold objects or see or hear or think, or how radio waves are changed into sound or light waves and these into radio waves. We have only theories, and we do not know whether our theories are true.

Even so, we do not know how the *kahunas* resurrect the dead. But we have no right to deny the fact that the *kahunas* can resurrect the dead. All we can say scientifically is that it is strange, or uncommon, or even extraordinary. But it is a fact; it occurs; it can be done. Only it is done in a way we do not, or science does not, understand.

We have no right, no logical or scientific or reasonable right, to label anything as false, just for the reason that it is strange, or uncommon, or extraordinary, or simply because we do not understand it. Clairvoyance is extraordinary, but it is a fact; so is clairaudience; so is telepathy; and so is precognition or prophecy.

We should learn to distinguish clearly between what is mysterious, though ordinary, and what is both extraordinary and mysterious. Thinking, or how we think, is ordinary; it is a common occurrence; but it is none the less mysterious. We do not know how we think.

On the other hand, *kahuna* resurrection is extraordinary. Like thinking, it is also mysterious.

Science, however, should not quarrel with fact; else it were not science. When fact is concerned, whether ordinary or extraordinary, mysterious or understandable, the duty of science is explanation and interpretation, not downright rejection or obstinate indifference. Science must explain. Science must, like philosophy, learn also to interpret.

The Kahuna Interpretation

The *kahunas* do not know modern psychological terms, but like the yogis of ancient India, they can teach us much about psychology. They are in possession of a system of secret knowledge, a science still unknown to modern man. This system, according to Mr. Long, is remarkable for two important reasons. In the first place, it works. In the language of modern science, it is pragmatic. It has the most salient characteristics of modern twentieth century experimental research, workability and satisfactory results. It works for the *kahunas,* at all places, at all times, and under whatever conditions. As such it is objective. It is, therefore, not faith or suggestion or hypnosis. It is science.

In the second place, it works not only for the *kahunas.* It works for all men, whether they believe it or not, no matter what their scientific beliefs or their religious convictions. As such, it possesses another distinguishing feature of modern experimental science, verifiability. It is not merely theory or hypothesis. It is fact.

Now, this science, this secret knowledge reveals one very important *fact*: namely, that man is consciousness, or better still, a soul.

This soul is energy of two kinds: one, the *unihipili,* has a powerful memory and never forgets. The other, the *uhane,* has a weak memory, but it has volition or will which it can use hypnotically, as well as the power of reason which it can use deductively and inductively. It is not difficult to recognize in the *unihipili,* the *unconscious* of modern depth psychology and in the *uhane,* the *conscious mind.*

But here the similarity between the *huna* and modern depth psychology stops. The *huna* science recognizes one fact that modern psychology regards as untrue — that the *unihipili* is detachable from the body and can be projected at will. Further, that it can insinuate itself into the body of another person and either obsess him, or vampirize him, that is, absorb his vital energy. By absorbing the vital energy of a person, the *unihipili* can bring about his death. Correspondingly, by discharging its vital energy into another person, it can heal his sickness.

By manipulating the occult force of *mana* the *unihipili* can insulate the feet from the most intense heat. This is the secret of fire-walking, both among the *kahunas* as among the Hindu or Mohammedan fakirs, such as Kuda Bux Khan, for example.

The important thing to note in the *huna* system is the complete distinction between the soul and the body. The soul, dual in aspect (*uhane-unihipili,* or conscious-unconscious), is one thing; the body is another. Death is the withdrawal of this dual soul from its body; resurrection is its return into it.

Dr. Brigham recognized this fact very clearly, as we can gather from his advice to Mr. Long.

"Always," he said, "keep watch for these things in the study of this magic: *There must be some form of consciousness back of and directing the processes of magic."* (Here is Dr. Brigham's recognition of the primacy of the soul or consciousness).

> There must also be some form of force used in exerting this control, if we can but recognize it. And last, there must be some form of substance, visible or invisible, through which the force can act.[15]

Should we give these statements of Dr. Brigham an Eastern interpretation, it would be something like the following:

The Atman (soul) can, by its force of will and thought (*ichchha-shakti* and *kriya-shakti,* respectively), manipulate the surrounding ether (*prana,* in all its various manifestations) and thus produce results upon whomever or whatever it pleases. The consciousness is Atman, the power is will-thought power, and the substance is ether or prana.

Whatever interpretation we give to the *huna* system, one thing stands indubitable: *it works,* and it works efficiently and effectively.

This pragmatic and highly workable psychological system points to the existence of the soul as a distinct, autonomous and self-integrating entity completely different from its body, detachable from it at will or at death, and returnable into it under certain conditions.

The Case Of Sotera Flandez

The resurrection of Sotera Flandez, mother of Delfin Batacan, one-time professor at the Far Eastern University, is not a lone example of the claims of resurrection in the Philippines. There are many.

This, however, is the only case I personally know about in which the parties concerned are people of integrity and who are willing to testify to the veracity of the occurrence. Furthermore, this seems to be the only case where the element of coincidence is highly improbable because of a confirmatory event at the end of the story.

Professor Batacan wrote the complete and unexpurgated story of the death and resurrection of his mother for me, thus:

> My mother, Sotera Flandez, was a school teacher. So was my father. Among those who took their three R's under her was one-time minority floor leader and Senator Cipriano P. Primicias.
>
> Mother had a weak heart. When my father's condition grew worse, the whole family left Manila and we moved to Alcala, Pangasinan, where my mother's folks had a house. A few days before father died, mother was transferred to my auntie's place, about a hundred yards away.
>
> On May 27, 1919 my father died. Mother wasn't told about it until the day of the burial. When she found out what happened she tried to bear her sorrow admir-

Evidence from the Phenomena of Death 221

ably. She steeled herself and was able to survive the constant threats of her weak heart until July 16th of the same year when at a little before twilight she passed away. Or so we thought.

There was the usual nocturnal vigil. Her "amigas," co-teachers and fellow-alumnae of "La Concordia" were all there.

I was seven then and as far as I can remember I had been reared in the town's convent. My brother Abelardo (now Airport Engineer of the Bureau of Aeronautics) was five and our sister, Avelina, was three.

Our Tia Martina, mother's only sister, had mother dressed in her favorite "terno" and on her out-stretched palms auntie placed mother's prayer book on her right hand and her book of novenas on her left. I remember this very vividly because I asked Tia Martina why.

I forgot to say that before mother's heart was supposed to have stopped, Rev. Augustin del Rosario was summoned and he administered to her extreme unction. On the morning of the 17th as mother lay there in her matrimonial bed, visitors and friends kept vigil; the carpenters were putting the finishing touches to her coffin, the "carro" was being readied with black satin ribbons and all. I was sitting close to mother's right. Several of her friends were in the hall. My Tia Martina had just left her chair on mother's left. It was a little past eleven (Dr. Jose Ampil Diaz glanced at his watch) when I noticed mother's prayer book being clutched by the fingers of her right hand. I looked at her left hand and there was a simultaneous and rhythmic movement of her fingers. Several of the people in the hall also saw what I saw. I was stunned. Not from fright. No, from joy! Why, *Mother was alive! She wasn't dead.*

"Nabiag ni Teray . . . . !" (Ilocano for "Teray is alive"). The shouting went up. The brave stayed. There was consternation with those frightened scampering for the nearest exit. By this time Tia Martina had rushed to the deathbed (now merely a bedside) and kept on calling mother's name: "Teray! Teray!" I kept on saying: "Nanay! Nanay!" ("Mother! Mother")

Mother was now clutching her books. Suddenly she opened her mouth and said: "M . . a . . m". Her voice was weak, hesitant, sepulchral. My auntie asked for "Water and spoon please." Again, mother's lips parted, saying, "Mam . . Mam." Tia Martina tremblingly poured the teaspoonful of water into mother's mouth. Slowly. One teaspoon. Two. Three teaspoons.

"Teray," my auntie kept on calling.

"Nanay," I kept on saying.

"Teray," her friends and classmates now joined the chorus of pleading voices.

Then she opened her eyes. She gazed at me (her eldest). She closed them again for a brief instant and then opened them and this time it looked to me as if she never wanted to close them again. "Hijo!" she cried as I hugged her. She gripped her sister's hand and said: "Manang!" (An Ilocano term for elder sister). She looked at the curious faces now converged all around her bed, some unbelieving, some frightened, all happy.

"Where are my other children?" She queried. Abelardo and Avelina were fetched. Her next question was: "Why am I dressed like this? And why are there so many people?" Tia Martina made the explanations as best she could.

Then when she was asked where she had been, it was mother's turn to tell her story. It was a long story. Briefly, it may be summed up, thus:

She went to a happy land, full of gladness and sunshine. There was a kindly old man with snow-white hair and snow-white beard. The road to and from that joyful place was a straight white road with white clean pebbles on the side and fresh green grass lining the way. She passed crystal clear brooks and streams. On the way, she saw her classmates at La Concordia, namely, Carmen, Pilaring, Rita, and others. She also saw my father. He was holding a broom. He was happy and contented. She said the old man didn't want her to leave. She said she insisted, pleading that she merely wanted to see her children again and to leave word with her Manang Martina on what to do with her two boys when she would return to the happy land. She said she was going to bring her daughter Avelina when she came back. The old man granted her request. So she was allowed to visit her folks. Her story dealt with a strange and unknown land; the people she met and saw have all been long dead.

She seemed visibly tired, and in between her labored breathing she kept continually glancing at the faces of those around her. Then she went on to explain why she tried to convince the "old man" with the snow-white beard to let her come back to see her children once more and to tell her sister Martina what to do with them. She promised the "old man" she was going back. Definitely. And she was to take her daughter Avelina with her. When my Tia Martina and mother's collegemates protested, she said very calmly: "My two dear boys are enough for Manang Martina."

"Why did you have to promise the 'old man' that you were going back?" they asked her.

"Only with that promise would he allow me to return," she explained.

And mother kept on talking of things and places and persons not of this world.

On the following morning she felt very much exhausted from uninterrupted story-telling. We, her dear children, were at her bedside. She kissed me first, then my brother Abelardo. Then she pressed close to her my sister Avelina.

She said a few more things to my aunt Martina on how to care for us "two boys."

Then she looked about the pale and ashen faces that watched her, now intently, intensely, and said:

"I am very tired. *I must sleep now.*"

It was nine-thirty, July 17, 1919.

And mother was dead. This time, really dead. The score of doctors who by now had flocked to our house made sure of that. True to her word my sister Avelina followed her to complete her promise to the "old man."

My sister died August 19 of the same year.

Analysis And Interpretation

Was Sotera Flandez really dead the first time, or was she only in a comatose state? It is not easy to tell because there is not sufficient basis for a decision.

The expected and usual argument of the dogmatic materialist would be that Sotera was not really dead as otherwise she would not have reawakened. In other words, she was only in a coma, a condition "of absolute unconsciousness during which the brain is totally refractory to excitation."[16]

This type of reasoning is, of course, thoroughly fallacious: Sotera was not really dead the first time since she woke up; therefore, the second time, she was really dead, because then, she did not wake up.

When is a person dead, then? When he does not wake up. And when does he not wake up? When he is dead. In logical parlance, we call this error in reasoning *circulus in probando* or arguing in a circle.

Whether or not Sotera was really dead the first time is not essential to me. It is not my aim to prove the reality of resurrection. It is my purpose to prove the existence of the soul.

One thing is certain in our case. Sotera entered into a *state of absolute unconsciousness,* whether of death or of coma. Death, as far as materialistic science is concerned, is an absolute state of unconsciousness; so is coma as far as physiology is concerned.[18]

If Sotera was in a *state of absolute unconsciousness,* how explain her experience on the "other side" which she related after waking up? How explain her "journey" to the happy land? How explain her meeting and conversation with the "kindly old man with snow-white hair and snow-white beard?" How explain her request to return to her family temporarily with the promise to go back to the "happy land" after seeing her children? In other words, *how explain her state of consciousness during all the time she was supposed to be dead or in coma, that is, in a state of absolute unconsciousness?*

Either we force our minds to accept this contradiction, *that is, regard Sotera as both dead and not dead, unconscious and conscious at the same time,* or admit the other more consistent, more coherent, more logical theory: namely, that the soul of Sotera, the real being, had withdrawn from the body, either through death or through coma, and had actually experienced the after-death plane, the higher dimensional world of *svapna.*

To avoid illogicality and confusion that may arise if we regard Sotera as being constituted only of her body, we have to agree to the following propositions:

1. That Sotera was all the time conscious on the other side, while her body was absolutely unconscious (dead or comatose, it does not matter) down here, as it were;

2. That if she were conscious on the other side, as her experience there clearly shows, she must be a conscious something, an experient, a soul, existing and energizing on the other side while her body on this side was completely inert in a state of absolute unconsciousness;

3. That death, therefore, is not, as is often supposed, really an annihilation, a destruction, but merely the withdrawal of consciousness or the soul from the body and its transfocalization into the after-death plane where it continues its life and experience in an unbroken state of self-consciousness.

Suppose, on the other hand, the objection should be raised that all the so-called experience of Sotera on the other side were really only hallucination, would it destroy our argument? For two valid reasons, it would not. On the contrary it would strengthen our position.

First, hallucination is a condition of consciousness. There can be no hallucination in a state of absolute unconsciousness. Therefore, the objection actually proves that Sotera was actually conscious during all the time her body was in a state of absolute unconsciousness. Who was having hallucinations? Who was conscious when Sotera was either actually "dead" or simply comatose? Our answer: The soul. The answer of materialism: either none or a contradiction.

Second, the experience of Sotera on the other side, if it were hallucination, was a most outstanding hallucination.

It was too serious, too solemn, too completely clear and veracious to be hallucinatory. Because when she woke up, she told the people that she came back to earth, not only to give her last instructions but also to tell them that she was taking her daughter, Avelina, with her to the other side. Everybody remonstrated. But she told them calmly that she would take Avelina with her. She died July 17, 1919.

Thirty-three days later on August 19, 1919, the three year old Avelina died.

Hallucination or actual experience? Let the reader judge for himself. When events become too coincidental, they cease to be accidental. So says the scientific Law of Probability.

References

[1] John Bigelow, *The Mystery of Sleep*, (New York: Harper and Brothers, 1903, 1946), p. 151.

[2] Alexis Carrel, *Man the Unknown*, (New York: Harper and Brothers, 1939) p. 82.

[3] C. J. Ducasse, "The Empirical Case for Personal Survival," quoted in *Body, Mind, and Death*, edited by Antony Flew, (New York and London: The Macmillan Company, 1964), p. 225.

[4] H. P. Blavatsky, *Isis Unveiled*, (London: Rider and Co., Paternoster House, F.C., Facsimile Edition, 1887), p. 15.

[5] C. W. Leadbeater, *The Astral Plane*, (Adyar, Madras, India: Theosophical Publishing House, 1941), pp. 1-2.

[6] Carl Jung, "The Reality of the Soul," quoted in D. D. Kanga, *Where Theosophy and Science Meet*, Vol. IV, p. 24.

[7] D. D. Kanga, *op. cit.*, p. 24.

[8] Evans-Wentz, *The Tibetan Book of the Dead or The After-Death Experience on the Bardo Plane, According to Lama Kagi Dawa-Samdup's Engish Rendering*. Second Edition, (London: Geoffrey Cumberlege. Oxford University Press, 1951.

[9] II Kings, IV, pp. 30-37.

[10] Mark, V, 39.

[11] Max Freedom Long, *The Secret Science Behind Miracles*, (Vista, California: Huna Research Publications) Second Edition, 1954.

[12] The Hawaiian word *huna* means "secret" and *kahuna* therefore, means "Keeper of the secret."

[13] Long, *op. cit.*, pp. 203-204.

[14] Edward H. Cotton, "Has Science Discovered God? A Symposium of Modern Scientific Opinion," pp. 3-4.

[15] Quoted by Long, *op. cit.*, p. 14.

[16] Carl J. Wiggers, *Physiology in Health and Disease*, (Philadelphia: Lea and Febiger, 1949) p. 212.

[17] *Ibid.*

Chapter 23

CONCLUSION

And now we rest our case; we pause for judgment.

The journey through science to reach the soul is ended.

Does the soul exist, as far as the facts of experience are concerned, as far as unbiased employment of the fourfold scientific method would allow?

Our answer is yes. The soul exists. There is in man a nonphysical element which alone can explain a multitude of phenomena concerning human life and behavior.

This alone can explain the nature of human consciousness, its primacy in all experience, its utter privacy, its selfhood and its continuity.

This alone can explain the nature of human thoughts and ideas, their metaphysical character, their relative indestructibility and permanency, their immediacy to consciousness and their complete inaccessibility to physical and chemical laws.

This alone can explain the mystery of perception: its absence in the dead, even if the apparatus of perception is intact; its presence in the somnambulist, even if its cerebral center is paralyzed; its modifiability by attention or by the will or by suggestion and its exaltation under conditions of complete brain inactivity.

This alone can explain the nature of memory, its persistence and immutability, its complete recoverability or revivability, its intensification under conditions of cerebral torpor or coma, and its operation even when the brain is either completely diseased or totally destroyed.

This alone can explain the various phenomena of sleep, the continuity of consciousness in sleep, and somnambulism and somniloquism.

This alone can explain the meaning and nature of dreams and the dream-consciousness, the significance of lucid dreams as well as of prophetic dreams, why mentality becomes exalted in the dream-state, the annihilation of time and space in the dream-consciousness, and the feeling of realism that accompanies the dream-condition.

This alone can explain the nature of death, of continued consciousness in coma, of the yogic state of *samadhi*, of the complete absence of life and thought in the corpse and of reported cases of resurrection of the dead.

This alone can explain the numerous phenomena of psychical research or parapsychology, such as the *psi* processes, including clairvoyance, telepathy, precognition or prophecy, and psychokinesis or the power of mind over matter and the more remarkable phenomenon of traveling clairvoyance or projection of consciousness.

This alone can explain the mysterious facts of hypnosis, such as extremes of anesthesia and hyperesthesia in the hypnotic state, the hyperactivity of memory, the sudden increase of intelligence, the vision of what is physically nonexistent and the utter blindness to what is physically visible under nonhypnotic conditions.

This alone can adequately and satisfactorily explain the humanity of man, the genuineness of human personality, the "creativity, autonomy, meaning, flexibility, and a host of other non-mechanical aspects of behavior."[1] Surely this alone can explain "love, creativity, self, growth, organism, basic need gratifications, self-actualization, higher values, being, becoming, spontaneity, play, humor, affection, naturalness, warmth, ego-transcendence, objectivity, autonomy, responsibility, meaning, fair play, transcendental experience, peak experience, courage, and related concepts."[2]

On The Other Hand

All these facts are completely inexplicable in terms of the materialistic theory that man is a purely physical being and that, therefore, all that he is and does comes from the brain or the nervous system.

Let us, for the sake of argument reduce the brain to its ultimate material constituents. What does it become? Atoms, as far as chemistry is concerned — atoms of carbon, of hydrogen, of oxygen, of different chemical elements.

By what trick of reasoning can the materialistic hypothesis convince any thinking man that these atoms are responsible for all the rich and multitudinous phenomena of life, thought, consciousness and action that are the primary characteristics of man?

Are atoms conscious? Do atoms think? Do they say "I"? Do they see, hear, taste, smell, feel? Do they sleep, dream, aspire? Have they ambitions, longings, hopes? Do they suffer, weep, curse? Do they smile? Do they laugh? What do they know of science, art, philosophy? How much of God do they know? Do they fear hell? Do they hold converse with Plato, Aristotle, Einstein? Do they hope for heaven? Are they good? Are they bad? Have they moral strivings? Do they long for perfection? Do they worship? What thoughts have they of beauty, truth, and goodness, what dreams of Eden, what hopes of the hereafter?

Organization Presupposes An Organizer

To attribute these richly varied and highly purposive functions and characteristics of the human organism to the *form* or *structure* which atoms and molecules take on, however, does not make the materialistic theory of man fare any better.

Organization presupposes an organizing or directive agency. If the functions of consciousness and thought are the products of the highly organized structure of material particles, who or what organizes them?

The answer is either intelligence or chance. If intelligence, then the soul-hypothesis becomes an empirical as well as a logical necessity, because, empirically and logically, we can associate intelligence only with a thinking, willing, self-directing conscious self, in other words, soul.

If chance, then materialism has to explain the onerous problem of how chance could produce intelligence as well as all the complex forms of behavior connected with it.

The fact is that this word *chance,* as used by materialists is just another way of expressing either ignorance or intellectual obstinacy. That all living, thinking, and self-directing beings, such as men, are due to the chance assemblage of mass particles in space is the most highly speculative and gratuitous piece of thinking that ever the materialistic thinkers can fabricate.

It will take chance, according to Lecomte du Nouy, approximately 10^{243} billions of years to manufacture a *single* molecule of high dissymmetry.

"But," he added warningly, "we must not forget that the earth has existed only for two billions of years and that life appeared about *one billion year ago,* as soon as the earth had cooled (10^9 years)."[3]

How could life appear on the earth 10^{243} billions years ago, when the earth, even the sun itself, did not exist then, since its age is only about 5 thousand billion years?[4]

But put intelligence somewhere, and the stupendous task of solar, planetary, biological, and psychological origination within a limited period of time ceases to be altogether impossible.

How long will it take chance, we venture to ask, to build one ordinary writing table, even granting that the materials are already there, nails, boards, hammer, and saw? The figure in years would be unreadable. But put a carpenter there, in addition, and the table will come into existence in about an hour or so.

Intelligence Presupposes Soul

Intelligence in man, therefore, necessarily implies soul. To think that man is only body is to suppose that this body can think, plan, will, love, choose, aspire, direct, desire, hope, imagine, remember, philosophize, worship.

In other words, that machine which the human body is, according to the materialistic theory, possesses the powers of thought, choice, will, imagination, perception, memory, deliberation, morality, and religion. Than this, there is no assumption more supposititious, no supposition more fanciful, and no fancy more vaporous.

Our Procedure Recapitulated And Concluded

We submit, therefore, that as far as our use of the facts of science as well as our employment of the fourfold scientific method of hypothesis is concerned, we have sufficiently and satisfactorily established a preponderance of probability in favor of the soul-theory as against the body-theory of human nature.

We have enumerated a number of indubitable facts — facts of consciousness, of memory, of sleep, of dreams, of death, of psychical research and parapsychology and of hypnotism and psychedelics. We have tried to analyze and explain these facts in terms of both the soul-theory and the body-theory, and have discovered that they are explicable *empirically, consistently, coherently, comprehensively,* only in terms of the view that man is essentially a nonphysical being in possession of will, thought, and action.

This nonphysical reality in man we advisedly call the soul.

Furthermore, we have shown that there are certain forms of human behavior which must be recognized as essentially and primarily manifestations of the inherent intelligence and spirituality of the soul. These are culture or knowledge, morality, and religion.

We can accept knowledge as real only insofar as it is a manifestation of a being capable of perception, thought, discrimination, and experience, and possessing, in addition, the powers of abstraction, conceptualization, generalization, and self-analysis. These, we have shown, are found only in an empirically real self or individuality, capable of saying, "I am." This individuality we call the soul.

We can accept morality only insofar as it is an expression of a being possessing free-will and the power of choice and self-determination. These, we have shown, are true only of an individuality nonmechanically determined as well as capable of assuming responsibility for its own motives and actuations. This individuality we call the soul.

And, finally, we can accept religion only insofar as it is a manifestation of spiritual faculties capable of virtue, worship, goodness, brotherhood, and ultimate perfection. These can be regarded as real only if man is essentially a spiritual being.

In other words, man must be regarded as a soul, a spiritual being, if we must find an explanation for humanity's ineradicable urge toward perfection or God. Man, the religious being, must be a spiritual being. He must be soul.

Scientific Fact

Scientifically, therefore, there is every reason to regard the soul as a scientific fact, just as we regard electricity as a scientific fact.

Naturally, our knowledge is incomplete. It should be incomplete, because our investigations have just begun. Apart from the fact that we know the soul to be non-physical, we know little about its basic nature, its origin and its potentialities and powers. It is, nevertheless, a fact, as much as electricity is a fact, even if the scientific knowledge of electricity, its basic nature as well as its source, is incomplete.

Electricity is a fact. So also is the soul a fact, but on different levels. Electricity is a physical fact. The soul, on the other hand, is a nonphysical, or a metaphysical, fact.

To say that electricity is a fact because we see its uses and manifestations, such as electric lights, electric cars, and a hundred and one electrical machines and apparatuses, is to argue from effect to cause. In other words, the tree must be known by its fruit.

Similarly, we can argue the existence of the soul on the basis of its effects and manifestations, such as thought, memory, perception, emotion, dream, hypnosis, and a hundred and one phenomena of the mind and consciousness.

In the first case, we have a whole series of physical electrical phenomena; in the other, we have a whole series of nonphysical psychological phenomena.

In fact, if we should argue further, we could even go to the extent of saying that the soul is a more indubitable fact than electricity because, empirically, the soul has the power of perceiving and knowing electricity, but electricity has no power of perceiving and knowing the soul. I can experience electricity; electricity cannot experience me.

The Duty Of Science

It is not for science to quarrel with fact. The function of science is research, investigation, and the extension, both horizontal and vertical, of the frontiers of human knowledge.

So far, science has been extending her horizontal frontiers. As a result, the knowledge of matter and energy has been tremendously enriched. As a further result, technological inventions for the improvement of man's physical welfare have multiplied.

In spite of almost countless material inventions designed for the amelioration of man's welfare, why is humanity, nevertheless, unhappy? Because man knows hardly anything about himself; his thoughts, his emotions, his motives, his desires. He does not know exactly what he wants, and his life is a battleground of confusion and conflict.

Science has not helped him advance his vertical frontiers. And here lies the primary duty of modern science.

Meden Agan

On the front of the ancient temple of Apollo at Delphi there were once inscribed those words of passionless wisdom which our learned but passion-bound modern humanity needs: *Gnothi seauton,* Know thyself and *Meden Agan,* Nothing in excess.

Science, it seems, has gone to excess in the investigation and study of material nature.

Can knowledge ever be in excess? Not absolutely; there can never be enough of knowledge. But relatively, yes, if only one of its aspects is over-emphasized to the complete neglect of its other aspects.

Science, it would appear, has been completely hypnotized by the bewildering facts of the material world: nothing is real except matter; nothing is factual, except the facts of the material universe.

In the study of matter, the intelligence that studies matter has been completely forgotten. There is even the preposterous attempt to reduce intelligence to matter; to regard the perceiver and experiencer of matter as the product of matter.

Evidence of the Existence of the Soul

This is the fantastic theory of the materialistic scientist, that man is nothing but a highly complex system of physico-chemical mechanisms — the corpocentric, cerebrocentric theory of human nature.

Gnothi Seauton

"Know thyself"; that now is the most important, the most legitimate, and the most urgent problem of modern science:

To know man as he should be known, in his entirety, as a whole, as an integer, unbiasedly and with sufficient insight and candor.

To know him as he is, a conscious being, thinking, perceiving, feeling, remembering, choosing, hoping, loving, aspiring, worshipping, building civilizations, creating sciences, creating philosophies, dreaming of immortality and perfection.

To know him as body, as animal, as passion, as lust; but, no less, to know him as soul, as spirit, as vision, as love.

To know him as he wallows in the mud; but, no less, to know him as he seeks the empyrean and scales the heights.

To know him as the ordinary senser, feeler, thinker, actor; but also to know him in his moments of exaltation when he shines with the glory of his future superhumanity.

To know him in his earthiness; to know him in his heavenliness.

To know him as body; to know him as soul.

To know him as a prisoner of time and space; to know him as a denizen of eternity.

To know him in his material crucifixion; to know him in his spiritual ascension.

To know him as a man; to know him as superman.

To know him in the tragedy of his passion; to know him in the vision of his perfection.

To know him in the mortification of his flesh; to know him in the transfiguration of his soul.

To know him, not as dust of the ground, but as the image and likeness of Divinity; not as a creature made out of nothing, but born from the very bosom of God; not as a slave of matter, but as a free citizen of the spiritual commonwealth; not as mortal body, but as immortal soul; not subject to the laws of death, but incorruptible through the eternity of Spirit.

To know him as a child of the Divine; hence, divine, not by special gift, but by legitimate inheritance; immortal, not by bestowal, but by inherent nature; perfecting and perfectible, not by any particular dispensation or privilege, but by divine lineage and divine sonship.

To know him thus, as very son of very God; and, then to help him unfold the dormant powers of both his body and soul; to help him up, by the process of intensive self-evolution toward his ultimate perfection; to create for him a vision of the universe that will enable him to expand his consciousness and attain the dream of his immortality; to make him realize his divinity, so he may also realize the divinity of others; and thus to bring about the actualization of the brotherhood of humanity predicated on the divine sonship of all men and the all-comprehending Fatherhood of God . . .

This is the duty of all true science, all true philosophy, all true religion.

And this, too, is the duty of all right-thinking and truth-loving men, be they philosophers, or scientists, or ministers, or just ordinary plain-living men of the earth.

References

[1] Quoted from the "Introduction," in Frank T. Severin's *Humanistic Viewpoints in Psychology*, (New York: McGraw Hill Book, Inc., 1965) p. xiv.
[2] *Ibid.*, p. xvi.
[3] Lecomte du Nouy, *Human Destiny*, (London: Longmans, Green and Co., Ltd., 1947,) p. 34.
[4] *Ibid.*, p. 32.

Appendix A

STRANGER-CHILD

Hear me, Child, and judge me rightly, if I tell the truth or lie,
In the heart of man is written sorrow of the earth and sky.
In the hour of many voices of the holy, silent night,
You were born to bring us tidings of great joy and rich delight.
"Lo! He comes," the Prophet told us, "He, the promised Prince of Love,
"Who shall make the sky an Eden for the Vulture and the Dove;
"And the earth where in the grasses creeping low the Serpent lies,
"With his magic wand of power He shall make a paradise."
Now we know the prophets told us but the hopes within their head,
For the earth and sky are bleeding with the bleeding drops of dread . . .
For the wolves steal in the darkness and surprise the sleeping sheep,
With the plunder of their footsteps and the carnage of their keep.
And I cry in tears commingled with disdain and bitter woe,
When I see the pomp of feasting in the yearly Christmas glow,
Hear the sounds of Christmas tidings as the long years come and go,
From the regions of the palm trees to the pathways of the snow.
Child of Love and Sweet Compassion (O the mockery of times!)
Thou art still a stranger to us, though we ring your Christmas chimes.

Appendix A

Lift our souls, O Stranger-Being, to the realms of lasting Light.
Great your vision, but your vision is beyond our human sight.
We are blind, O Stranger-Being, call us, guide us from the wild!
Hail, to Thee, but to us worldlings, Thou art still a Stranger-Child!

by Benito F. Reyes

(Published in the *Philippine Free Press,* Manila, Dec. 22, 1934)

Appendix B
HOW A DREAM INSPIRED THE POEM "KUBLA KHAN"
by Samuel Taylor Coleridge (1772-1834)

The following fragment is here published at the request of a poet of great and deserved celebrity (Byron) and, as far as the author's own opinions are concerned, rather as a psychological curiosity, than on the ground of any supposed poetic merits.

In the summer of the year 1797 the author, then in ill health, had retired to a lonely farmhouse between Porlock and Linton, on the Exmoor confines of Somerset and Devonshire. In consequence of a slight indisposition, an anodyne had been prescribed, from the effects of which he fell asleep in his chair at the moment that he was reading the following sentence, or words of the same substance, in "Purcha's Pilgrimage": "Here the Khan Kubla commanded a palace to be built, and a stately garden thereunto. And thus ten miles of fertile ground were inclosed with a wall." The author continued for about three hours in a profound sleep, at least of the external senses, during which time he had the most vivid confidence that he could not have composed less than from two to three hundred lines; if that indeed can be called composition in which all the images rose up before him as things, with a parallel production of the correspondent expressions, without any sensation or consciousness of effort. On awaking he appeared to himself to have a distinct recollection of the whole, and taking his pen, ink and paper, instantly and eagerly wrote down the lines that are here preserved. At this moment he was unfortunately called out by a person on business from Porlock, and detained by him above an hour, and on his return to his room, found, to his no small surprise and mortification, that though he still retained some vague and dim recollection of the general purport of the vision, yet, with the exception of some eight or ten scattered lines and images, all the rest had passed away like the images on the surface of a stream into which a stone has been cast, but, alas! without the after restoration of the latter!

> Then all the charm
> Is broken — all that phantom-world so fair
> Vanishes, and a thousand circlets spread,
> And each mis-shapes the other. Stay awhile,
> Poor youth! who scarcely dar'st lift up thine eyes —
> The stream will soon renew its smoothness, soon
> The visions will return! and lo, he stays
> And soon the fragments dim of lovely forms
> Come trembling back, unite, and now once more
> The pool becomes a mirror.
>
> S.T.C.

KUBLA KHAN

In Xanadu did Kubla Khan
A stately pleasure-dome decree:
Where Alph, the sacred river, ran
Through caverns measureless to man
   Down to a sunless sea.
So twice five miles of fertile ground
With walls and towers were girdled round;
And there were gardens bright with sinuous rills,
Where blossomed many an incense-bearing tree;
And here were forests ancient as the hills,
Enfolding sunny spots of greenery.
But oh! that deep romantic chasm which slanted
Down the green hill athwart a cedarn cover!
A savage place! as holy and enchanted
As e'er beneath a waning moon was haunted
By woman wailing for her demon-lover
And from this chasm, with ceaseless turmoil seething,
As if this earth in fast thick pants were breathing,

A mighty fountain momently was forced:
Amid whose swift half-intermitted burst
Huge fragments vaulted like rebounding hail,
Or chaffy grain beneath the thresher's flail:
And 'mid these dancing rocks at once and ever
It flung up momently the sacred river.
Five miles meandering with a mazy motion
Through wood and dale the sacred river ran,
Then reached the caverns measureless to man,
And sank in tumult to a lifeless ocean:
And 'mid this tumult Kubla heard from far
Ancestral voices prophesying war!
   The shadow of the dome of pleasure
   Floated midway on the waves;
   Where was heard the mingled measure
   From the fountain and the caves.
It was a miracle of rare device,
A sunny pleasure-dome with caves of ice!
   A damsel with a dulcimer
   In a vision once I saw:
   It was an Abyssinian maid,
   And on her dulcimer she played,
   Singing on Mount Abora.
   Could I revive within me
   Her symphony and song,
To such a deep delight 'twould win me,
That with music loud and long,
I would build that dome in air.
That sunny dome! those caves of ice!
And all who heard should see them there,
And all should cry, Beware! Beware!
His flashing eyes, his floating hair!
Weave a circle round him thrice,
And close your eyes with holy dread,
For he on honey-dew hath fed,
And drunk the milk of Paradise.

Appendix C
THE PHENOMENA OF REINCARNATION

In presenting the case for the existence of the soul by the use of the scientific method, it is important to bear in mind the idea that proof increases in strength in proportion to the amount of evidence presented. The more examples cited, the more convincing.

One of the most universally accepted beliefs in Asia among its millions upon millions of people is the idea of reincarnation. Reincarnation, as a doctrine, regards the soul as distinct from the body which it occupies from birth to death. Belief in reincarnation thus implies belief in the existence of the soul. Therefore, any evidence in favor of reincarnation supports the case for the existence of the soul. The basic question for our purpose here is still the same, however, namely, which can better explain reincarnation, the cerebrocentric body-theory or the psychocentric soul-theory?

It is not the purpose of this book to argue the case for reincarnation, except insofar as doing so also endorses the case for the soul. For this reason, some well-authenticated cases of reincarnation are cited here. There are many such cases in the ancient literature of India, China, and the Near East, such as the story of the great Hindu philosopher Shankaracharya who left his body temporarily to occupy the body of a king newly dead, as recounted beautifully in chapter V of L. Adams Beck's well-known book, *Oriental Philosophy*;[1] the popular Chinese story, "The Tale of Chienniang" and the lovely narrative poem, "The Tale of Meng Chiang," both of which may be read in Lin Yutang's *The Wisdom of China and India*;[2] and the story of John the Baptist in the Bible whom Christ identified clearly as the Old Testament prophet reincarnated.[3] Two very recent cases, however, are unusually interesting, that of Bridey Murphy and that of Karman Shanti Devi. Only the case of Shanti Devi will be recounted here, inasmuch as that of Bridey Murphy has been well-publicized.

The Case Of Shanti Devi

The case of Shanti Devi as recounted in Swami Sivananda's book *What Becomes of the Soul After Death,* published by the Divine Life Society, Hongkong, 1958, is certainly one of the most celebrated cases of "recalled reincarnation" on record now. It was reported officially about thirty-two years ago by a locally-formed committee of learned and competent men in Delhi and was much publicized in leading local and foreign newspapers.

Shanti Devi was born on October 12, 1926. As a little girl, she had vivid recollections and memory of her previous life from 1902-1925 at Muttra, India, and also details of incidents, events, and experiences with her husband of a previous life, Pundit Kedar Nath Chaubey. Her parents, unbelieving as they were, dismissed Shanti Devi's narrations of her past life as the jabberings of a child and deeply wished that the recollections would be erased from her memory as she grew. The child, however, became more insistent on recollecting more of her past life, and even succeeded in prevailing upon her parents to take them to the city of her previous birth, where she could show them her old house as well as other details of her previous incarnation.

At Delhi, where the initial interview on the case was held and where the people intimately associated with Shanti Devi in her previous life in Muttra were called, the girl showed instant recognition of them and made very satisfactory answers to questions they asked her. She immediately recognized Pundit Kedar Nath Chaubey, her claimed husband of a previous life, and their ten-year old son, who came along with Pundit Kedar Nath's present wife. She was visibly moved to tears at the sight of them. She also recognized Pundit Kanji Mal, who gave her the initial interview at Delhi, as the younger cousin of her husband. She gave a description of their house at Muttra, named the roads and streets leading to it, and described the temple of Dwarkadhish, the Vishrant Ghat. She also made mention of some money, about a hundred rupees, which she had hidden and which she had vowed to give to the temple of Dwarkadhish. As a result of all these, and Pundit Kedar Nath Chaubey's confirmation of the veracity of Shanti Devi's recollections and statements and his acceptance that she is indeed the same soul, that of his first wife who had died at Muttra, the party composed of the investigation committee, Pundit Kedar Nath Chaubey's group, Shanti Devi and her parents, left for Muttra. Shanti Devi shouted with joy as the train steamed into the Muttra Station and as she got down from the train she identified in the crowd an elderly man in typical Muttra dress as Babu Ram Chaubey, the elder brother of her husband. She led the party to her former house from the railway station and at the Dharmashala at Muttra she identified the "brother" of her previous birth, and her "uncle-in-law."

In the courtyard of her former house, she looked for the well which was now covered with stone. She also dug up the hole where she kept hidden the money she vowed to give to the Temple of Dwarkadhish. Not finding it there, she felt dismayed. Pundit Kedar Nath confessed he had taken the money from there after the death of his former wife, now the girl Shanti Devi. She was also taken to her "parents'" house where she recognized them and where both the girl and her "parents" sank into continued sobs, making parting most difficult. At the Vishrant Ghat, she unfolded many more surprises and details of her past life to the investigating committee and to the others, who by now were all agreed of the accuracy and veracity of Shanti Devi's recollections and memory of her previous birth.

References

[1] L. Adams Beck, *The Story of Oriental Philosophy* (New York: Farrar and Rinehart Inc., 1928).

[2] Lin Yutang, *The Wisdom of China and India* (New York: The Modern Library, 1942).

[3] Matthew 17:9-13.

BIBLIOGRAPHY
I. BOOKS

Abhenanda, Swami. *How to Be a Yogi.* The Ramakrishna Vedanta Society, Calcutta.

Akhilananda, Swami. *Hindu Psychology, Its Meaning for the West.* Harper and Brothers Publishers, New York and London, 1946.

Alfven, Hannes. *Worlds - Antiworlds: Antimatter in Cosmology.* W. H. Freeman and Company, San Francisco and London, 1966.

Angeles, Sixto de los. *Legal Medicine.* Pobre Press, 267 Solana St., Manlia, Philippines, 1934.

Barton, William E. *My Faith in Immortality.* Red Label Reprints, New York, 1926.

Beck, L. Adams. *The Story of Oriental Philosophy.* Farrar and Rinehart, Inc., New York, 1928.

Benjamin, A. Cornelius. *An Introduction to the Philosophy of Science.* The Macmillan Co., New York, 1937.

Bergson, Henri. *Mind-Energy,* translated by H. Wildon Carr. Copyright, 1920, by Henry Holt and Company, Inc., New York. Copyright, 1948, by H. Wildon Carr.

Besant, Annie. *Thought Power, Its Control and Culture.* The Theosophical Publishing House, Madras, London and Wheaton, Illinois, 1968.

———. *A Study in Consciousness, A Contribution to the Science of Psychology.* The Theosophical Publishing House, Madras, London, and Wheaton, Illinois, 1967.

———. *The Self and Its Sheaths.* Theosophical Publishing House, Madras, London, and Wheaton, Illinois, 1895.

———. *Psychology.* Second Edition. Theosophical Publishing House, Los Angeles, 1919.

———. *Thought-Forms.* The Theosophical Publishing House, Madras, London, and Wheaton, Illinois, 1969.

——— and Leadbeater, C. W. *Man, Whence, How, and Whither.* The Theosophical Publishing House, Madras, London, and Wheaton, Illinois, 1967.

Best, Charles Herbert and Norman Bucke Taylor, *The Physiological Basis of Medical Practice*. The Williams and Wilkins Company, Baltimore, 1961.
Bigelow, John. *The Mystery of Sleep*. Harper and Brothers Publishers, New York and London, 1946.
Blavatsky, H. P. *Isis Unveiled*. Rider and Co., London, Facsimile Edition, 1887.
Brightman, Edgar Sheffield. *A Philosophy of Religion*. Prentice Hall, Inc., New York, 1946.
Bucke, Richard Maurice. *Cosmic Consciousness, A Study in the Evolution of the Human Mind*. Introduction by George Moreby Acklom. E. P. Dutton and Company, Inc., New York, 1948.
Burtt, Edwin A. (ed). *The English Philosophers From Bacon to Mill*. The Modern Library, New York, 1939.
Carew, John Eccles. *The Neurological Basis of Mind*. The Clarendon Press, Oxford, 1965.
Carrel, Alexis. *Man the Unknown*. Harper and Brothers, New York, 1939.
Carrington, Hereward. *The Psychic World*. G. P. Putnam and Sons, New York, 1937.
Cashman, John. *The LSD Story*. A Fawcett Gold Medal Book, Greenwich, Connecticut, 1966.
Chase, Stuart. *The Tyranny of Words*. Harcourt, Brace and Company, New York, 1938.
Clarke, Ide Clyde. *Men Who Woudn't Stay Dead*. Bernard Ackerman Inc., New York, 1945.
Clegg, Robert Ingham. *Mackey's Symbolism of Freemasonry, Its Science, Philosophy, Legends, Myths and Symbols*. The Masonic History Company, Chicago, New York and London, 1921.
Cohen, Morris R. and Nagel, Ernest. *An Introduction to Logic and the Scientific Method*. Harcourt, Brace and Company. New York, 1934.
Cotton, Edward H. (Editor). *Has Science Discovered God? A Symposium of Modern Scientific Opinion*. Thomas Y. Crowell Company, New York, 1931.
Dampier, Sir William Cecil. *A Shorter History of Science*. The Macmillan Company, New York, 1945.

Das, Bhagavan. *The Science of the Self.* The Theosophical Publishing House, Madras, London, and Wheaton, Illinois, 1938.

Das, Bhavagan. *The Science of Peace. An Attempt at an Exposition of the First Principles of the Science of the Self,* Adhyatman-Vidya. The Theosophical Publishing Society, Madras, London, and Wheaton, Illinois, 1904.

Dechanet, J. M. O. S. B. *Christian Yoga.* Harper and Row, Publishers, New York and Evanston, 1960.

DeRopp, Robert S. *Drugs and the Mind.* Grove Press, Inc., New York, 1957.

Durant, Will. *The Story of Philosophy.* Garden City Publishing Co., Inc., New York, 1943.

Edwards, Paul (Editor). *Body, Mind, and Death.* With an introduction by Antony Flew. The Macmillan Company, New York, 1964.

Evans-Wentz, W. Y. *The Tibetan Book of the Dead or The After-Death Experiences on the Bardo Plane,* According to Lama Kazi Dawa-Samdup's English Rendering. Second Edition. (Geoffrey Cumberlege,) Oxford University Press, London, 1951.

Freud, Sigmund. *A General Introduction to Psychoanalysis.* Garden City Publishing Co., Inc., New York, 1943.

Fuller, A. G. *A History of Philosophy.* Henry Holt and Company, New York, 1945.

Fulton, John F. (Editor). *Howell's Textbook of Physiology.* W. B. Saunders Co., Philadelphia and London, 1949.

Gaddis, Vincent H. *Mysterious Fires and Lights.* David McKay Company, Inc., New York, 1967.

Garbedian, H. Gordon. *Major Mysteries of Science.* Garden City Publishing Co., Inc., New York, 1933.

Gardner, E. L. *The Nature and Function of the Soul.* Theosophical Publishing House, Madras, London and Wheaton, Illinois, 1946.

Gates, Arthur. *Elementary Psychology.* The Macmillan Co., New York, 1936.

Heidbreder, Edna. *Seven Psychologies.* D. Appleton Century, New York and London, 1933.

Bibliography 247

Hibben, John Grier. *Inductive Logic.* Charles Scribner's Sons, New York, 1904.

Hocking, William Ernest. *The Meaning of God in Human Experiences.* Yale University Press, New Haven and London, Fourth Printing, 1963.

Hodson, Geoffrey. *The Science of Seership.* Rider and Company, London.

Huxley, Aldous. *Collected Essays.* Bantam Books Inc., New York, 1966.

Huxley, Julian S. *The Science of Life.* Doubleday, Doran and Co., New York, Four Volumes, Vol. IV, 1931.

Jacobi, Jolande. *The Psychology of C. G. Jung.* Yale University Press, New Haven and London, 1962.

James, William. *The Varieties of Religious Experience.* Longmans, Green and Company, New York, 1902.

Janet, P. *The Major Systems of Hysteria.* The Macmillan Co., New York, 1907.

Jastrow, Joseph. *Freud, His Dreams and Sex Theories.* The World Publishing Company, Cleveland and New York, 1946.

Jinarajadasa, C. *The Nature of Mysticism.* Theosophical Publishing House, Madras, London, and Wheaton, Illinois, 1934.

Joad, Cyril Edwin Mitchinson. *Introduction to Modern Philosophy.* Clarendon Press, Oxford, 1958 (Reprint).

Joseph, H.W.B. *An Introduction to Logic.* Clarendon Press, Oxford, 1906.

Jung, Carl G. *Man and His Symbols.* Doubleday & Company Inc., New York, 1964.

———. *Memories, Dreams, Reflections.* Pantheon Books, New York, 1961, 1962, 1963.

Kanga, D. D. *Where Theosophy and Science Meet, A Stimulus to Modern Thought.* A Collective Work. Four Volumes. The Adyar Library Association, Adyar, Madras, India, 1949.

Kleitman, Nathaniel. *Sleep and Wakefulness.* The University of Chicago Press, Chicago and London, 1963.

Landis, Carney and Marjorie Bolles. *Textbook of Abnormal Psychology.* The Macmillan Company, New York, 1947.

Late Inmate of the Glasgow Royal Asylum for Lunatics at Gartnaval. *The Philosophy of Insanity.* With an Introduction by Frieda Fromm-Reichmann. Greenberg Publisher, New York. 1947.

Leadbeater, C. W. *The Astral Plane.* Theosophical Publishing House, Madras, London, and Wheaton, Illinois, 1968.

Leuba, James. *A Psychological Study of Religion.* The Macmillan Company, New York, 1912.

Lin Yutang. *The Wisdom of China and India.* The Modern Library, New York, Seventh Printing. c. 1942.

Long, Max Freedom. *The Secret Science Behind Miracles.* Huna Research Publications, Vista, California, 1948, 1954.

Matson, Floyd W. *The Broken Image.* George Braziller, New York, 1946.

McDougall, William. *Body and Mind: A History and A Defense of Animism.* The Macmillan Co., New York, 1911.

Mill, John Stuart. *A System of Logic.* Longmans, Green Publishing Co., London, 1952.

Moore. Benjamin. *The Origin and Nature of Life.* Home University Library, Henry Holt and Company, New York.

Muldoon, Sylvan. *Psychic Experience of Famous People.* Aries Press, Chicago, 1947.

Nevius, Warren Nelson. *The Meaning of the Moral Life, An Introductory Discussion of Theoretical and Historical Ethics.* Noble and Noble, New York, 1930.

Nouy, Lecomte du. *Human Destiny.* Longmans, Green and Company, Ltd., London, 1947.

Ouspensky, P.D., *Tertium Organum, The Third Cannon of Thought, A Key to the Enigmas of the World.* Translated from the Russian by Nicholas Bessaraboff and Claude Bragdon. Third American Edition, Alfred A. Knopf, New York, 1945.

Patrick, George Thomas White. *The World and Its Meaning, An Introduction to Philosophy.* Houghton Mifflin Co., Boston and New York, 1925.

Payne, Phoebe. *Man's Latent Powers.* Faber and Faber Ltd., London.
Penfield, W. and Jasper, H., *Epilepsy and the Functional Anatomy of the Human Brain.* Little Brown Co., Boston, 1954.
Pillsbury, W. B. *The Essentials of Psychology.* The Macmillan Company, New York, 1930.
Plato, *Great Dialogues of Plato.* Mentor Books, New York, 1956.
Prince, Morton. *The Unconscious.* The Macmillan Company, New York, 1929.
Reyes, Benito F. *An Introduction to Logic and the Scientific Method.* Far Eastern University, Manila, 1947.
Rhine, J. B. *The Reach of the Mind.* William Sloane Association, Inc., New York, 1947.
Roberts, William Henry. *The Problem of Choice, An Introduction to Ethics.* Ginn and Co., New York, 1941.
Robinson, Daniel Sommer. *The Principles of Reasoning.* A. Appleton Century Co., New York and London, 1947.
Row, T. Subba. *Esoteric Writings.* Theosophical Publishing House, Madras, London, and Wheaton, Illinois, 1931.
Russell, Henry, Norris Dugan, Raymond Smith, and John Quincy Stewart. *Astronomy, A Revision of Young's Manual of Astronomy.* Ginn and Company, New York, 1926.
Runes, Dagobert D. *The Dictionary of Philosophy.* Philosophical Library, New York, 1942.
Sartre, Jean-Paul. *Existentialism and Human Emotions.* Wisdom Library, New York, 1957, p. 53.
Severin, Frank T. (Editor). *Humanistic Viewpoints in Psychology.* McGraw Hill Book Company, New York, 1965.
Sivananda, Swami. *What Becomes of the Soul After Death?* Divine Life Society, Hongkong, 1958.
Smart, Harold R. *The Logic of Science.* D. Appleton and Co., New York and London, 1931.
Solomon, David (Editor). *LSD - The Consciousness-Expanding Drug.* G.P. Putman's Sons, New York, 1964.

Startling, Ernest Henry. *Principles of Human Physiology.* 13th Edition. Edited by Hugh Davson and M. Grace Eggleton, Lea and Febiger, Philadelphia, 1962.

Stebbing, L.S. *A Modern Introduction to Logic.* Methuen and Co., Ltd., London, 1930.

Stromberg, Gustaf. *The Soul of the Universe.* David McKay Company, Philadelphia, 1948.

Suner, Augusto Pi. *The Bridge of Life.* The Macmillan Co., New York, 1951.

Tillich, Paul. *The Courage to Be.* Yale University Press, New Haven, 1959, p. 124.

Tsanoff, Radoslav A. *Ethics.* Harper and Brothers, New York and London, 1947.

Warren, Howard C. *Dictionary of Psychology.* Houghton Mifflin Company, The Riverside Press, Cambridge, 1934.

Washburn, Margaret Floy. *The Animal Mind, A Textbook of Comparative Psychology.* The Macmillan Company, New York, 1936.

Watts, Alan W. *The Joyous Cosmology.* Vintage Books, New York, 1962.

Wiggers, Carl John. *Physiology in Health and Disease.* Lea and Febiger, Philadelphia, 1949.

Winton, F. R. and L. R. Bayliss. *Human Physiology.* 5th Edition. Little Brown Co., Boston, 1962.

Woods, Ralph (Editor). *The World of Dreams, An Anthology.* Random House, New York, 1947.

Yogananda, Paramahansa. *Autobiography of a Yogi.* The Philosophical Library, New York, 1946.

II. OTHER SOURCES

Battersby, H. F. Prevost. "A Clue to Magic," *Round Robin.* Vol. IV, No. 4, April-May, 1948, pp. 21-24.

Duval, M. "Hypothese sur la physiologie des centres nerveux. Theorie histologique du sommeil." *C. R. Soc. Biology,* 47:74-76, 86-87, 1895.

Gaddis, Vincent H. "With Brain Destroyed They Live and Think!" *Fate,* Vol. I, No. 2, Summer, 1948. pp. 76-83.

Graham, R. P. "Science and the Soul." *Fate*, 1:96-99, Spring, 1948.
Hodson, Geoffrey. *The Mystery of Death. A Message to the Bereaved.* New Zealand Section of the Theosophical Society, Auckland, New Zealand, 1945.
Hogarth, Peter J. "The Physiological Basis of Memory," *Advancement of Science.* 22, April, 1966.
Keeton, M. T., "Some Ambiguities in the Theory of the Conservation of Energy," *Philosophy of Science,* Vol. 8, No. 3, July, 1941.
Layne, N. Meade. "The Cloud of Witnesses," (From Vincent H. Gaddis's Introduction to *Psychic Experiences of Famous People*). *Round Robin,* Vol. IV, No. 4, April-May, 1948, pp. 13-14.
Leadbeater, C. W. *The Chakras.* A Monograph. Theosophical Publishing House, Madras, London, and Wheaton, Illinois, 1968.
Lepine, R. "Theorie mecanique de la paralysie hypnotique, du somnambulismo, du sommel natural et de la distraction." *C. R. Soc. Biol.,* 47:85-86, 1895.
Reyes, Benito F. *What is Death?* Manila: Philippines, 1938.
Rhine, J.B. "The Reach of the Mind." A Condensation. *The Readers Digest.* Vol. 52, No. 310, February, 1948, pp. 129-142.
Philippine Free Press, Manila, Dec. 22, 1934.
The Scotsman, "On edge of death: record of out of the body experience: brought back to life." February 27, 1937, p. 16, columns 3-4.
The Theosophical World. Adyar, Madras, India: The Theosophical Publishing Society. Vol. 2, No. 7, July, 1937.

INDEX OF NAMES

Abercrombie, Dr., 145-146
Adams, W.S., 206
Adriano, P., 139
Ageo, G., 189, 190
Aksakof, A.N., 160
Alfven, H., xix
Alpert, R., 64
Arnold, M., 11

Backman, A., 144
Balfour, W., 159
Baraduc, Dr., 159
Barrett, W., 159
Batacan, D.F., 215
Bates, W.H., 158
Bayliss, L.E., 73
Beaufort, 115
Bender, H., 44
Berger, Hans, 177
Bergson, H., 79, 159, 203
Beringer, Dr., 196
Besant, A., 95, 105
Bigelow, J., 209
Binet, 143
Boehme, 26
Bolles, M., 141, 142
Bond, F.B., 159
Boodin, J.E., 206
Bottazzi, F., 160
Bouilland, Prof., 160
Bowers, E., 158
Bozzano, E., 160
Bragdon, C., 158
Brath, S., 159
Brigham, W.T., 215, 216, 219
Brightman, E.S., iii, xv, xix, 57, 58, 69, 70, 71, 90
Broad, C.D., 69, 203
Brofferio, A., 160
Brown, R.T., 189, 190
Brown, W., 158
Bruno, G., 52
Bucke, R.M., 6
Bull. T., 158
Burr, H.S., 206
Butler, N.M., 158

Cajal, 118
Cannon, A., 159
Carington, W., 159
Carpenter, E., 6
Carrel, A., 3, 24, 158, 172, 210
Carrington, H., 158
Cashman, J., 194
Cayce, E., 131
Challis, J., 159

Chambers, R., 159
Charcot, 145, 159
Chase, S., 2
Chiapelli, Prof., 160
Chuang, T., 131
Coates, J., 160
Coleridge, S.T., 140
Comstock, D.F., 158
Copernicus, 51, 52, 53, 56
Corning, J.L., 130
Coues, E., 159
Crawford, J.W., 159
Crookes, W., 159
Curie, Marie, 159
Curie, Pierre, 159
Curney, E., 44

d'Albe, E.E.F., 159
Darget, C., 159
Darwin, C., 159
Das, B. 98-99
D'Assier, A., 160
Davis, R., 79
Davy, H., 159
Dechanet, J.M. 26, 63
Dellane, Dr., 160
DeMorgan, A., 159
Denton, W., 159
de Rochas, A., 159
Descartes, 32, 59, 75, 127
Devi, S., 242-243
Diderot, 33
Dreisch, H., 160
Ducasse, C.J., 83, 174-175, 184, 212
Dunne, J.W., 159
Du Prel, C., 105, 108, 114-115, 144
Durville, H., 159
Duval, M., 118

Eddington, A., 206
Einstein, A., 205
Ellis, H., 137, 159, 193, 198-199
Emerson, 11
Exner, 118

Farigoule, L., 159, 165
Fauventy, C., 159
Feire, P., 159
Fere, 143
Fichte, I.H., 160
Figuer, L., 159
Fiske, E., 159
Flammarion, C., 130, 159
Flandez, S., 215, 220-223, 224, 225
Flew, A., 212
Flournoy, Th., 160

Index of Names

Fodor, N., 159
Freud, 127, 130, 136
Frick, H.L., 172
Fulton, J., 76
Fukari, Prof., 160

Gaddis, V.H., 77, 158, 205
Gage, P., 77
Galileo, 52
Gedder, A., 181
Geley, G., 78, 79-80, 159
Geresa, G., 159
Gibier, P., 159
Gibson, E.P., 172
Gilbert, J., 158
Ginsberg, A., 64
Gould, Dr., 78
Gould, R.T., 159
Graves, R., 64
Greenwood, J.A., 169
Grinard, E., 159
Gully, J.M., 159
Gurdjieff, G.I., 205
Gurney, E., 159
Guye, C.E., ix, 47, 49, 50, 58

Haas, W., 160, 214
Haddock, Dr., 144
Hamilton, T.G., 160
Hamilton, W., 66
Hamsun, 123
Hannesor, C., 160
Hare, K., 158
Hart, H., 158
Hartley, D., 130
Hartman, 127
Harvey, W., 120
Henry, C., 159
Hobart, 120
Hobbes, 12, 32
Hocking, W.E., 63
Hodgson, R., 158
Hodson, G., 161, 165-166, 214
Hofmann, A., 64, 193
Hogarth, P., 110
Hollingsworth, H.L., 129
Hommel, F., 160
Howell, J., 117
Hufeland, Dr., 78
Hujer, K., 206
Hume, D., 93, 175
Husserl, E., 87
Huxley, A., 64, 193, 202, 203, 205
Hyslop, J.H., 158

Jacobsen, 75
James, W., 45, 63, 158, 192, 193, 205
Janet, P., 44, 124, 125
Jennings, 101-102
Joad, C.E.M., 159

Johnson, S., ix
Johnson, W.B., 158
Joseph, H.W.B., 102
Jung, C.G., 6, 35, 130, 131, 214

Kaempffert, W., 169
Kant, 84
Kardec, A., 159
Keeton, M.T., 175
Kilner, J.W., 159
Kleitman, N., 117
Koning, P.W., 159

Labadie, J., 159
Ladd, 130
Lancelin, C., 159
Landis, C., 141, 142
Larkin, E.L., 158
Leadbeater, C.W., 55, 214
Leary, T., 64
Leibnitz, 84
Lepine, R., 118
Lescarboura, A.C., 158
Leuba, J.H., 63
Lewin, L., 193
Lincoln, 46
Lirenensis, V., 46
Lobroso, C., 160
Locke, J., 84, 85
Lodge, O., 159
Long, M.F., 214, 215, 219
Loomis, 120

Macario, Dr., 160
Macfarlane, J.M., 87
Maeterlinck, M., 138
Martin, D., 170
Maslow, A.H., xviii
Mather, K.F., 216
Matta, J.L., 159
Mattieson, E., 160
Mayo, H., 159
MacDougall, Prof., 172
McDougall, D., 158
McDougall, W., 6, 45, 158
Meinong, 87
Mesmer, 165
Mill, J.S., 40
Moore, B., 87
Montesquieu, 33
Morgan, T.H., 206
Moselli, Prof., 160
Moulton, F.R., 206
Moureau, B.M., 144
Mucchi, Dr., 160
Muldoon, S., 158, 179
Mumford, L.C., 31
Murphy, B., 242
Murphy, G., 159, 212
Myers, F.W.H., 113

Index of Names

Nicholls, F.L., 159
Niel, P., 161
Nielson, H., 160
Nouy, Le Compte du, 24, 47, 230

Ochorowicz, Dr., 160
Oesterreich, C., 160
O'Neil, J.J., 158
Osmond, H., 195
Osty, E., 159
Ouspensky, P.D., 6, 81, 83, 87, 88, 138, 139, 159, 177, 184
Ouvrien, M., 165

Paramahansa, Y., 63, 184
Patacsil, V.B., xix
Patanjali, xviii
Paulsen, F., 83
Pavlov, 117
Paz, B., 161-162
Pieron, 117
Pictet, P., 160
Pillsbury, W.B., 110, 129, 140
Podmore, F., 159
Powell, E., 159
Pratt, J.G., 169
Preston, E.W., 165
Price, H.H., 63
Price, H., 159
Prince, M., 125, 158
Prince, W.F., 158
Prins, D.H., 145, 156
Ptolemy, 51, 52
Pyle, Dr., 78

Rankine, A.O., 159
Rayleigh, Lord, 159
Reichenbach, B.V., 160
Reichmann, F.F., 123
Reiss, B., 170
Reyes, B.F., x, xiii-xv, xx, 140, 162-165, 236-237
Rhine, J.B., 14, 15, 23, 24, 26, 27, 44, 50, 63, 127, 139, 147, 153, 158, 161, 166, 168, 169, 170, 171, 174, 177, 184, 214
Richet, C., 26, 144, 155, 214
Rivers, W.H., 130
Robertson, L., 159
Rosett, J., 130
Rousseau, JJ., 33
Russel, H., 87

Salumbides, V., 162
San Benito, M., 160
Schiaparelli, G., 160
Schleiermacher, 10
Schrenck-Notzing, B.V., 160
Schwab, F., 160

Seiling, H.M., 160
Shaker, N.S., 159
Shaw, W., 79
Shepard, 117
Sherman, H., 158
Sherrington, C., 83
Sidgwick, H., 159
Sivananda, S., 242
Smith, B.M., 169
Smith, H., 200
Soal, S.G., 159
Spencer, H., 110
Sponsler, O.L., 206
Stace, W.T., 200
Stanford, T.W., 158
Stanley, H.M., 160
Stokes, C., 158
Stribic, F.P., 170
Stromberg, G., 205
St. Theresa, 26
Stuart, C.E., 169
Stuart, C.B., 158
Surya, C.W., 78, 79, 159
Swedenborg, 26

Thompson, A., 181
Taylor, W.J.L., 158
Tyrrell, G.N., 63
Tuttle, H., 159
Tillyard, J., 160
Tenhaeff, 159, 179
Thouless, R.H., 63, 173

Valery, P., xviii
van Eeden, F., 135, 136, 137, 138, 159, 179
Vazzani, Prof., 160
Vogt, C., 81
Voltaire, 33

Wallace, A.R., 159, 160
Warrick, F.W., 159
Warren, H.C., 141
Wasson, G., 193, 197
Watson, 5
Watters, R.A., 158
Watts, A.W., 64
Whymant, N., 158
Wiggers, C.J., 74, 125
Wilkins, H., 158
Winslow, Dr., 105, 107
Winston, F.R., 73
Wood, F.H., 159
Wundt, W., 130
Wyld, G., 158
Wyld, R.S., 158

Zelst, V., 159
Zollner, J.C.F., 160

INDEX OF SUBJECTS

abnormality, definition of, 123
after-death world, 214
agreement, method of, 102
anosognosia, 74
antimatter, xix
antiserotonin, 193
apparitions, 155
Atman, 7, 75, 219, 220
Atma-Vidya, 28

Baconion Method of Varying the Circumstance, 102
behavior, 5, 33, 34
Berger rhythm (EEG), 75, 177, 120-121
body, 9, 12, 13, 15, 22, 33, 61, 64, 67, 95, 96, 98, 118, 121, 133, 139, 140, 151, 175, 177, 183, 203, 230, 231
body,
  as instrument of expression, 203
body-hypothesis (see also corpocentric attitude) 64, 174, 231
body-psychology, 13-16
Brahmarandra chakra, 75
brain, 14, 18, 61, 69-70, 74, 79, 81, 87, 88, 89, 90, 97, 98, 100, 103, 110, 114, 121, 126, 132, 133, 134, 142, 151, 152, 173, 177, 183, 185, 202, 227, 229
  as organ of mind, 153
  Berger rhythm (EEG) and, 177
  cerebration and, 185
  consciousness and, 76-78, 92, 111-112, 184, 202
  dream consciousness and, 134
  eliminative function of, 203
  fibrillation and, 183
  memory and, 100-102
brain-thought relations, 81-91
  theories on, 82-85

cerebrocentric attitude, xvii, 15, 23, 44, 61, 124, 152, 203, 234
  on ideas, 89
  on man, 15, 23, 61, 142, 147, 152, 174, 234
cerebrum, 83, 84, 85
clairvoyance, 26, 44, 50, 127, 144, 156, 160-166, 168, 172, 174, 175, 176, 228
  definition of, 160-161
  experiments on, 165,166, 169-170
  hypnosis and, 165
  inborn, 161-162
  spontaneous, 161-165

clairvoyance, traveling, 26, 61, 75, 144, 179-192, 195, 228
  Geddes' report on, 181-183
  other terms for, 180
  psychedelic phenomena and, 195-197
  the author and, 186-190
coherence, 56, 57, 58
coma, 152, 153, 224, 227
communism, 19, 20
consciousness, 1, 2, 3, 4, 28-29, 61, 62, 66-99, 100, 102, 103, 111, 114, 118-119, 133, 134, 175, 197, 202, 205, 213, 220, 227, 229
  anatomical structure of, 89
  as epiphenomena of brain, 92, 202
  assumptions about, 73-76
  characteristics of, 184-185
  classification of, 28-29, 120
  cosmic, 6, 120
  death and, 213, 224
  function of, 229
  four-dimensional, 6, 139
  indefinability of, 66
  identity and continuity of, 67, 95-97
  memory and, 102-103
  sleep and, 120-122
  without brain, 76-78
  subliminal, 6, 98
Copernican theory, 52
corpocentric attitude, 34, 72, 234
correspondence, 56, 57
cryptopsychism (see psychical research)

Darwinian principle, 17
delirium, 186
democracy, 20
determinism, 13
difference, method of, 87, 102
dissociation, theory of, 125
dreams, 61, 107, 119, 126, 129-140, 156, 228, 238-240
  definition of, 129, 137
  lucid, 135, 137, 138
  prophetic, 26, 135, 139
  theories on, 129-131
dream-consciousness, 228
  brain and, 134
  nature of, 132-134
  soul-consciousness and, 134-135, 138-139

economic determinism, 21, 22

Index of Subjects 257

education, 14
educational problem, 14-16
ego, 6, 59, 86, 95, 98, 103, 134
electrical theory of life, 208
energy conservation, law of, 62, 112, 175, 211
epiphenomenalism, 3, 90, 184
epiphenomenon of brain,
  consciousness as, 92, 202
  mind as, 3, 14, 79, 114, 153, 177
ethical postulates, 13
ethics, 12-14
existence, modes of, 87, 89

fact, 41, 45-50
fibrillation, 152, 183
forgetting, 104
Freudians, 6
fugue, 125

geocentric hypothesis
  (see Copernican theory)
Gestaltists, 6
Guye's principle, (see also scale of observation) ix, 47-48, 49, 50, 56, 58

hallucination, 62, 130, 132, 156, 181, 185, 186, 188, 203, 204, 226
  consciousness and, 205
hashish, 192
heliocentric hypothesis,
  (see Ptolemic theory)
Huna science, 218, 219
Hunter College experiment, 170
hypnosis, 145, 228
  clairvoyance and, 165
  defined, 141
  exaltation of the senses in, 143-144
  memory and, 145, 147-148
  physiological activity under, 151-153
hypnotism, 61, 63, 69, 107, 108, 115, 119, 130, 141-154
  blocking of vision in, 150-151
  meaning of, 141
hypophenomenalism, 184

"I am", 58, 59, 68, 98, 103, 112, 133, 180
ideas, 84-90, 93
  cerebrocentric theory of, 89
  characteristics of, 89-90
  existence of, 88-89
  nature of, 89-90
  sensations and, 84-85
  theory of, 82-85
immortality, 16
induction, 40-41

inductive reasoning, 40-41
interference, law of, 113
intuition, 55, 56

kahuna, 215, 216, 217
kaluluwa, 11
kamaloka, 138, 214
kamarupa, 138

levitation, 156
Lirenensis' maxim, 46
lysergic acid diethylamide (LSD), 64, 192-194

man, 3, 31-37, 43, 65, 84, 93, 95, 118, 119, 185, 195, 204, 219, 227, 232, 233
  cerebrocentric view of, 15, 23, 61, 142, 147, 152, 174, 234
  corpocentric theory of, 173, 174, 234
  dehumanizing of, 31-33
  materialistic theory of, 147, 228, 229
  mechanical view of, 29
  physicalistic view of, 157
  proper study of, 35
  sad state of, 21-23
  soul-theory of, 175
  the Unknown, 175
memory, 4, 61, 62, 73, 78, 100-116, 122, 145, 147, 153, 157, 227
  a soul-function, 115, 122
  brain and, 100-101
  brain theory of, 109-115
  conscious, 106
  consciousness and, 102
  definition of, 110, 148
  exaltation of, 107-109
  hypnosis and, 145, 147-148
  permanence of, 104-107
  perseveration theory of, 113
  revival of, 105-106
  unconscious, 106
mental state, 97, 174
mescaline, 64, 192, 198-199
metapsychics (see also psychical research), 26, 157, 214
  definition of, 155
  branches of, 155
mind, 2, 4, 14, 25, 34, 61, 74, 84, 89, 98, 100, 103, 104, 114, 128, 150, 153, 171, 173, 177
  as epiphenomenon of brain, 3, 14, 79, 114, 153, 177
Mind-at-Large, 203
minimum meaning, principle of
  (see also Occam's Law), 65
morality, 12-13, 157

258 Index of Subjects

mysticism, 26, 55, 56, 61, 63, 200-201

Occam's Law, 65

parapsychology (see also psychical research), 26, 155, 228
  outline of, 156
parsimony, law of, (see Occam's law)
Pearce-Pratt experiment, 176
perception, extrasensory (ESP), 15, 44, 47, 50, 61, 156, 168-178
  definition of, 168
  experiments on, 176
personal survival, 212-213
personality, 2, 12, 16, 29, 34, 43, 67, 68, 69, 86, 87, 89, 94, 98, 100, 112, 119, 132, 133, 140, 156
  dissociation of, 125
peyote, 64, 192
philosophy, xiv, 21, 24, 218, 235
physiology, 1, 2, 5, 28, 72, 73, 86, 111, 178
  definition of, 73
physiological psychology, 72
politics, 20
pragmatism, 56, 57
precognition, 50, 139, 169, 174, 175
  experiments on, 171
presentiments, 155
primitivism, fallacy of, iii
probability, principle of, 41-42, 43, 167, 226
prophecy (see also precognition), 139
psi, 142, 147, 174, 175, 177, 178, 179-180, 185, 228
  characteristics of, 176-177
psilocybin, 192
psychedelic phenomena,
  exaltation of the senses and the mind in, 197-199
  examples of, 195-201
  its resemblance to yoga and mysticism, 200-201
  nature of, 193-195
  other terms for, 195
  traveling clairvoyance and, 195-197
psychedelics, xvii, xviii, 61, 64, 192-208
psychic science (see psychical research)
psychical research (see also metapsychics and parapsychology), 26, 61, 63, 69, 155-191, 214, 228
  categories of, 155-156
  definition of, 155
  names in, 158-160

psychoanalysis, 34, 36, 63, 104
psychokinesis (PK), 168, 174, 175, 228
  experiments on, 171-172
psychological physiology, 72
psychological reorientation, 34-37
psychology, 1, 2, 12, 16, 18, 27, 28, 61, 72, 76, 111, 178
  abnormal, 123
  classroom, 2
  definitions of, 4-5
  Eastern and Western, 28-29
  ethics and, 12-14
  history of, 1-2, 26
  humanistic, xvii, xviii, 37
  physiology and, 72-73
  "third force" in, 34, 35, 36-37
  Ptolemic theory, 52
purusha, 7

raps, 155, 156
reduction, fallacy of (see also fallacy of primitivism), 111
reincarnation, 241-243
  cases of, 242-243
  soul and, 241
reintegration, process of, 137
religion, xiv, 10-12, 18, 21, 178, 231, 235
  confusion on, 18
  science and, 29-30
remembering, 106
resurrection, 216
  cases of, 214-216
  kahuna, 215-216, 217, 218
  of Sotera Flandez, 220-223
Rhine experiments, 169-172, 176

samadhi, xviii, xix, 209, 210
satori, xviii
scale of observation (see also Guye's principle), 44, 47, 58, 82, 204
science, 21, 25, 38, 43, 45, 46-47, 59, 64, 172, 173, 178, 218, 233
  duty of, 24, 218, 233, 235
  fallacy of, 46-47
  new idea of, xix
  problem of, 234-235
  religion and, 29-30
  the soul and, 43-44
  scientific dogmatism, 25
  scientific evidence, 51-55
    meaning of, 51
  scientific inference, 54
  scientific method, ix, 34, 38, 39-40, 43, 51, 54
self, 3, 34, 58, 59, 67, 68, 90, 94, 95, 103, 126, 132, 133, 134
  minimum, 71
  theories of, 60

Index of Subjects 259

self-experience, 56-57
sense-experience, 56-57
serotonin, 193
situation believed-in, 59, 69, 70
situation experienced, 59, 69, 70
sleep, 61, 62, 107, 117-128, 137, 209, 211, 227
  consciousness and, 12-122
  death and, 211
  definition of, 118-119, 137, 211
  EEG record and, 120-121
  stages of, 210
  theories on, 117-118
sleep-consciousness, 120-122
society, 21
confusion in, 19
somnambulism, 26, 119, 122-127, 175, 227
  cases of, 126
  nature of, 124-125
somnambulist, defined, 124
  personality of, 125
somniloquism, 26, 119, 122, 127, 227
soul, ix, xiv, 8, 25, 27, 28, 33, 34, 37, 45, 46, 47, 49, 50, 54, 64, 65, 69, 75, 87, 89, 94, 95, 100, 103, 113, 114, 121, 122, 125, 126, 128, 133, 134, 137, 151, 153, 175, 178, 179, 185, 203, 225, 227, 230, 232
  abolition of, 4-6
  as identical and continuous self-consciousness, 98-99
  Eastern concept of, 7, 9-10
  in *Huna* science, 218-219
  hypotheses regarding, 60, 61
  other terms for, 6-7, 11
  pineal gland and, 75
  rejection by science, 38
  Western concept of, 9-10
  use of the word, 1, 6, 7

soul-concept, 38, 39
soul-hypothesis, 64, 174, 175, 229
soul-problem, ix, 8-23
  legitimacy of, 8-16
  religion and, 10-12
  urgency of, 17-23
spiritualism, 214
subconscious, 6, 106, 122, 125, 127, 136, 151, 155
sushupti, 29, 120, 121
svapna, 29, 120, 121, 126, 132, 136, 137, 224

tardigrada, 210
telekinesis, 156
telepathy, 26, 44, 50, 144, 156, 168, 171, 172, 175, 176, 228
  experiments on, 171
teonanacatl, 197
thermodynamics, first law of, 62, 104
thought, 81, 82, 157, 184
  brain and, 81-83
truth acceptance, 55, 56-57
turiya, 29, 120
Turner-Ownbey experiment, 171, 176

uhane, 218, 219
unconscious, 113, 122, 127, 155, 209
unihipili, 218
universe,
  materialistic theory of, 39, 43
  naturalistic theory of, 173
University of Colorado experiment, 170

Vedantist, 7

yoga, xix, 7, 26, 61, 107, 204, 209, 210
  definition of, 63

SOME QUEST BOOK TITLES

THE DOCTRINE OF THE SUBTLE BODY IN WESTERN TRADITION, by G.R.S. Mead

THE FUTURE IS NOW, by Arthur W. Osborn

THE MANIFOLD AND THE ONE, by Agnes Arber

THE MYSTERY OF HEALING, edited by Adelaide Gardner

THE PSYCHIC SENSE, by Phoebe D. Payne and Laurence J. Bendit

PSYCHISM AND THE UNCONSCIOUS MIND, edited by H. Tudor Edmonds

THE SCIENCE OF YOGA, by I.K. Taimni

THE TRANSFORMING MIND, by Laurence J. Bendit and Phoebe D. Bendit

For a complete descriptive list of all Quest Books write to:

QUEST BOOKS
P.O. Box 270, Wheaton, Ill., 60187